Dickens and Creativity

Also by Barbara Hardy:

Literary Criticism
The Novels of George Eliot: A Study in Form
The Appropriate Form: An Essay on the Novel
The Advantage of Lyric
Dickens, The Later Novels: Writers and their Work
The Moral Art of Dickens
The Exposure of Luxury: Radical Themes in Thackeray
Tellers and Listeners: The Narrative Imagination
Charles Dickens: Writers and their Work
Particularities: A Reading of George Eliot
Forms of Feeling in Victorian Fiction
A Reading of Jane Austen
Narrators and Narration: Collected Essays
Henry James, The Later Novels: Writers and their Work
Thomas Hardy: Imagining Imagination
Dylan Thomas: An Original Language
George Eliot: A Critic's Biography

Books Edited
Middlemarch: Critical Approaches to the Novel
Critical Essays on George Eliot
Daniel Deronda by George Eliot
The Trumpet Major by Thomas Hardy
A Laodicean by Thomas Hardy
Not So Quiet ... by Helen Z. Smith

Autobiography, Fiction and Poetry
Swansea Girl
London Lovers
Severn Bridge: New and Collected Poems
The Yellow Carpet: New and Collected Poems

Dickens and Creativity

Barbara Hardy

continuum

Continuum
The Tower Building   80 Maiden Lane, Suite 704
11 York Road   New York
London SE1 7NX   NY 10038

www.continuumbooks.com

British Library Cataloguing-in-Publication Data
A catalogue record for this book is available from the British Library.

ISBN: 978-08264-9526-6 (hardback)
      978-18470-6459-2 (paperback)

Library of Congress Cataloguing-in-Publication Data
A catalog record for this book is available from the Library of Congress.

Typeset by YHT Ltd, London
Printed and bound in Great Britain by
Biddles Ltd., King's Lynn, Norfolk

In affectionate memory of my grandfather William John Abraham who gave me my first Dickens, *A Christmas Carol,* and my grandmother Florence Mary Abraham, née Jones

Contents

Acknowledgements ix

Note on Editions xi

Preface xiii

1 A Career and its Context 1

2 Dickens Discusses Creativity 19

3 The Awareness of Art in *Sketches By Boz, Pickwick Papers, Oliver Twist, Barnaby Rudge, The Old Curiosity Shop* and *The Chimes* 31

4 The Artist as Narrator in *Doctor Marigold, David Copperfield, Bleak House* and *Great Expectations* 45

5 Talkative Men and Women in *Pickwick Papers, Nicholas Nickleby, Martin Chuzzlewit* and *Little Dorrit* 61

6 Imaginative Extremes, Negations and Norms 71

7 Subversions and Oppositions 87

8 Crises of Imagination in *Oliver Twist, A Christmas Carol, Dombey and Son, Bleak House, Hard Times* and *The Lazy Tour of Two Idle Apprentices* 97

9 Forecast and Fantasy in *Little Dorrit* 109

10 Creative Conversation in *Hard Times, Great Expectations* and *Our Mutual Friend* 127

11 Assertions of Style: Rhythm and Repetition in *A Tale of Two Cities* and *Our Mutual Friend* 137

12 Shakespeare in Dickens: *David Copperfield* and *Great Expectations* 145

13 Dickens in the Twentieth Century 157

Sources 175

Index 179

Acknowledgements

I am very grateful to the following: Miranda El-Rayess for reading and criticizing the manuscript and helping with references, checking and proofs; Amanda Jones for help with proofs; Michael Slater for creative conversation over many years, for answering questions, reading part of the book, and sharing his knowledge of Dickens; my other Dickensian colleagues Steven Connor, Sally Ledger and Andrew Sanders for Dickens talk; Janet El-Rayess for reading and criticizing the book; Merivan Coles and Tony Poynton for reading part of the book and giving advice; Isobel Armstrong, Martin Dodsworth, Beryl Gray, Julia and Kate Hardy, Debbie Harrison, Sam Hynes, Bill Nathan and Leonee Ormond for help of many kinds; Kate for the Matisse anecdote; Simon Richards and Nathan Hardy for advice about computers; students of Birkbeck and Royal Holloway and members of the Dickens Fellowship; the British Library, the libraries of London University, Birkbeck College, the Dickens House Museum and the Brompton Road and Hornton Street branches of Kensington and Chelsea libraries. I have listed works used in this book but I am indebted to many Dickens scholars and critics not acknowledged here.

Note on Editions

I have used the Clarendon edition of Dickens's novels (Oxford: Clarendon Press, 1966–97) for *Oliver Twist* (ed. K. Tillotson), *The Mystery of Edwin Drood* (ed. M. Cardwell), *Dombey and Son* (ed. A. Horsman), *Little Dorrit* (ed. P. Sucksmith), *David Copperfield* (ed. N. Burgis), *Martin Chuzzlewit* (ed. M. Cardwell), *Pickwick Papers* (ed. J. Kinsley), *Great Expectations* (ed. M. Cardwell) and *The Old Curiosity Shop* (ed. E. Brennan).

I have used the Oxford Illustrated edition (London: OUP, 1948–55) for *Bleak House* (intro. O. Sitwell), *A Tale of Two Cities* (intro. J. Shuckburgh), *Our Mutual Friend* (intro. E. Salter Davies), *Barnaby Rudge: A Tale of the Riots of 'Eighty* (intro. K. Tillotson) and *Hard Times* (intro. Dingle Foot) and *Nicholas Nickleby* (intro. Sybil Thorndike).

I have used the Penguin edition of *The Christmas Books*, ed. M. Slater, Harmondsworth: Penguin, 1971.

I have used the Pilgrim edition of *The Letters of Charles Dickens*, ed. M. House, G. Storey et al., vols 1–12, Oxford: Clarendon Press, 1965–2002; cited as *Letters*.

I have used *Dickens's Journalism*, ed. M. Slater and J. Drew, vols 1–4, London: Dent 1994–2000; cited as *Journalism*.

I have used the New Arden edition (Second Series, London: Methuen), for Shakespeare's plays and sonnets.

Preface

In my book *The Moral Art of Dickens*, as its title suggests, I was interested in the way Dickens combined art and moral appeal. I am always aware that Dickens's passionate and scrupulously researched social concern is at the heart of his life and writing but in this book I concentrate on an aspect of his work which has attracted very little attention: his interest in processes of the creative mind, which he called the imagination, the fancy and the inventive capacity.[1]

He sometimes mentions the subject of imagination explicitly and directly but more often reveals his ideas in ways that are embedded in his characters and stories and are complexly reflexive.[2] He did not set out to study imagination, fancy, invention, inspiration, narrative, or generative form, in the conscious and systematic way he investigated workhouses, prisons, schools, charity, working-class leisure, emigration and hospitals, but creativity was his subject. Like many other artists he scrutinized his art as he practised it, sometimes commenting personally and suggestively on experience, like A. E. Housman, who told a learned Cambridge audience that he was inspired by beer at lunch followed by a walk.

Dickens gives some account of his writing and working habits as he feels the need to explain them to his wife and friends, or as he is struck with a new idea or gives up an old one or stuggles to find a title or get on with a novel or is surprised or puzzled by what is going on in his mind and on the paper. Quite early in his writing career his ideas about art, invention and composition also show themselves as they are assimilated in his descriptive and reflective sketches, for instance when he – or his surrogate narrator – looks at what he calls 'the still life' of the streets and is – or seems – suddenly inspired by a suit of clothes to imagine its owner and his history, presenting the reader first with the idea and then with the execution. When he starts writing his novels, which were all serials and nearly always composed hand to mouth, the subject of creativity is revealed in conscious or unconscious observations of fancy, imagination and the unconscious mind, placed in the language and psyche of his characters, who are all – or nearly all – created to dream, fantasize, invent, foresee, remember, report, and tell their stories, in ordinary or in extraordinary conditions. Throughout his career he invents narrators to frame serial stories who are given individual characteristics or placed in particular situations which motivate their story-telling function, characters like the recluse Master Humphrey, the Uncommercial Traveller who deals in 'fancy goods', the good gossiping landlady Mrs Lirriper. More profoundly and thoroughly he imagines characters who tell their own life-story, or a large part of it, at length, like David Copperfield or Esther Summerson, portraits of the highly motivated narrator, one a professional and the other an amateur. Other major characters with less conspicuous narrative roles are often revealed by their stories, for instance Arthur Clennam, Amy Dorrit and Lizzie Hexam. Characters who play much smaller parts also have their story to tell, because the narrative imagination is everywhere, in sensitive tellers like Polly Richards or Jenny Wren and unlikely people like the crusty bachelors Jarvis Lorry and Mr Grewgious, and the bony spinster Miss Pross, who claim to have no scrap of imagination or poetry in them. And there are their opposites, extremists of imagination like Mrs Nickleby and Mrs Gamp, great talkers whose stories and styles are the richer for being wild, loose and disordered, and more pathologically bizarre fantasists like Barnaby Rudge and John Jasper, all created as creators of original languages with a freedom and subversion we associate with modernism. And there are the fantasies we all experience when what we call reality is made strange by illness, drowsiness or dream. What is brilliant in Dickens – a genius ignorant of metaphysics and aesthetics – is his personal, informal, non-conceptualizing way of generalizing or defining imagination, delirium, spontaneity, control, passive and active creativity, lateral thinking, creative wonder, the half-conscious or unconscious mind.

In a different category, there are awkward characters who seem to go against the grain of the moral or the story, like Chuckster in *The Old Curiosity Shop*, Uriah Heep and Miss Wade, who show or suggest that the creative artist needs to imagine discord and subversion rather as the experimenting scientist needs to disprove his hypothesis.

What Dickens thinks about the creative mind is often shown or implied in his characters' conversations, which are often models of an interplay or exchange with otherness and also of what Matthew Arnold called the dialogue of the mind with itself. I have also discussed certain moments of mental and affective crisis, where an effort or concentration or lapse of imagination is illuminated, for instance in a guilty murderer, a distressed wife, an imaginative child. I have discussed passages in two novels, *A Tale of Two Cities* and *Our Mutual Friend*, where rhetoric or poetic effect is so assertive and conspicuous as to make form apparent, self-aware, reflexive, substantiated as the subject of art and not only its means and manner.

I have looked at discussions and images of creativity across a range of Dickens's fiction but more closely analyzed the explicit and implicit presentation of creative mind in one work, *Little Dorrit*, because it strikes me as a great social novel which is also exceptionally introspective, and because I wanted to slow down my survey and give an isolated and detailed reading of a single novel.

Finally, one aspect of Dickens's creativity is what we have come to call intertextuality, in his case largely confined to the assimilation of one writer, Shakespeare, the artist who for him – a writer not widely or deeply read, not conventionally educated in the classics like Thackeray, or self-educated in many subjects and languages like George Eliot – represented literary history, model, and tradition. Reversing the process of intertextual exchange, I conclude with a selective account of Dickens as a creative inspiration, in his turn, for later novelists, some traditional and some high modernist.[3]

Although I begin the illustration of Dickens's interest in creativity by concentrating chiefly on early letters, sketches and novels, I treat the subject thematically, picking examples across the range of writing, so in my first preliminary chapter I set his career in a briefly sketched and selective biographical context, looking at the fiction in chronological order to say something about his development as a novelist, and also to make evaluative and analytic comment which goes beyond the subject of creativity, and to place some sketches and stories, with all the novels, in the context of relevant and important events in their author's life.

Notes

[1] The terms 'fancy' and 'imagination', firmly and famously distinguished by Coleridge in the *Biographia Literaria*, were almost always used by Dickens interchangeably, as synonyms, though there is the odd discriminatory nuance, as when he praises Charles Reade's *Griffith Gaunt* for 'a brilliant fancy, and a graceful and tender imagination' (*Letters* 11, 317). Philip Collins examines the subject in 'Queen Mab's Chariot among the Steam Engines; Dickens's Fancy' (*English Studies*, no. 42, 1961); I discussed his essay and Dickens's interest in creativity in an unpublished paper, 'Dickens Imagining Imagination', at Philip Collins's retirement conference in 1986, and in lectures given over many years at Birkbeck College's annual 'Dickens Day', begun by Michael Slater and continued by Sally Ledger.

² Edmund Wilson in 'The Two Scrooges' in *The Wound and the Bow* was the
first critic to use Freud and relate Dickens's creativity to his childhood trauma,
though in his fiction Dickens himself shows an implicit awareness of such
connection between a psychic wound and creativity. John Butt and Kathleen
Tillotson wrote a scrupulously illustrated account of his compositional methods in *Dickens at Work*; Robert Garis drew attention to the self-dramatizing art
in *The Dickens Theatre*; Michael Slater has a chapter on 'Fancy' in his *Intelligent
Person's Guide to Dickens*; Richard Lettis has two volumes, on *Dickens's Aesthetic*
and *Dickens on Literature*, generally restricted to explicit reference; John Carey's
The Violent Effigy is deeply and amusingly concerned with Dickens's imagination; in *The Night Side of Dickens* Harry Stone is concerned with Dickens's
creativity, and with imaginative extremes, but with not with their self-
awareness.

³ Dickens and other Victorians have been seen by some post-structuralist
critics as creating the enclosed, authoritarian and simply mimetic forms of
what has been called the classic realist novel, a politicized construct which
bears little relation to the self-conscious and self-analytic art of Dickens,
George Eliot, Thackeray – who first interested me in the reflexive awareness of
Victorian fiction – or any important novelist of the period known to me. One
irony of literary history is that the Victorian multiple plot and its omniscient or
nearly omniscient narrator have been compared adversely with the artistic
concentration and multi-vocalism of writers like James Joyce, who himself drew
attention to Dickens's influence on English literature, nowhere seen more
powerfully at work than in Joyce's own experimental and subversive language.

Chapter 1

A Career and its Context

On 7 February 1812, in 13, Mile End Terrace, Portsea, Portsmouth, Charles Huffam Dickens was born, second child of John, clerk in the Navy Pay Office, and Elizabeth, née Barrow; his siblings included a brother and sister who died young, a beloved elder sister, Frances or Fanny, Letitia with whom he had less in common but to whom he was always kind, especially after her husband died, Frederick or Fred, Alfred a successful civil engineer, and Augustus who left his wife and went to Canada with another woman, and like Fred caused Dickens some anxiety. In Dickens's childhood the family moved to London then down to Chatham and the dockyards, Kent marshes and river Medway which inspired landscape and action in *Great Expectations* and some of the 'Uncommercial Traveller' sketches. Charles was a small and ailing child who enjoyed books, acting, joking and singing, and wrote a couple of tragedies when he was eight or nine. The eighteenth-century novels and *The Thousand and One Nights* (or *The Arabian Nights* as Dickens always called it) which he read when young made a lasting impression which helped to shape his imagery, his rambling constructions and the adventurous wanderings of many characters.

Dickens's schooling was desultory. He went to a dame-school and to William Giles's school in Chatham but his education was interrupted in 1822 when the family moved back to London, to live in Bayham Street, in a poor part of Camden Town, and he became a household drudge, cleaning boots and going to the pawnshop, while Fanny was winning prizes at the Royal Academy of Music – though he never held it against her. John Dickens's financial situation went from bad to worse and he ended up in the Marshalsea debtors' prison; Charles went reluctantly and miserably into solitary lodgings and to work in a blacking factory owned by a relative, James Lamert, suffering the trauma of shame, a 'secret agony' kept from everyone except his friend John Forster, and perhaps his wife. He forgave his irresponsible eloquent father in benign Micawber but recalled him more bitterly in William Dorrit. He never forgot that his mother had wanted him to resume his detested work after he left because of a family disagreement. The solitude and humiliation he felt when he was 11 or 12 – of course many children of his time and class started work at that age – began his fearful, compassionate, amused and excited discovery of London's mean streets, its great filthy river, its crime, drunks, prostitutes, crowds and lonely people, which all go into the creation of Oliver Twist, Fagin, the Artful Dodger, David Copperfield and the terrible children Ignorance and Want in Scrooge's Christmas dream. In London's humanity Dickens found his own, and the discovery was painful and creative.

The family fortunes recovered a little, and for two years Dickens went to the Wellington House Classical and Commercial Academy kept by William Jones, to be re-made as a shabby school and an ignoramus master for David Copperfield, who is also granted a vaguely superior academic education at Dr Strong's. Dickens left school at 15 to work for Charles Molloy in Symond's Inn, and later for Ellis and Blackmore of Raymond Buildings. His clerk's experience goes into the office scenes of *A Christmas Carol, Great Expectations* and *Edwin Drood,* and his critique of the law into nearly all the novels.

Perhaps inspired by his father who was making a fresh start as a reporter, Charles studied shorthand, began reporting at Doctors' Commons, in 1832 joined the *True Sun,* and in 1834 the *Morning Chronicle.* As parliamentary reporter he began to form his low opinion of English representative government, an opinion which grew steadily lower in spite of the two Reform Acts passed in his lifetime. Feeling his lack of education he read history and the classics of English literature in the British Museum Reading Room.

His first passionate and long-lasting love was for Maria Beadnell, and their relationship went on for four years, ending unhappily, perhaps because of her fickle flirtatiousness and her parents' opposition. She is often linked with Dora Copperfield but though the novel's courtship raptures may reflect her attractions and the young Dickens's strong feelings, the character Forster called 'the book Dora' develops subtly and understatedly in fictions of everyday living, loving, adjusting and suffering, which have nothing whatever to do with Maria. Dickens always insisted that his novels were true to life and perhaps critics have accepted his view too avidly. In 1855 Maria eagerly re-entered Dickens's life as the unattractive middle-aged Mrs Henry Winter and inspired her dis-appointed old flame to create Flora Finching, though voluble Flora also owes much to an old literary stereotype in Chaucer, Shakespeare and Sheridan, not to mention her close predecessors Mrs Nickleby and Mrs Gamp.

Like Defoe, Thackeray and George Eliot, Dickens learnt the novelist's trade as a journalist, though his first published work was fiction, 'A Dinner at Poplar Walk', included in *Sketches by Boz* as 'Mr Minns and his Cousin'. It is a neat sketch of drab snobbish genteel middle-class life with a mildly amusing civil-servant hero who hates children and dogs. The more promising early work is in 'Street Sketches' (*Morning Chronicle*) and *Sketches of London* (*Evening Chronicle*), also collected in *Sketches by Boz*: their intimate warm tone, incisive social particularity and precisely specified time and place are admirable but he does even better in the later sketches 'Newgate' and 'Meditations in Monmouth Street', which also show a more developed psychology and a narrative urge. Dickens was writing for fairly radical papers, and obviously found their politics congenial as his own sympathy and sociological imagination were beginning to fuse with his story-telling and his interest in people.

He met Catherine Hogarth through her father George, editor of the *Evening Chronicle*, and they were engaged in 1835 and married in 1836 just after the first number of *Pickwick Papers* (1836–7). When the publishers Chapman and Hall asked Dickens to supply a text for a series of sporting illustrations by the popular artist Robert Seymour he expanded the scope of its story and thought of Mr Pickwick. After the first number the unfortunate Seymour committed suicide and the artwork was taken over by Hablot Knight Browne, who took the pseudonym 'Phiz' to go with 'Boz', the name based on Dickens's little brother Augustus's mispronunciation of his nickname 'Moses', from Goldsmith's *Vicar of Wakefield*. Dickens loved inventing nicknames for his children, and his characters' names often work with the comic aptness or ineptness of nicknaming.

The serialized *Pickwick* begins as an episodic novel with farcical scenes and comic or dark inset stories of no great merit, but it becomes more intense and concentrated. In the fourth number Dickens thought of Sam Weller and developed the Cockney double act of Sam and his father Tony (perhaps *Steptoe and Son* is a modern equivalent) and later the novel acquires social point as Pickwick is involved in a breach-of-promise case where the plaintiff, Mrs Bardell, is egged on by a firm of wicked lawyers. The story takes a serious turn in the Fleet prison, fascinatingly used as a testing-place for character and a microcosm of misery and social injustice. Dickens is learning to combine as well as contrast his pathos and his fun.

Oliver Twist was serialized in the first magazine edited by Dickens, *Bentley's Miscellany* (1837–9), and overlapped with *Pickwick*. It is in no way an immature work but a tense and concentrated construction, a model

for the later expansive novels as it combines a story of crime and punishment with social criticism, comedy and a romantic love-story. The
narrative boldly simplifies character and action in a moral fable, by-
passing plausibility of detail (for instance in the language of the
foundling Oliver) and indicting the heartless bumbling bureaucracy of
baby-farming and the new Poor Law (1834). The love-story is sentimental
but the *crime passionel* a thrilling social and psychic drama of violence and
corruption, with fence and gang-leader Fagin, 'bully' Sikes, prostitute
Nancy and a wonderful mixed gang of thieves. Dickens exploited the
horror of a brutal murder and Sikes' grim accidental self-execution in
his last public readings, making audiences faint and his own pulse-rate
rise.

The first child, Charles, was born to the young couple in 1837, just
before the first instalment of *Oliver*, and five months later Dickens was
stunned by the sudden death of Catherine's sister Mary, at 17. She was
living with them and died in Charles's arms after a theatre trip, making
him postpone the next numbers of *Oliver* and *Pickwick* and write his
affection and grief into beautiful frail Rose Maylie, whose life he threa-
tens and then spares.

Oliver overlapped with the episodic *Nicholas Nickleby* (1838–9) which
satirized the already notorious Cheap Schools of Yorkshire. Dickens and
Phiz carried out undercover investigations which inspired the comic and
horrifying Dotheboys Hall and its foul master, Squeers, like Dingley Dell
and Sam Weller, places and characters combining strong caricature with
vivid individuality, to become mythical – and in this case good propa-
ganda too. Everyone is driven by greed: the crime-story cleverly involves
Squeers with the more subtly drawn villain Ralph Nickleby, who like
Sikes is larger than life but realistic enough to suggest a process of social
corruption, while at the comic extreme there are the aspirant Kenwigses
– often quoted by their author – and the perfectly yoked sparring-part-
ners Mr and Mrs Mantalini. There is free hilarious comic play, of a kind
Dickens never dropped, in the Crummles theatre company and their
unforgettable Infant Phenomenon. The romantic story is thin but the
trio of Madeline Bray, her mercenary father and the repulsive miser-
suitor Gride, forms an erotically sharpened image of the Victorian
marriage market. Nicholas is given one or two moments of pity and
insight, surprising and rather erratic but not to be wished away.

In 1840, Dickens devised a plan to make a change for himself and his
readers, a weekly periodical where Master Humphrey was the frame
narrator and keeper of papers, with a clock-case depository for the
stories. But readers weren't keen on the fragmented links or the tales,

and not beguiled by a very class-conscious revival of Pickwick and the low Wellers, shadows of their former selves, unpropelled by plot or action and introducing Sam's unattractively winking, drinking and smoking small son. Never at a loss, the improvizing author spun out an earlier idea for a short story into the long novel *The Old Curiosity Shop* (1840–1), first kept within the framework of *Master Humphrey's Clock* but eventually published on its own, with Humphrey kept as an anonymous initiating narrator and also a wounded artist inspired like Dickens by trauma, night, solitude, London streets and a curious obsession with inanimate objects. Narrator and narrative are the better for the removal of Humphrey's original undramatic full life-story and the arrival of his new seat of imagination: the antique-shop which gave a name to the most popular and the most sentimental of Dickens's novels.

Dickens was an uneven genius, often writing badly – sloppily, sensationally, coyly, cosily, superficially, self-indulgently and falsely, and his medley works on and off: Quilp is unsurpassed for gross harsh high jinks; the love-interest is a sprightly sub-plot featuring poetic wine-bibbing Dick Swiveller who is saved by and saves the super-intelligent skivvy, his Marchioness; there is good crude satire of the law; the vivid road-narrative with comic images and humours of Punch-and-Judy troupe, giants, stilt-walkers, performing dogs and flexible waxworks, is impromptu and rambling but perfectly in tune with the opening theme of curiosity and curiosities. The doomed angelic Little Nell broke tender hearts on both sides of the Atlantic but Oscar Wilde famously quipped that it took a heart of stone not to laugh at her death. Even that part of the story contains telling tropes and scenes like the early image of youth surrounded by dark twisted old things, the grim episode of industrial life where Nell and her grandfather are sheltered by a poor workman at a blast-furnace, and the topical scene of frightening industrial riot.

Next in *Master Humphrey's Clock* emerged more scenes of riot for *Barnaby Rudge* (1841), another postponed item in Dickens's tangle of early commissions, and a thoroughly researched chronicle of the anti-Catholic Gordon Riots (1780), in which he satirized religious extremes – though giving a fair portrait of the fanatical Lord George Gordon. As in *The Old Curiosity Shop* he indirectly reflects or refers to the contemporary riots of Midlands cotton-workers and brickmakers, contemporary threats of violent revolution violently put down. Marx predicted that Great Britain was the only European nation which might achieve social justice without violence but the fear of revolution was a very real thing for many of its citizens, and deeply felt by Dickens and Thomas Carlyle.

The love-interest in *Barnaby Rudge* is feeble, but there is uproarious –

though by modern standards politically dubious – fun in the caricatures of Sim Tappertit, a subversive apprentice, and Miggs, a skinny sycophantic maid. At one extreme of the social spectrum there is the chillingly heartless Sir John Chester, and at the other his rough illegitimate outcast son Hugh and Dennis the hangman in whom Dickens indulged his taste for morbid physical detail and his distaste for public executions and – in a more qualified way – capital punishment. Dennis's perverse brooding over condemned prisoners in the stormed Fleet prison, his conflict between a gloating sensual pride in his trade and a dread of discovery, and his last frantic bodily struggle against his own hanging, are disgusting and knowing. Sharing the centre with Dennis as a pathological study is mad wild Barnaby, a poetic and sympathetic figure sometimes related to Wordsworth's Idiot Boy and to Scott's David Gellatley in *Waverley* but in fact bearing no resemblance to either of these characters – who are also quite unlike each other – in speech, mind or personality, and distinct in his articulate energy and creative self-awareness.

In January 1842 Dickens left for a three-month trip to the United States and Canada with Catherine, leaving their children to be looked after by their friends the Macreadys and Fred Dickens. He reported the pleasures and pains of their voyage and travels in letters to Forster which went into *American Notes* (1842) and the novel *Martin Chuzzlewit* (1842–4). Letters, travel-book and fiction alike all show the writer's disappointment at the manners and customs of a democratic republic of which he had high hopes. Dickens's richly miscellaneous critique combines fastidious objections to tobacco-chewing, spitting and lack of privacy, with social disapproval of solitary confinement in prisons, slavery, and the absence of international copyright law which meant that Dickens suffered from lost royalties and pirated reprints which were often inaccurate and abridged. He saw absolutely no reason not to complain publicly and as his tour was widely publicized even his fans were outraged by what they interpreted as ingratitude and cupidity. His criticism is depersonalized in *Martin Chuzzlewit* but this did not mean that American readers were not offended.

The novel shows with strong squalid realism the exploitation of immigrants in the swamps and shacks of 'Eden' where Martin is converted from egoism to unselfishness by a combination of fever, disillusion and the self-sacrifice of too-good-to-be-true Mark Tapley. The change of heart important in so many of the novels is here schematic rather than plausible but it does help to individualize the young gentleman-hero. The two chief villains are superb: Pecksniff is a caricature as comically horrifying as Molière's Tartuffe, and a physical presence too, with a creepy sexual predatoriness all his own which almost shakes a little life into the tedious young heroine Mary Graham, and Jonas Chuzzlewit is a sexually sinister husband whose guilty self-horror and divided identity may owe something to Poe's 'The Telltale Heart' but in perverted thrills is pure Dickens. The blends are extraordinary. Mercy modulates shockingly from comic flirtatious Pecksniff daughter to realistic abused and terrified Chuzzlewit wife, and infinitely various Mrs Gamp is a social indictment of Victorian monthly nurses, a new Mrs Malaprop and a brilliant liar set to work for the plot's tension and surprise. Some of Martin's transatlantic adventures are surprisingly and improbably transferred from the novelist to his less talented hero but the dreary landscape of the swamp-settlement with its deadly miasma, dilapidated buildings, sick and dying people, is a wasteland with many meanings.

A Christmas Carol (December, 1843) is Dickens's best portrayal of the change of heart. It uses the psychological short-cuts of fantasy and the economy of fable, its villain-hero magically reformed by dreams and ghosts and naturally re-integrated by memory, joining past to present in a sympathetic return to the pains and pleasures of childhood and youth: the story subtly shows Scrooge urged by dream-trauma to care for himself and for his neighbour as himself. The humour of the ghost-story is seriously frightening: Scrooge jokes to keep his spirits up in Marley's presence and Dickens amuses us and makes our flesh creep at the same time – the character reflecting his author's craft. Dickens knows why and when to withdraw humour too, as Scrooge sees in his own unmourned grave and desecrated bare deathbed – chilling metonymy – the future of unloving and unloved man.

The next Christmas story, *The Chimes* (1844), uses a similar supernatural machinery and the same device of a story with two endings. The fantasy is used for a new and scathing topical satire, striking 'a great blow for the poor' by specific and topical attacks on real recognizable politicians and magistrates who had deplored the extravagance, feckless fun and despair shown by the lower classes (an attitude Dickens destested and attacked strongly in articles as well as fiction). The chimes were inspired by church bells in Genoa, where Dickens took his family to live in 1844–5, for domestic economy and a personal Grand Tour. A direct result of the Italian journey was *Pictures from Italy* (1846), a chronicle more informative about the social scene than art and architecture, with anti-Catholic animus and anti-Papal satire, imaginative variations of pace, feeling and style he imaginatively re-characterized for William and

Amy Dorrit, and an extraordinary chapter, 'An Italian Dream', about Venice, the city he described as 'beyond imagination' and said became 'a bit' of his 'brain' from the day he first saw it.

Chuzzlewit is usually praised as the first novel with thematic unity but its change of heart is narrated not enacted, and its humour of Selfishness imposed rather than embodied, as is clear when we compare it with *Dombey and Son* (1846–8), which may have gained from the exercise of compression and the release of poetry in the *Carol*. *Dombey* is another novel turning on a ruling passion – Pride. It is dramatized, judged, punished and cured in a patriarchal figure who compounds both pride and power as capitalist, father and husband. But Dombey is more than a type: he is a psychic whole, his humanity first violently suppressed then violently released. His second wife, Edith, has a more sympathetic pride, and his son Paul is one of the most interesting examples of the Dickensian pathetic sick child, whose vision, poetry and innocence seem to come from another world to challenge his society's values with a piercing, almost Swiftian, clarity as he asks: 'What is money?' (Ch. 8).

With a central character like Dombey the novel scarcely needs a villain but one is supplied in the deep devious Carker who has the mannerisms and features of a melodramatic evil-doer – like a set of flashing white teeth – but is a sexually and politically felt threat to women, and satisfactorily put down, with the husband he hoped to cuckold, in a wonderfully imagined woman's retaliation, before he meets his death in one of the best railway melodramas in Victorian fiction.

Dickens is beginning to use poetry with daring and freedom, outside his dream-fables. The novel's prevailing symbols – the sea and the railway – are manipulated with conscious and unconscious point as they represent nature and civilization, powerful in destruction and creativity. Leaving realism far behind, Dickens boldly and with deliberated obscurity anticipates Paul's death in the child's poetry of a moonlit sail like a beckoning arm out at sea (Ch. 12), and Carker's in images of 'a visionary terror, unintelligible and inexplicable, associated with a trembling of the ground, – a rush and sweep of something through the air, like Death upon the wing' (Ch. 55).

The weak spot in the novel is the heroine Florence Dombey, affecting and politically significant as neglected daughter and defended by some partisans as a fairy-tale figure, but I think too conventionally romantic and far from magical – so unlike Paul – when she grows up into love and marriage but invariably spreads girlish sweetness and softness as she leads us to the happy ending.

Dickens called *David Copperfield* (1849–50) his 'favourite child', and it is his own in a special sense. In the late 1840s he began a memoir, decided not to finish it and put some of its reminiscence into this novel – his old neglected solitary days, the degradarion of the blacking factory (translated to a wine warehouse), bad school, prison, office, shorthand, reporting, courtship of Maria Beadnell, and his career as writer. But as in other Victorian autobiographical novels, like *Jane Eyre, Pendennis* and *The Mill on the Floss*, the most biographical and personal parts are drawn from the author's early years; there is a high proportion of invented material; and actual people and events are changed in the company and contexts of fiction. No doubt it was satisfying to kill off one wife and imagine a better but both Mrs Copperfields were imaginary, even if the sad disappointed feeling of disparity in marriage was real enough. David is a neglected bookish boy who becomes a novelist but he is far more passive, far less mercurially charismatic and far less socially engaged than his author. The book is more formally inventive and modulated than earlier novels: the repeated 'Retrospects', with their accelerated narration and present tense, are finely and confidently created for a novel of memory; the narrator's presence is varied according to his role; the combination of comedy with pathos in Betsy Trotwood, Dora, Mrs Micawber, Miss Mowcher and the young David, is fresh in nuance and feeling: because we find these people funny our sympathy or pity is restrained; because we find them pitiable they transcend humorous type. The story of Nature and human nature in David's Alpine resurgence, after the deaths of Dora, Steerforth and Ham, is vague and conventionally high-toned and an apparent emulation of Wordsworth, drawing attention to its banal description and sentiment. The iambic pentameters that often mark Dickensian intensities do not help: 'seeking out Nature, never sought in vain'. But there are fine moments: in the chapter called 'Tempest', when Ham dies to save the man he does not know is Steerforth, the human and inhuman turbulence sound together and sound true. The Strong marriage stretches plausibility to breaking point and Agnes is universally acknowledged to be ludicrously angelic – worse than Nell because she is an angel in the house who survives – but Peggotty and Barkis are humane comic figures, delicately changed by marriage and aging; Betsy grows beyond stereotype, her history told with suggestive restraint; Dora Copperfield is a woman character rare in Dickens, a charmer made charming and an object of desire made desirable; the Micawbers are so good that their triumphant emigration is more or less acceptable (except to G. K. Chesterton); Uriah Heep makes our flesh creep and makes us examine and qualify our revulsion, to understand like David why the Heeps are what they are. (Chesterton insists that Dickens does not show the effects of social conditions but I think he is wrong.) Into the novel went old and new social concerns, the interest in prison reform, and a new knowledge of emigration and prostitution developed from his work with the philanthropist Angela Burdett-Coutts at Urania Cottage, a home for homeless women which he managed for ten years, in a practical and humane way: inmates were mostly ex-prisoners who had committed theft and other offences but he met women who had been seduced, and perhaps prostitutes, and helped to plan emigrations to Australia, where, like Martha, the women sometimes re-married. (Not that Martha or Emily are realistic characters; their expressed attitude is dully and invariably pure and they do not have inner lives like Elizabeth Gaskell's seduced women.)

1851 was a difficult year, personally and socially. Dickens's troublesome but much loved father and his 8-month-old daughter Dora both died suddenly, when Catherine was taking a cure at Malvern for some nervous trouble. He disliked the triumphalist Great Exhibition and left town to avoid visiting enthusiasts. The mismanagement of the Crimean War shocked the nation. No surprise that the next three books, the 'Condition of England' novels, are bleak and melancholy. *Bleak House* (1852–3) experiments in voice and point-of-view, combining two storytellers, a contented good woman remembering her past and an impersonal ungendered narrator addressing the present in pity and anger. Esther has some of the excessive virtue of Agnes but the novel shows how her wounded childhood is healed in a self-subduing service. Verbless sentences establish a London fog in a substantial and portentous beginning, and the blend of comic and grim feelings condemns Chancery and makes the Spontaneous Combustion scene tense and physically shocking. Sir Leicester Dedlock is a gentleman with a heart of gold who opens out under our eyes, to fall sick and forgive without affective exaggeration or high style. We move dramatically from past to present tense. The satire which functioned locally in *David Copperfield*, like the Doctors' Commons scenes, is integrated in narrative and drama, character and action, comedy and tragedy, and the fog symbol extends a common metaphor to a large social significance – because of Dickens's developing art but also because of a new political grasp. This novel of multiple action surveys poverty, pollution, slum housing, monetary greed, class-war, the misrule of Law, Church, Civil Service, Parliament, all those heartless institutions run by a money-making establishment. The unifying energy has its source in the observed network of social cause and effect, fact becoming fiction. Chesterton said, only half-ironically, that the novel would please modern aesthetic critics, and his praise of political depth and artistic unity contrasts with Forster's dislike of the sustained sombre mood and symbolism and his preference for the 'incidental' satire in earlier novels. Some defects in the novel are political, like the sexism in the conception of Mrs Jellyby and Mrs Pardiggle, but the dislike of such 'telescopic philanthropy' was a general and topical concern not primarily anti-feminist. Esther's role as good housekeeper is placed in relation to England's bleak houses and bad housekeeping, and relieved if not entirely excused by her authorial function.

Dickens not only contributed to periodical journals but from time to time edited his own, for a week or two in 1846 taking on *The Daily News*, and in 1850 *Household Words*, a two-penny weekly which he part-owned and edited, publishing his articles and fiction and fixing his imprint by radical revision of other writers. One contribution was a weekly serialization of *Hard Times* (1854) a satirical novel which he knew resembled its predecessor Elizabeth Gaskell's *Mary Barton*, probably realizing that his knowledge of the industrial city, in this case Preston alias Coketown, was much less intimate and specific than hers. He knew his knowledge of strikes was not helped by one brief visit, and indeed he presents trade unionism superficially and unsympathetically, with the working-class 'scab' Stephen Blackpool, his alcoholic wife and apolitical friend Rachel melodramatically assembled – though interestingly involved in the villainy of mis-educated Tom Gradgrind. There are interesting characters in his love-story: insufficiently ground-down Louisa Bounderby née Gradgrind, lovelessly married to raucous Bounderby, who invents a history of his poor neglected childhood, and James Harthouse, her would-be seducer, a subtly sympathetic successor to Steerforth and Carker. Gradgrind is a Benthamite killjoy, educational theorist and another case of repression and conversion. Like railway, prison, river and city slums, the Coketown smokestack brilliantly joins industrial fact and symbol, a psychological metaphor for Louisa and a social metonymy for the reader. The tight action owes something to weekly serialization, something to concentrated social theme.

Shaw said *Little Dorrit* (1855–7) was more seditious than Marx's *Capital*, perhaps because it traces the corruption of a profit-motive in every heartless institution, firm, factory, government and civil service department. Chesterton and Forster said everyone in *Bleak House* is in a fog and everyone in this novel is confined in prison or lost in the Circumlocution Office – much the same thing – stuck there like damned souls in Dante, not because of sins but because of muddle, injustice and profiteering that are *Nobody's Fault* – the novel's old ironic working title. There is satire, pity and anger but no diagnosis: love is shown as the answer to some individual problems but not a social solution. Shaw was nearly right but Dickens was not Marx. Perhaps he was Kafka, who admired and emulated him. *Little Dorrit* is remarkable for its central woman figure, too individualized to be mythical, more creative than Esther, not a love-object for the author and arguably the most imaginative character Dickens imagined. She is matched with a time-worn melancholy lover in Arthur Clennam, with whom at the end she goes back down into the city streets and uproar, without the consoling faith or hope that transforms the symbolism and simplifies the politics of *Bleak House*. Amy Dorrit is Dickens's strongest woman but neither romantic nor romantically empowered: the novel given her maiden name for a title has no closure and her happy marriage is no social metonymy.

Dickens's marriage had been under a strain for some time – from the first month, if we believe what he wrote to Angela Burdett-Coutts (*Letters* 7, 632). In the late 1850s an occasional feeling of restlessness, variously explained, grew more disturbing, while the old unhappy feeling associated with Copperfield's sense of 'disparity' in his marriage became habitual, as Forster notes in a chapter of his biography reticently entitled 'What Happened At This Time'. Dickens most unfairly complains to Angela Burdett-Coutts that Charles has inherited his mother's inertia (*Letters* 7, 245). And then he falls in love.

He had always thrown himself into private and semi-public theatricals for good causes, and when professionals had to take parts first played by his daughters, for a public production of Wilkie Collins's *The Frozen Deep* (1857), he met the 18-year-old actress Ellen Ternan, and not long after partitioned off the marital bedroom, moved into his dressing-room and began thinking about a separation from his wife. He was 45. Furious at gossip about his relations with Ellen and with his sister-in-law Georgina Hogarth – who lived with them and helped with the children and housekeeping – he decided Catherine should move to a house near Camden Town, with Charles as companion and an allowance of £600 a year. The break-up of their marriage was made unpleasantly public when Dickens published a defensive letter in *The Times* and *Household Words*, a good example of accusing by excusing. There was a breach with his friend Mark Lemon, and with Bradbury and Evans for refusing to publish his letter in *Punch*, the end of *Household Words* and the beginning of *All the Year Round*.

At first he spoke tolerantly of Catherine and their incompatibility but when gossip spread he held her family responsible and became implacably hostile, telling Angela Burdett-Coutts, who tried to intercede, that Catherine was an uncaring mother, and sending his manager Arthur Smith an aggressive and self-righteous letter about her faults, which was published – according to Dickens 'violated' without his knowledge – in the *New York Tribune* and other papers.

There were ten children: baby Dora died in 1851 and Walter in 1863, serving in India; Charles went to Eton, studied in Germany for a business career, and despite his father's disparagement of his lack of ambition, joined *All The Year Round* and took on its editorship after Dickens's death; Mary or Mamey was the home daughter, housekeeping with her aunt Georgina and having an active social life; Kate married Charles Collins, then Carlo Perugini, and was like them both an artist; Francis joined the Canadian Mounted Police; Alfred emigrated to Australia and in later years lectured on his father; Henry, the only graduate, became a judge; Edward or Plorn was briefly an MP in Australia and then a rabbit inspector; Sydney was in the navy and died at sea. Dickens seems to have been more affectionate to daughters than sons, at his best when the children were young and fun to play with. Long after his death Kate told Gladys Storey that her father did not 'give a damn' about the children when the marriage ended, and that he was a wicked man – she may have been thinking of his rejection and accusation of her mother rather than his infidelity.

It was an infidelity of which there is no proof, though we know Dickens bought property for Ellen, visited her in England and France, told some friends and relatives about her and referred to her in letters to his co-editor and friend W. H. Wills during the last tour in 1869 to America as his 'Darling' and 'the patient' – affectionately nicknamed after her arm was hurt in a Staplehurst train accident, in June 1865, travelling with Dickens and her mother. Dickens suffered lasting nervous effects from the crash, in which he threw himself into efforts to help distressed and injured fellow-passengers.

Critics have tried to find images of Ellen in the novels, in disdainful or cold heroines like Bella and Estella, and echoes of her name in Bella, Estella and Helena Landless, but similarly named Little Nell and haughty Edith Dombey precede Ellen. There is a tender, barely-veiled and erotic allusion to her in *The Lazy Tour of Two Idle Apprentices* (serialized in *Household Words*, 1857) and co-written when he and Wilkie Collins took a trip north because Ellen was acting in Doncaster during Races Week. In an odd medley of arch detail, like 'little lilac gloves' and 'winning little bonnet', with ecstatic images from the *Arabian Nights* and the St Leger, the rhapsodical Francis Goodchild (Dickens) dreams of a timeless moment which suspends the running horses and the sands of time in 'everlasting autumn-sunshine' and in the company of an 'unknown' golden-haired 'Angel' (Chapter the Fifth, *Journalism* 3). Another *Household Words* piece, 'Please to Leave Your Umbrella', about a visit to Hampton Court, contains another coy coding, the 'little reason' for the narrator's good humour, with 'whom' he shared his umbrella and wishes were with him as he writes (*Journalism* 3). He wrote to his friend Wills about a 'little riddle'. Dickens could not resist such thinly disguised indiscreet hints in these early days. Amy Dorrit is a quietist creation, not at all erotic; a thoughtful girl wearing her old prison dress to visit her love, she is much younger than the middle-aged man who calls her 'Little'; it is like a premonition of the love affair that was to come, no doubt because in it Dickens obliquely expressed his melancholy, desires and need.

A schematic critic might ask how Dickens could follow the muted realism of *Little Dorrit*: he did so by writing a novel about another country and another time, *A Tale of Two Cities* (1859). It teeters at times on the verge of costume drama, its 'translated' French is stiff and strained, its lovers are a stereotyped romantic pair, though Lucie has a few individual traits and Sidney Carton is interestingly nonchalant as he sees the better and follows the worst, though his love and heroism are highly romanticized. The crowd scenes of suffering and violence are good, knitting was never the same after Madame Defarge, and the storming of the Bastille is a new historical and symbolic variation on the prison image. A striking linguistic feature is a conspicuous pattern of poetry, which runs through the novel and intensifies crisis, for instance in the strange secret murder of the callous Marquis, the narrative of 'the mender of roads', and the great formal inset of Manette's Bastille letter.

Next, Dickens turned back to autobiographical form – the form of *Copperfield*, which he re-read to avoid repetition. Pip of *Great Expectations* (1860–1) is wounded like David, by a bad mother-figure – his sister who brings him up by hand and sticks needles on her bosom and in her bread – and by Estella who mocks him into class-shame. He is wounded but healed by the illiterate loving blacksmith Joe who focuses his shame, and by the convict Magwitch for whom he steals, accruing fresh guilt. The gratitude of Magwitch becomes a burden and new shame but in the end Pip is able to give him the pity and love he expects and deserves. Pip's career has to be ordinary so like Jane Eyre or Esther Summerfield he is a first-person narrator with no literary profession but is made imaginative enough to tell his tale. Joe and Magwitch are two of Dickens's best virtuous people, Jaggers and Wemmick as close to virtue as Dickensian lawyers can be, the malignant Orlick motivated enough not to be quite motiveless, Miss Havisham a disturbingly particularized grotesque, and Estella a heroine who could have figured without flourish in the unhappy ending Dickens intended and who is convincing in the quiet happy ending Bulwer Lytton persuaded him to adopt. Like *Dorrit* and unlike the other books, *Great Expectations* sounds no sentimental or melodramatic false notes, but is harmonious, like its poetic blacksmith.

Our Mutual Friend (1864–5) is like the Condition of England novels in theme, form and symbolism, its metonymy the dustheap, its subject the cash nexus, its landscape the traffic, tides, locks, bridges, pollution, danger and beauty of the Thames. The satire of the Veneerings, the new rich, uses the rigidity and animation of objects which always fascinated Dickens but with a new anthropology of the conspicuous consumption he may have learnt to scrutinize and symbolize more sharply from the example of Thackeray. The novel's poetry has strong rhythms and repetitions like *A Tale of Two Cities*, in even more ritualized and sustained patterns, again locally assertive and self-aware. There is the old insistence on domestic bliss, and a weak hero in Rokesmith, who is given an important long narrative retrospect which is awkwardly placed and barely motivated, and his courtship and marriage with Bella are disappointingly conventional. Bella's aggression, her assumption of mercenariness and her change of heart, helped by Boffin's impersonation of a hard-hearted miser – about which critical opinion is divided – are new and fascinating but Bella's disclosure of her pregnancy is incredibly arch and she dwindles into 'the doll in the doll's house' she so wanted not to be. The story of Lizzie Hexam and the languid gentleman Wrayburn is more thoughtfully done, and treats problems of sex and class with conviction and originality. The strange young–old dolls' dressmaker Jenny Wren is the most radiantly creative and harshly human of Dickens's children.

Dickens's late years were spent on strenuous reading tours, one in America and others in England, one in 1868–9 which his doctors stopped, the last in 1870. His last novel, *The Mystery of Edwin Drood* (1870), written in ill-health and much possessed with death and the grave, was interrupted halfway through by the death of its author. If it was overpraised by Forster who said it showed Dickens's power at its best, it is new in its concentration and plain style. The writing is sparer than usual, the timescale contracted and the locations confined to a few places in Cloisterham (Rochester) and London. There is no central figure except John Jasper and almost every character has – or would have had – a part in the story of crime and punishment, with the probable exception of the London landlady Mrs Billikin, one of several exuberant comic characters like Miss Twinkleton and the self-important husband Sapsea. The odd and unusual thing about *Edwin Drood* is that it is makes no large central critique of society: there is good incidental satire in the philanthropist Honeythunder, but Dickens's habitual compassion and anger are absent, dropped in fatigue, disillusion or new experiment. He left a fair amount of information about his intentions – fascinatingly ignored by enthusiastic inventors of new endings, not to mention new plots. John Jasper, leading a double life, was destined to end in a condemned cell telling a formal life-story like that of Miss Wade or Manette, but strangely detaching himself from his acts, as if they were not his, with 'temptations … to be dwelt upon as if, not he the culprit, but some other man, were the tempted' (Forster Bk. 11, Ch. 2). If we remember the murderer Jonas Chuzzlewit, unmanned by guilty dissociation, expecting to see himself in his bed, and fearful of himself, we get some idea of what we missed. The mystery is cleverly plotted, the disappearance of Drood prepared with an intricately laid trail, graveyard setting, false suspect, disguised professional detective, decrepit amateur spy, Shakespearean chorus of drunken sexton and Deputy the wild devil-boy hired to stone him, clues like a gold watch and chain, a ring and a heap of quick-lime. Rosa Bud and Edwin Drood are enlivened by their interestingly developed discovery that they are not in love, supplying motive for a murder which turns out to be unnecessary – ironies of timing are subtle. The good lawyer Grewgious is one of those Dickensian eccentrics who grows into a subtle and changing character, and Durdles the sexton is a comic in a morbid setting, and with a vital role. The artist Luke Fildes did some strong suggestive illustrations, in which Princess Puffer and her opium den are more erotic than the text suggests.

Described as a sad man by Annie Fields, the wife of his American publisher, Dickens clearly suffered – as of course Ellen must have done too – from the clandestine and illicit relationship, whatever its nature. But his last years were lightened by hospitality and sociability at Gad's Hill, his country house on the Dover road between Rochester and Gravesend, which he dreamed of possessing when he was a boy, and he died there in the country of his boyhood. Georgina was the last member of the family to speak to him before he collapsed at dinner after a working day. (A plausible report that he collapsed while with Ellen Ternan at Peckham and was taken unconscious or dead to Gad's Hill has prompted Claire Tomalin to construct a conjectural scenario: see her 'Postscript' to *The Invisible Woman*, 1991.)

His grave is in Westminster Abbey though he had wanted to be buried in Rochester or Cobham, but that proved impossible; he had the unostentatious funeral he wanted. He left a sizeable fortune, some ungracious words in his will about Catherine's allowance and his expenses, a mixed reputation as a man, and fame rivalling Shakespeare's.

When he was at the height of his powers, in 1855, Dickens wrote to his old love Maria Beadnell, now Mrs Henry Winter, in a defensive explanation of an artist's protection of time and privacy:

> I hold my inventive capacity on the stern condition that it must master my whole life, often have complete possession of me, make its own demands upon me, and, sometimes for months together, put everything else away from me. If I had not known long ago that my place could never be held, unless I were at any moment ready to devote myself to it entirely, I should have dropped out of it very soon. All this, I can hardly expect you to understand – or the restlessness and waywardness of an author's mind ... Whoever is devoted to an Art must be content to deliver himself wholly up, and to find his recompense in it. (*Letters* 7, 583–4)

But this is only part of the truth about his career. He was an exceptionally wide-ranging and energetic worker, with more than a devotion to art, with several careers. He was not only a novelist but a man of the theatre, directing, acting, and inventing his own performance-art in the readings which allowed him to act out prose fiction. He never stopped being a reporter, piercingly observant, joining investigative journalism with personally felt and meditative essays, as well as becoming an editor and publisher. Egoist and altruist, from deep personal need and thoughtful human sympathy, he was an earnest social reformer who used his brilliance as novelist, journalist, editor and public speaker, to show the motive and need for progress, to lay a tender hand, as he said, on his hard times. He was consistent and honourable in his distaste for patronage and conventional honours, a public man but never a political man. He came to despair of political means and institutions, though now and then he turned pragmatically to use them. He began and ended as someone who cared about suffering and wanted to raise public consciousness and change society, at least the part of it he knew and could touch. He would interest us much less if he had not been a very great artist but the novelist's art was never enough for his teeming imagination and energy.

Chapter 2

Dickens Discusses Creativity

The critic and biographer John Forster, one of Dickens's closest friends, remembers the time when Dickens was still working on *Pickwick Papers* and becoming engrossed in *Oliver Twist*:

> ... it was delightful to see how real all its people became to him. What I had indeed to notice in him at the very outset of his career, was his indifference to any praise of his performances on the merely literary side, compared with the higher recognition of them as bits of actual life, with the meaning and purpose on their part, and the responsibility on his, of realities rather than creatures of fancy. (Forster, Bk 2, Ch. 1)

Dickens often insisted – and sometimes wove the insistence into the fabric of his fiction – that he was concerned with truth to life, not 'the literary side', and his comments on other arts like painting, and a minor art to which we might expect an interesting response from him, that of pantomime, are aesthetically and intellectually disappointing. From time to time, however, he writes spontaneously as an artist fascinated by his personal experiences of artistic creativity, perhaps the more strikingly because of a naive fresh wondering strain in the contemplation of his own imaginative processes.

He writes about them in an entirely personal way, usually in letters to close friends like Forster and in later years Mrs Richard Watson, and sometimes in correspondence with contributors to his weekly periodicals *Household Words* or *All the Year Round*, but in his early days when he wrote to Catherine Hogarth during their engagement. As far as I know, the first mention of his imaginative life comes in a letter to her, and the discussion or explanation is both an intimate confidence and evidence of their obvious difference in experience. In this letter he insists – and refers to other occasions when he has insisted – on his special need to devote time and energy to writing even if it means forgoing her company. He sets before her the experience of creative urgency, writing excitedly about day-and-night professional pressures and an inner state of compelling inspiration:

> As I have frequently told you ... my composition is peculiar; I can
> never write with effect – especially in the serious mode – until I have
> got my steam up, or in other words until I have become so excited with
> my subject that I cannot leave off ... (*Letters* I, 97)

He writes best in an inspired and exalted state which he must submit to
without rest or interruption, and he emphasizes concentration, absorption and the feeling of being taken out of himself in a demanding
imaginative activity he cannot totally control or predict and must pre-
serve at all cost. The explanation is personal and informal in style but
seriously relevant to the start of his career, and he is aware of genre and
technique – 'my serious mode' – as well as creative excitement.

Once or twice he writes to Catherine about particular pieces of writing, for instance telling her that he hopes to get into his creative 'state'
with a piece on Newgate, one of the best early sketches, and on another
occasion, which I shall come back to in more detail, mentioning his
'extraordinary' idea for 'The Black Veil', a story written specially for the
collected *Sketches by Boz*. These are two good pieces that stand out among
more run-of-the-mill social observations. When Catherine was dying she
asked for his letters to her to be given to the British Museum so that the
world, which had read his public and biased account of their separation
in 1858, would know that he loved her once. He had denied that they
ever had any common interests but she was the recipient of these intense
confidences about the habits and urges of an artist.

The 'peculiar' process he describes so simply and unsophisticatedly is
an imaginative abandonment to the unconscious mind, the suppression
of intellect and rational will, the self-generative composition described
empirically by artists before – and after – Freud and later psychologists
elaborated the concept of the unconscious. (Dickens uses the word
'unconscious'.) He is clearly articulating the same experience as he starts
on each new novel, but at different times he refers to different physical
and psychological particulars, like the various inspirations he found in
walking, night, meditation, solitude, water, and crowded city streets.

A mention of the capacity to absorb himself in creative experience
comes in a letter about *Barnaby Rudge* at a time when he was suffering
from two separate causes of distress, one physical, a painful fistula
operation, and the other emotional, the decision to give up his intention
to be buried next to his sister-in-law Mary Hogarth. He writes to Forster,
as he did to Catherine, feeling free to admit his sense of being a special
case but on this occasion with an astonishing detachment as he recognizes the compulsions of art, during a suffering which bore:

... a terrible, frightful, horrible proportion to the quickness of the gifts you remind me of. But may I not be forgiven for thinking it a wonderful testimony to my being made for my art, that when, in the midst of this trouble and pain, I sit down to my book, some beneficent power shows it all to me, & tempts me to be interested, & I don't invent it – really do not – *but see it*, and write it down ... (*Letters* 2, 411)

As in the letters to Catherine, the sense of being surprised by self is itself a striking testimony to the experience of artistic compulsion, the submission to what he feels as an external power, an irresistible and involuntary inspiration, evoking wonder.

The experience is discussed in George Henry Lewes's article 'Dickens in Relation to Criticism' (*Fortnightly Review*, Feb. 1872) where he speaks of Dickens's 'hallucinatory powers', saying Dickens told him that he heard his fictional characters distinctly speaking. Forster disliked Lewes's word 'hallucinatory', cites Scott, claims that all writers of genius to whom their art has become second nature may experience what the 'vulgar' call hallucination, but denies that hallucination can account for it (*Letters* 2, 411 n.). Lewes and George Eliot were good friends with Dickens, and he visited them shortly before he died, but Lewes was a sophisticated psychologist and critic genuinely amazed by Dickens's combination of genius with an intellectual lack of reflective capacity and historical interest – and tacitly comparing his mind with the psychological imagination and large culture of George Eliot. Forster was understandably touchy and jealous, also no doubt because Lewes did not mention the first volume of Forster's biography of Dickens, just published. Forster attacked Lewes strongly in his third volume.[1]

In fact Dickens anticipates what George Eliot – whom Lewes had not met when he first met Dickens and they talked about creative experience, and whom Dickens was not to meet for almost 20 years – was to say about her creative process. The experience of relaxing cognition was described by her intimate friend Herbert Spencer who had discussed with her the unconscious element in his own psychological and sociological problem solving (*Autobiography*, pp. 399–401). Her sense of 'a "not herself" which took possession of her', of feeling 'her own personality [as] merely the instrument through which this spirit, as it were, was acting', was recorded by her husband, John Cross (*George Eliot's Life*, vol. 3, pp. 424–5). She described how the idea for her first story and its title, 'The Sad Fortunes of Amos Barton', came while she was lying in bed in a state of relaxed consciousness, as her 'thoughts merged themselves in a dreamy doze' (G. S. Haight, *George Eliot. A Life*, p. 206).

She would of course have talked to Lewes about this and other aspects of creativity but unlike Spencer he did not write his own life-story and unlike Cross did not write hers. Like Dickens, she reports hearing characters talk, telling her publisher John Blackwood that a 'weight upon her mind' when writing *Romola* was a feeling that 'Savonarola and his friends ought to be speaking Italian instead of English' (Haight, 349). For the crucial dialogue of Rosamond and Dorothea in *Middlemarch,* she waited to hear the voices, deliberately not planning ahead and leaving the scene to unpremeditated composition. Dickens and George Eliot both use the image of 'simmering' to suggest a relaxed unhurried unforced process: Dickens speaks of 'simmering' ... 'over a slow fire'. (*Letters* 4, 577) and when writing *Daniel Deronda* George Eliot tells Blackwood that she is 'simmering towards another Big book' (*George Eliot Letters* 5, 454). The tautology in Dickens's slow fire may reflect his interest in food as consumer, whereas George Eliot knew how to cook. He used another cooking image when he said 'I come home stewing "Little Dorrit" in my head' (*Letters* 8, 12).

In a letter to Forster about development of characters in *Martin Chuzzlewit,* Dickens enlarges on his sense of unconscious process:

> As to the way in which these characters have opened out, that is, to me, one of the most surprising processes of the mind in this sort of invention. Given what one knows, what one does not know springs up; and I am as absolutely certain of its being true, as I am of the law of gravitation – if such a thing be possible, more so. (*Letters* 3, 441)

The characters are unnamed but described by Forster as 'the most prominent' in the novel, and may be Jonas Chuzzlewit and Mrs Gamp as Forster implies or Pecksniff and Tom Pinch as the Pilgrim editors suggest: all these characters open out and develop in interrelationships, and the important thing is the author's awareness and articulation of dynamic development. Again, Dickens is surprised by the way his own imagination works: there are other similar examples. For instance, he became aware of his habit of falling into iambic pentameters in his prose and mentions it as an unconscious process (*Letters* 4, 114), and in a later letter about his story 'The Battle of Life' he says he falls into blank verse when in 'earnest', a comment echoing the remark to Catherine about feeling creative excitement when in his serious mode (*Letters* 4, 114).

There is no philosophical or cultural reference of the kind we find in the better-read Thackeray or George Eliot, and the nearest approach to critical generalization occurs when he is giving editorial advice to other writers and alludes to his own experience. Rejecting a story by R. H. Mason submitted to *All the Year Round,* he criticizes what he thinks a willed over-explicit treatment of characters:

> ... it is not enough to say [of characters] that they were this, or that. They must shew it for themselves, and have it in their grain. Then, they would act on one another, and would act for themselves whether the author liked it or no. As it is, there is not enough reason for you writing about them, because they do nothing and work out nothing. (*Letters* 6, 87)

There is a similar reference in friendly advice to Jane Brookfield about her novel *Only George* in which the critical editor found more telling than showing:

> ... you constantly hurry your narrative (and yet without getting on) by telling it, in a sort of impetuous breathless way in your own person when the people should tell it and act it for themselves. My notion always is, that when I have made the people to play out the play, it is, as it were, their business to do it, and not mine. (*Letters* 11, 160)

Jane Brookfield was an intimate friend of Thackeray, and a fascinating bonus in this letter is Dickens's unconscious or deliberate echo of the words that end *Vanity Fair,* 'for our play is played out'.

Dickens makes similar objections to conspicuous and over-deliberated art in the novels of his friend and collaborator Wilkie Collins, admired by modern critics for his sophisticated elaborations and variations of narrator. Discussing *The Woman in White*, he criticizes Collins's 'disposition to give an audience credit for nothing – which necessarily involves the forcing of points on their attention', admits he finds it hard to suggest an editorial cut because the habit seems to belong so integrally to Collins's 'habits of thought and manner of going to work', but invokes his own very different method:

> ... the three people who write the narratives in these proofs, have a DISSECTIVE property in common, which is essentially not theirs but yours; and ... my own effort would be to strike more of what is got, *that way*, from them by collision with one another, and by the working of the story. (*Letters* 9, 194–5)

But when at a later point he thinks about collaborating with Collins he unselfconsciously emphasizes his own submission to the creative unconscious: 'I have very odd half-formed notions' ... 'in a mist' ... 'of something that might be done that way' (*Letters* 9, 195). When he read Collins's *The Moonstone* he made similar criticisms of what he found intrusively self-conscious art.

In another letter to Forster about *Barnaby Rudge* he explains a vivid physical simile put in the mouth of the minor character Solomon Daisy to express his sensitive response to the Gordon rioters: 'It came upon me with a kind of shock, as if a hand had struck the thought upon my forehead.' Forster probably objected to the brilliant explanatory image as more characteristic of the novelist than of simple Daisy because Dickens writes defensively: 'Solomon's expression I meant to be one of those strong ones to which strong circumstances give birth in the commonest minds' but he told Forster to 'Deal with it as you like' and Forster left it (*Letters* 2, 411). In spite of 'the commonest minds', Dickens is probably drawing on his own affective experience in expressing Daisy's shock by the catachresis of two clashing body images, forehead literal and hand metaphorical, but the interest lies in his awareness of an image correlative – and his willingness to discard it.

He repeats the sudden inspiration for an ordinary mind, and in another strong metaphor, when he makes Joe Gargery a poet, at least on one occasion: 'Whatsume'er the failings on his part, Remember reader he were that good in his heart.' Joe looks on his creation and finds it good: 'I made it ... my own self. I made it in a moment. It was like striking out a horseshoe complete, in a single blow.' If Dickens is having fun at Joe's expense at least he lets his character share his own serious pleasure and wonder in making: 'I never was so much surprised in my life – couldn't credit my own ed – to tell you the truth, hardly believed it *were* my own ed' (*GE*, Ch. 7).

In Genoa, Dickens complained of finding it hard to write, because he is on holiday but also because he is feeling the 'absence of streets and numbers of figures':

> I can't express how much I want these. It seems as if they supplied something to my brain, which it cannot bear, when busy, to lose ... a day in London sets me up again and starts me. But the toil of writing, without that magic lantern, is IMMENSE! ... My figures seem disposed to stagnate without crowds about them. (*Letters* 4, 612–13)

In his Leslie Stephen Lecture, 'The Name and Nature of Poetry', as I mentioned in the Preface, A. E. Housman told a learned Cambridge audience how inspiration would come after a sedative pint of beer with lunch and a long relaxed solitary meditative afternoon walk. In the first sentence of *Death in Venice*, Thomas Mann's artist Gustav Aschenbach sets out for a long solitary walk, exhausted and over-stimulated because 'the productive mechanism in his mind, – that *motus animi continuus* which according to Cicero is the height of eloquence – had so pursued its reverberating rhythm that he had been unable to halt it even after lunch, and had missed the refreshing daily siesta ... And so ... had left the house hoping that fresh air and movement would set him to rights'.

The inspiration of walking is often mentioned by Dickens, usually associated with the city streets and crowds. Sometimes he stresses his need for night-time, as in one of the 'Uncommercial Traveller' articles, 'Night Walks', where he describes in great detail the therapeutic effect of merging his restlessness with the restlessness of city streets, when 'a temporary inability to sleep, referable to a distressing impression, caused me to walk about the streets at night, for a series of several nights'. It is a full creative episode:

> In the course of those nights, I finished my education in a fair amateur experience of houselessness. My principal object being to get through the night, the pursuit of it brought me into sympathetic relations with people who have no other object every night in the year ...
>
> The restlessness of a great city, and the way in which it tumbles and tosses before it can get to sleep, formed one of the first entertainments offered to the contemplation of a houseless people. (*Journalism* 4)

The Traveller, the frame-narrator closest to the author in experience, voice and affect, is not referring directly to creative work but he makes an explicit link between personal need and empathy, demonstrating it with great energy. The identification of his restlessness and his 'amateur' houselessness with the unrest and real homelessness of city outcasts is dramatized: the personal 'I' becomes the collective 'We'; the first lower-case 'houselessness' is poetically transformed by sympathetic irony to the companionable 'Houselessness'; the adjective 'houseless' is elaborated in moving metonymies. The key words are ritualistically repeated in the compassionate scenes that unfold: the 'fits and starts' of late drunks, police and cabs in the Haymarket and East End give way to a stillness in which 'the yearning of the houseless mind would be for any sign of company' and 'the houseless eye looked out for lights in windows', there is 'a furtive head' in a doorway, a 'houseless shadow' on the road to Waterloo bridge, a cheerful tollkeeper, and the suicide-haunted river, on which 'the very shadow of the immensity of London seemed to lie oppressively'. The description that follows is a conflation of several night-walks, when the Traveller observes outcasts of the past and present: he moves with topographical exactitude from one of the 'great deserts' of theatre-land, where the Traveller feels 'much as a diver might, at the bottom of the sea', through Newgate prison and Debtor's Door. There the wanderer imagines 'hundreds of wretched creatures ... mercilessly swung out of a pitiless and inconsistent world, with the tower of yonder Christian church of Saint Sepulchre monstrously before their eyes'. Then he modulates from a morbid, comic and technically informed meditation on Dry Rot to one of his most imaginative speculations about the mind:

> From the dead wall associated on those houseless nights with this too common story [of the criminal Horace Kinch], I chose next to wander by Bethlehem Hospital; partly, because it lay on my road back to Westminster; partly, because I had a night-fancy in my head which could be best pursued within sight of its walls and dome. And the fancy was this: Are not the sane and the insane equal at night as the sane lie a dreaming? (*Journalism* 4)

In a later passage the Traveller is strangely moved to contemplate the vast population of the dead, like Dickens's admirer James Joyce, who put the same bizarre thought into the head of another city wanderer, Leopold Bloom, in *Ulysses*. It is a startling and bizarre example of the way Dickens's imagination was stirred in well-known places made unfamiliar by night:

> in those houseless night walks – which even included cemeteries where the watchmen went round among the graves ... it was a solemn consideration what enormous hosts of dead belong to one old great city, and how, if they were raised while the living slept, there would not be the space of a pin's point ... for the living to come out into. Not only that, but the vast armies of the dead would overflow the hills and valleys beyond the city ...

In a letter about *Little Dorrit* to his friend Mrs Watson, he writes creatively about his writing and walking moods, excitedly imaging this habitual restlessness and need for solitude, both mentioned during reading tours and theatrical trips as well as times of concentrated composition. Here

he is less surprised than amused at finding a familiar experience so hard
to fathom, and once again there is more going on than walking:

> You know my state of mind, as well as I do ... How I work, how I walk,
> how I shut myself up, how I roll down hills and climb up cliffs, how the
> new story is everywhere – heaving in the sea, flying with the clouds,
> blowing in the wind – how I settle to nothing, and wonder (in the old
> way) at my own incomprehensibility. (*Letters* 7, 703–4)

Sometimes the restless feeling and need for wandering show a mind
trembling uncertainly on the brink of apprehension, in insight and
language reminiscent of William James's account of attempting to
retrieve memory or thought, what Joyce brilliantly calls 'almosting'.
Dickens writes, 'This is one of what I call my Wandering days, before I
fall to work. I seem to be always looking at such times for something I
have not found in life, but may possibly come to, a few thousands of
years hence, in some other part of some other system' (*Letters* 6, 721).
This feeling is related to the old unhappy unrest of Copperfield, and
hints at domestic discontents but it also records subtle apprehensions of
the creative mind.

There are other passing recognitions of the unforeseen and
impromptu element in creativity: 'Just after I had sent the Messenger off
to you yesterday concerning the toll-taker memoranda, the other idea
came into my head – and, in the most obliging manner, came out of it'
(*Letters* 6, 835); and when meditating *Little Dorrit*: 'I am in the first stage
of a new book which consists in going round and round the idea, as you
see a bird in his cage go about and about his sugar before he touches it'
(*Letters* 7, 571–2). He also wrote about the Dorrits, 'I am not quite
resolved but I have an idea of overwhelming that family with wealth.
Their condition would be very curious' (*Letters* 7, 701). He wrote to his
old friend the actor Charles Macready in terms recalling the early
account of creative absorption to Catherine: he can only manage a short
letter because his new serial *Great Expectations* starts on 1 December:
'When I have done my day's work, I rush into the air and take fierce
exercise; the pen once laid down, – is leaden and not feathery – to take
up again that day' (*Letters* 9, 327).

But not all Dickens's creative moods were restless. One of the
Uncommercial Traveller's most relaxed reminiscences, 'Chatham
Dockyard', begins with a meditation on tranquillity:

There are some small out-of-the-way landing-places on the Thames
and the ... Medway, where I do much of my summer idling. Running
water is favourable to day-dreams, and a strong tidal river is the best of
running water for mine. I like to watch the great ships standing out to
sea or coming home richly laden, the active little steam-tugs ... the
fleet of barges that seem to have plucked their brown and russet sails
from the ripe trees ... the heavy old colliers ... the light screw barks
and schooners ... Watching these objects, I still am under no obligation to think about them, or even so much as to see them, unless it
perfectly suits my humour. As little am I obliged to hear the plash and
flop of the tide, the ripple at my feet, the clinking windless afar off, or
the humming steam-ship paddles ... (*Journalism* 4)

This is detachment, movement and harmony. As on other occasions, he
begins by locating or generalizing an initial inspiration to compound the
sense of beginning. He locates the seat of inspiration in the running
water, and his sensuous vivid reflections flow on dreamily, given order by
sets of imagery: the river sounds of splash, flop, ripple, clinking and
humming are succeeded later in the passage by riverside shapes, jetty
and tidemarks in mud, and the region's animals, sheep, cattle, gulls,
crows and a heron. Then he sums up, not definitively but dreamily:

Everything within the range of the senses will, by the aid of the running water, lend itself to everything beyond that range, and work into
a drowsy whole, not unlike a kind of tune, but for which there is no
exact definition.

The introductory set piece ends as it began with a general reflection,
describing a unifying and harmonizing urge, felt in a state of relaxed
consciousness. The conclusion is both analysis and illustration, and its
pleasant vagueness – 'not unlike a kind of tune' and 'no exact definition'
– typically modest, almost naive but precise enough. Here is the close
observer of outer scene and inner life.

Another attractive discussion and example of creative preliminary,
with a very different subject, presents an idea which was never realized.
He is meditating a theme for the weekly magazine which replaced
Household Words and was about to become *All the Year Round*, toying with
the idea of a dominant narrator and a title for the paper in which most
contributions were to be anonymous, virtually collaborative, editorially
influenced or controlled. He is in the preliminary state in which ideas
are 'floating' though they seem to be 'settling down into orderly

arrangement'. He is afraid of sounding foolish but willing to try out the
chaotic images on Forster:

> I do a great injustice to my floating ideas (pretty speedily and com-
> fortably settling down into orderly arrangement) by saying anything
> about the periodical now ...
>
> Now to bind all this together [poetry, original and selected matter],
> and to get a character established as it were which any of the writers
> may maintain without difficulty, I want to suppose a certain SHADOW
> ... a kind of semi-omniscient, omnipresent, intangible creature ...
> cheerful, useful, and always welcome ... I want him to loom as a fan-
> ciful thing ... I think the importance of the idea is, that once stated on
> paper, there is no difficulty in keeping it up. That it presents an odd,
> unsubstantial, whimsical, new thing: a sort of previously unthought-of
> Power going about. That it will concentrate into one focus all that is
> done in the paper ... just mysterious and quaint enough to have a sort
> of charm for their [people's] imagination, while it will represent
> common-sense and humanity. I want to express ... that it is the Thing
> at everybody's elbow, and in everybody's footsteps ... everyone's
> inseparable companion ... Now do you make anything out of this?
> which I let off as if I were a bladder full of it, and you had punctured
> me ... I have a lively hope that it *is* an idea ...' (*Letters* 6, 621–3)

Floating ideas float an idea of fancy – the fanciful thing – of mystery,
elusiveness and Power, (a shadow related to shadow images in the
novels, images of imagination in *Little Dorrit* and *A Tale of Two Cities*) and
the meditation also revives his 'beneficent Power' in the letter to Forster
about forgetting physical and emotional pain in the excitement of
writing (*Letters* 2, 411). It is a good example of Dickens projecting an
Other – friend, judge, critical super-ego. The 'bladder full of it' which
could be 'punctured' combines a sense of plenitude with fear but he
clings to a hope, 'that it *is* an idea'. Forster apparently rejected the
shadow but the first number of *All the Year Round* speaks of a 'light of
Fancy' so the Shadow was a creative shadow which presided over the
venture. Such ambivalence was preliminary and productive, part fiat,
part hypothesis to be proved or disproved by the creative method.
Dickens's preliminaries would often be changed, revised and erased
before an end was reached: they were necessary beginnings that were just
beginnings, because you must start somewhere, before you make
another start, let alone an end.

He wrote to Forster about the beginning of *Great Expectations*:

For a little piece I have been writing – or am writing; for I hope to finish it today – such a very fine, new, and grotesque idea has opened upon me, that I begin to doubt whether I had not better cancel the little paper, and reserve the notion for a new book ... it so opens out before *me* that I can see the whole of a serial revolving on it, in a most singular and comic manner. (*Letters* 9, 310)

The little paper was obviously cancelled and he went on to plan in more detail first a 20-number novel then a weekly serial when Charles Lever's *A Day's Ride* was so unpopular that sales of *All the Year Round* fell off. Dickens wrote to Forster and to Lever about the need 'to shape the story for these pages' (*Letters* 9,19; 321) and later told Forster 'I have made the opening. I hope, in its general effect exceedingly droll' and later speaks of bringing together 'a child and a good-natured foolish man' and 'in relations that seem to me very funny' (*Letters* 9, 325). The child grew to man's estate, the good-natured man turned out less foolish, actually not foolish at all, the social and psychological relations of man and boy much more than funny, and the novel grew new and unforeseen relationships, with many other characters. Out of a little that he knew at the start, grew a complex novel.

The process described pragmatically through particulars of story and character was grasped and finely generalized by Bulwer Lytton – a much better critic than he was a novelist, and like Lewes aware that Dickens was 'no metaphysician' – when he wrote about Dickens in his journal: 'he takes care of his own fame refreshing it if it seems to fade'; 'He understands the practical side of authorship beyond any author'; and 'He ... detects oddities and out of them invents original creations ...' (*Letters* 12, 718 n.).

Matisse said if your picture wasn't working, you should take out the bits that did work. Dickens wrote to George Craik with advice for his daughter who had literary ambitions and became a writer: 'Patience, attention, seclusion, consideration, courage to reject what comes uppermost and to try for something better below it – these are the stones *I* have found in the road, and have learnt to pave the road with' (*Letters* 6, 689).

Notes

1 See Rosemary Ashton, *G. H. Lewes. A Life*, Oxford: OUP, 1991.

Chapter 3

The Awareness of Art in *Sketches By Boz, Pickwick Papers, Oliver Twist, Barnaby Rudge, The Old Curiosity Shop* and *The Chimes*

In stories and essays collected for *Sketches by Boz* (1836), reprinted pieces from *The Old Monthly Magazine, Morning Chronicle, Evening Chronicle,* and *Bell's Life in London,* with two tales written specially for the collection, the novelist moves from facetious short story to his individual documentary style in 'Scenes' and 'Characters' where observation of places and their inhabitants tends to generate some element of narrative. These sketches also show an early awareness, casual and intermittent but often striking, of the creative processes mentioned in his letters.

This awareness is usually that of the dominant narrator, as in 'The Parlour Orator', first published in December 1835. At the end of this sketch the narrator dismisses his characters, toys lightly with the possibility of deducing a different story from the inn where the scene was set, pauses on the brink of fantasy and then pulls back:

> If we had followed the established precedent in all such instances, we should have fallen into a fit of musing, without delay. The ancient appearance of the room – the old panelling of the wall – the chimney blackened with smoke and age – would have carried us back a hundred years at least, and we should have gone dreaming on, until the pewter pot on the table, or the little beer chiller on the fire, had started into life, and addressed to us a long story of days gone by. But, by some means or other, we were not in a romantic humour; and though we tried very hard to invest the furniture with vitality, it remained perfectly unmoved, obstinate, and sullen. Being thus reduced to the unpleasant necessity of musing about ordinary matters, our thoughts reverted to the red-faced man, and his oratorical display. (*Journalism* I, *SB*, Characters 5)

The *occupatio,* telling the kind of story he would have told if he had told

it, is a good non-committal form for the artist's dilemma: is the fault
inside or outside, in mood or materials? The rhetoric goes beyond a joke
as it draws attention to the observation of ordinary life which is the
expressed purpose of the *Sketches*. The writer is making a distinction
between styles and forms, and dramatizing the creative process itself,
starting, stopping and hypothesizing in the playful self-analyzing permutations and lapses of mimesis we associate with Joyce, Beckett and
Calvino, though here in unadventurous language and dealing with less
exciting subject matter.

The self-generated excitement with subject described to Catherine
and Forster was not 'peculiar' but it seemed so to the young self-
educated and not at all widely read journalist turning his powers of
observation on his own mind. Here the very lack of interesting subject
lays bare the reflexive structure, as the narrator sees his inventive capacity at work, and moves back to inspect and demonstrate. We see this self-
consciousness working on more interesting material for 'Meditations in
Monmouth Street'. The street was 'the only true and real emporium for
second hand wearing apparel' – its shops are smarter now but some still
specialize in antique fashion – and the narrator hits on the conceit of
deducing character and story from old clothes, as he tried to do with the
room and furniture in the old inn, but here in a more excited mood or
finding less obviously romantic material:

> We love to walk among these extensive groves of the illustrious dead,
> and to indulge in the speculations to which they give rise; now fitting a
> deceased coat, then a dead pair of trousers, and anon the mortal
> remains of a gaudy waistcoat, upon some being of our own conjuring
> up, and endeavouring, from the shape and fashion of the garment
> itself, to bring its former owner before our mind's eye. (*Journalism* I,
> *SB*)

The sketch makes up for lack of individual characters by the creative
personality of the writer, self-illustrative in ways unmistakably Dickensian: the exuberant narrator is fascinated by the still-life of the street
and proceeds to 'invest' it with 'vitality' and all the time watching his
animation develop. His discussion of fantasy is often wildly comic, as he
regards what he is imagining with a kind of detachment and the zany
touch he makes his own and shares with some great clowns:

> We have gone on speculating in this way, until whole rows of coats
> have started from their pegs, and buttoned up, of their own accord,

round the waists of imaginary wearers; lines of trousers have jumped
down to meet them; waistcoats have almost burst with anxiety to put
themselves on; and half an acre of shoes have suddenly found feet to
fit them, and gone stumping down the street with a noise which has
fairly awakened us from our pleasant reverie, and driven us slowly away
... (*Journalism* I, *SB*)

You can feel the verve and play as fantasy develops from mere statement
of creative habit, to action, satisfied conclusion and the final crazy
awakening from reverie because of the noise of his own creations. Its
self-consciousness is like Charlie Chaplin's, in setting up a delighted
complicity. In the personifications but explicit too – 'of their own
accord' – the narrator registers a knowing submission to the comic
powers.

Next comes a more sustained and lively narrative as the fantasist starts
off again by speaking vaguely of fitting boots 'on an ideal personage'
then letting the idea become dynamically conscious as he moves from
inspiration – a set of garments belonging to one man – to what he calls
'autobiography'. The story gets serious. There is a sense and style of
irresistible impetus but he cautiously considers calling the inspiration 'a
fantastic one', briefly reflects on the theme, uses a writing image to
imagine a 'man's whole life ... written legibly on those clothes' then lets
himself go. Light-hearted play becomes a coherent and sad story: a
lifetime's clothes, from blue tight boy's suit to convict's garments, con-
jure up child, mother, wife, children, degeneration, crime and death.
The comic clothes-play could not last and we see how he works himself
into the 'more serious mode' he mentioned to Catherine as he
explained his creative impetus and absorption. At the end there is a
hesitant, provisional hovering between alternatives, 'banishment or the
gallows', and the uncertainty makes a closure as the narrator returns
from tale to teller. As he moved from the comic animated shoes into the
tragic life-history – interesting in its own right – he moves back to
comedy, finding a cellarful of footware, fitting a jolly character into a
pair of boots and restoring his own 'naturally cheerful tone' for a comic
finale:

... to our unspeakable astonishment, we perceived that the whole of
the characters, including a numerous *corps de ballet* of boots and shoes
in the background, into which we had been hastily thrusting as many
feet as we could press into the service, were arranging themselves in
order for dancing ...

He is joking but also seriously astonished by the fantasy that has taken over: the entire action is self-generative and spontaneous creation and also wondering and understated self-analysis. It is not simply spontaneous: the self-awareness is intelligent and we sometimes see the narrator thinking twice, consciously making a reality-check before fancy takes flight. This early attempt to set fantasy in a context of reality is exotically repeated at the end of his career in the first paragraph of Edwin Drood when a dreamer becomes conscious that his fragmentary images are not real, but here Dickens nonchalantly traces real-life sources of the fantasy and authenticates them by place-names: 'This was the very man after our own heart; we knew all about him; we had seen him coming up to Covent Garden in his green chaise cart' ... and 'we ... recognised the very girl who accepted his offer of a ride, just on this side of Hammersmith suspension bridge'. It is self-delighting, like Joe Gargery or God on the seventh day, 'We had been looking on at this little pantomime with great satisfaction.' Serious subjects, delicately treated.

Though the fantasies begin consciously with curious cool observation, the imagination 'gets up steam' to become absorbed in the (seeming) reality of the story, and is then brought back to earth by his stamping shoes, or when he is interrupted by an old lady at the top of the cellar steps (so not in the Cruikshank street-scene) whom he 'must have been staring at for half an hour' in 'the depth of ... meditations', so provoking her to hope sarcastically, 'you'll know me agin, imperence!' Dickens's self-analysis and reflexive awareness are so laid back, so jokey and so embedded in particulars that the terms 'analysis' and 'reflexive' are too abstract and heavy, but the conceptual implications of his unconceptual writing are crystal clear and by no means naive.

The imaginative invention is realistic and fantastic; it needs that close observation of life on which David Copperfield will pride himself, but it takes off, self-generative, conscious and unconscious – as Coleridge said about the poetry of Donne and Dryden – 'the wheels take fire from the mere rapidity of their own motion' (*Biographia Literaria*, Ch. 17). Sam Weller has his streetwise version of this brilliant image when he says he 'runs on like a new barrow with the vheel greased' (*PP*, 10). The gap between Coleridge and Dickens (who would not have read the *Biographia*) might be filled by Thackeray, who lets the wise, highly educated, widely read and articulate Esmond, also an author, observe 'there are a thousand thoughts lying within a man that he does not know till he takes up his pen to write' (*The History of Henry Esmond*, Vol. 2, Ch. 1).

The conscious demonstration is less explicit in 'The Pawnbroker's Shop' which presents an implicit image of social conditioning, describing three sets of women, divided conveniently in three booths or compartments of the shop: a mother and daughter pawning a forget-me-not ring, a prostitute moved to tears as the ring and the girl recall her own innocent past – in the manner of Holman Hunt's painting 'The Awakening Conscience' – and a wrecked old woman at the end of the line, all three sections delineated by the speculative observer and fore-caster who abstracts from vivid visualized particulars – and reinforced by the wonderful illustration of Cruikshank – to infer the future in self-effacing style, telling us that one woman's 'attire ... bespeaks her sta-tion', as a writer quietly present: 'a feeling similar to that we have described' (*Journalism* I, *SB*, Scenes).

There is one example – really three in one – of a sustained generative process at work in a number of sketches, stories and novels. When Dickens was writing 'A Visit to Newgate' he told Catherine he was having difficulty in arranging and even remembering materials from his visit three weeks earlier. He struggled, and the result was one of the most graphic and intense 'Scenes', with good plain writing and a smooth modulation from general to particular – the particular in type rather than individual. For an even earlier sketch, 'The Old Bailey', re-named as 'Criminal Courts', he had touched on Newgate in a first paragraph describing its outside but in 'A Visit To Newgate' he goes inside the prison to tell a story which is psychologically specific, horrifying and compassionate. This in its turn generated the more particularized and inventive plot and characters of 'The Black Veil', not comparable with the mature work and let down by a comforting conclusion, but more interesting than facetious stories like 'Mr Minns and his Cousin' and rightly described to Catherine as a 'singular' story with 'an extraordinary idea' (*Letters* 1, 98). It is about a mother who makes a cryptic engage-ment with a doctor to see her 'dying son', without saying this will be after he is hanged. The mystery and sensational solution are internalized: the anxious novice doctor, whose point of view is dominant, puzzles over the enigma of the appointment, and the climax is harrowing but humane as the cut-down body is produced and the mother's project shown to have a bizarre but real reason. The story is morbid in plot and psychology but particularized: the black veil has a clever double meaning, and the narrative has a concentrated and individual point of view.

As the editors of Volume I of Dickens's *Letters* remark, 'The Black Veil' has developed from the generalized and externally observed treatment of crime and punishment in 'Criminal Courts', which reports on a man about to be executed, and the 'Visit to Newgate' in which character is individualized by a dream sequence on the eve of execution. There are also links with the meditation in Monmouth Street where the old clothes tell the history of a criminal. The self-sourcing is complex and there are later connections too: as Forster points out, the Newgate scene looks ahead to Fagin's death cell and the trial of the Artful Dodger – though Fagin and the Artful are much more individual and complex – and the generative trail includes scenes in *Pickwick Papers* and is itself a serial history of conscious and unconscious developments in Dickens. At various points in the sequence Dickens was clearly aware of doing a reconstruction from memory and being gripped by an original idea, and in all the variations he continues the animation of objects, a literary conjuring act by a man who loved doing magic tricks at his children's parties.

The awareness of art also shows itself in formal and technical terms. Throughout *Sketches by Boz* we find the word 'fancy', and, less frequently, 'imagine', both used to signal invention and speculation. Boz is surprised to find that the imaginary construction of a mother's care and grief, from a diminutive clean coat, is as moving as actual everyday suffering: he can 'imagine' and 'know' that it is fiction and yet feel 'as much sorrow when we saw, or fancied we saw – it makes no difference which – the change that had begun to take place now, as if we had just conceived the bare possibility of such a change for the first time' (*Journalism* I, *SB*, Scenes 6).

There is the art term 'still life' which he puts in inverted commas in his account of Seven Dials in *Sketches by Boz*, where it contrasts strongly with Cruikshank's animated character piece featuring a brawl, which shows nothing of 'the "still life" of the subject' (*Journalism* 1, Scenes 5). He uses it in *Pickwick Papers* to describe Lant Street, in the great phrase, 'the still life of the street' (Ch. 32). He returns to it in *The Old Curiosity Shop* when Dick Swiveller wonders at 'the still-life' in the Brasses' office. With a shade of irony Dickens adopts the painting term to indicate socially significant objects, to make a distinction between things and people, and to emphasize without irony the aspect of perception discussed in *The Old Curiosity Shop* whose narrator is inhibited in human relations and fascinated by objects.

In *Pickwick Papers* Dickens jokes about 'poetry' – which he himself could never write – in the kind of rude literary satire which created poetical characters in *Sketches by Boz* but is here placed in narrative and character for Sam Weller's love-story. Sam's father Tony thinks poetry 'unnat'ral' and approves the plain style of compliment in Sam's valentine, 'you *are* a nice gal and nothin' but it', 'because there ain't no callin' names in it – no Wenuses' (*PP*, 33). He fears Sam 'werges on the poetical' in comparing the lasting impression Mary made on him to 'a likeness . . . took by the profeel macheen . . . altho' it *does* finish a portrait and put the frame and glass on complete with a hook at the end to hang it up by and all in two minutes and quarter', but is dismissed offhand with Sam's 'No it don't'. He judges the ending 'rayther a sudden pull up' and is answered, 'she'll vish there wos more, and that's the great art o' letter writin'' (*PP*, 32). This low-life practical criticism of rhetoric and reader-response may seem patronizing, and perhaps is a little, but it is comic too.

The most subtle display of artistic awareness in this not very subtle novel is the virtue of its rambling form: Dickens multiplies narrative and draws attention to its acts and arts. The sprawling novel consists not only of loosely linked episodes but also of stories within stories – Chinese puzzle construction or emboxed narrative or ring composition – insets of different lengths and genres. It derives from the miscellaneous structure of *The Arabian Nights, Don Quixote* and the English eighteenth-century novels, new-tuned to Dickens's purpose. (As it had been tuned to suit Swift and Voltaire.) The compounding self-assertion includes rather tedious Gothic insets like 'The Stroller's Tale' and 'The Madman's Story', the Bagman's grotesque tale of the talking chair, and the feeble love-story 'The Parish Clerk', by Sam but edited by more literate Pickwick. (*The Pickwick Papers* is very class-conscious.) Some insets are 'papers' to be read aloud, or silently, within the novel. Some are oral set pieces like Sam's long tall stories of the man who loved crumpets, and the buttons in the sausage machine, and his less incredible election-tale about Tony Weller tipping 'woters' into a canal. There are Sam's ironic one-sentence anecdotes, and Jingle's quick compressions. The bagman tells 'The Bagman's Story', told to him by his bagman uncle, and the dismal man's 'Stroller's Tale' is a stroller's tale which contains another. The book is an anthology of narrative which can seem naive – especially since nearly all the serious inset stories are weak or over-sensational – but also an elaborate construction of narrative which is complexly reflexive, a slung-together sequential arrangement and a Chinese puzzle construction within the sequence, foregrounding structure and story-telling in forms that anticipate twentieth-century dislocation, experiment and play.

Oliver Twist is a more straightforward narrative, with little literary reference apart from a discussion of melodrama which draws attention to the structure. It starts with a technical discussion in simple language:

> It is the custom on the stage: in all good, murderous melodramas: to
> present the tragic and the comic scenes, in as regular alternation, as
> the layers of red and white in a side of streaky, well-cured bacon ...
>   Such changes appear absurd; but they are not so unnatural as they
> would seem at first sight. The transitions in real life from well-spread
> boards to death-beds, and from mourning weeds to holiday garments,
> are not a whit less startling; only, there, we are busy actors, instead of
> passive lookers-on; which makes a vast difference. (Ch. 17)

Dickens talked of creative stews and simmering and here another
kitchen image, 'streaky bacon', describes the convention and also
enables the transition of scene and character as we leave Fagin's ken for
Oliver's birthplace. The whole passage is characteristic of Dickens, as he
argues that what seems unrealistic in art is really lifelike, then moves to a
comment on the emotional life which seems obvious but – no doubt
unconsciously – draws attention to his drama of emotional reversal, very
strong in this tight and tense novel.

Two scenes of some psychological interest probe borderline states of
mind and connect with Dickens's descriptions of the unconscious element in creativity. George Henry Lewes apparently asked him about
some episode in *Oliver Twist* and he replied, 'how it *came*, I can't tell. It
came, like all my other ideas ... ready made to the point of the pen – and
down it went' (*Letters* 1, 403). In the last chapter I quoted his image of
the leaden or feathery pen, and like the simmerings, Dickens's creative
pens are another link with George Eliot, who often used the image of a
pen with a life of its own to describe her own and her characters' less
than conscious creativity.[1] If the *Pilgrim* editors are right in thinking that
the passage which impressed Lewes is 'Oliver Sleep-Waking', where in a
dream or a half-dream Oliver sees Fagin and Monks outside his window,
it is interesting that Dickens said he had hit on it unconsciously, since
the scene itself is about the lapse or lowering of consciousness:

> There is a kind of sleep that steals upon us sometimes, which, while it
> holds the body prisoner, does not free the mind from a sense of things
> about it, and enables it to ramble at its pleasure. So far as an over-
> powering heaviness, a prostration of strength, and an utter inability to
> control our thoughts or power of motion, can be called sleep, this is it;
> and yet we have a consciousness of all that is going on about us, and if
> we dream at such a time, words which are really spoken, or sounds
> which really exist at the moment, accommodate themselves with sur-
> pising readiness to our visions, until reality and imagination become

so strangely blended that it is afterwards almost a matter of impossibility to separate the two. (Ch. 34)

This is not about artistic creation but it observes the blend of real experience with invention, and of freedom with control, in a cluster of insights by an observant reporter and an artist capable of wild surreal fantasy.

There is an even subtler description of mind in a half-conscious state in an earlier episode – the other scene Lewes might have asked Dickens about – where Oliver is observing Fagin, who thinks he is asleep:

Although Oliver had roused himself from sleep, he was not thoroughly awake. There is a drowsy state, between sleeping and waking, when you dream more in five minutes with your eyes half open, and yourself half conscious of everything that is passing around you, than you would in five nights with your eyes fast closed, and your senses wrapped in perfect unconsciousness. At such times, a mortal knows just enough of what his mind is doing, to form some glimmering conception of its mighty powers, its bounding from earth and spurning time and space: when freed from the restraint of its corporeal associate. (Ch. 9)

Here too Dickens is not talking directly about creativity but about a release of the mind from normal attention, a relaxation of will in a 'half conscious' state, which is of course not exclusive to creative invention but is what Dickens emphasizes when he is describing it. The most interesting detail is 'the glimmering conception of its mighty powers', because it is articulated in terms that go beyond Oliver's consciousness to suggest the artist's awareness of his creative imagination. Here too the psychological observation is redundant to the situation and character which generate the generalization but don't need it, as if Dickens fortunately forgot Oliver and the novel in discovering this experience of the artistic self. The passage is one of several articulate moments of creative awareness, made almost in passing, both consciously and unconsciously self-referential. Form and content are intricated in these passages where Dickens is making an observation about a character's strange state of mind, then inadvertently touching on the creative unconscious and the involuntary development of ideas, not in an abstract discussion of art but in the course of observing a particular mental process in his fiction, creating a commentary which is also an example.

In *Barnaby Rudge* there is much mention of 'imagination', as a commentary on character, but also as fragmentary creative awareness edging its way towards thematic generalization. Every person and every creature in the novel, including Grip the raven, is endowed with imagination, to suggest the consistent story and drama of inner creative life – occasionally its absence – which enlivens the novel's psychology and constitutes an interesting aspect of the characters' interaction. The subject of imaginative life is not consistently related to the revolutionary theme, but there are many occasions where the connection is suggested, and Dickens rewrites history to embody ideas of fantasy, sometimes of madness.

Kathleen Tillotson prefers Dickens's gentler lunatics like Mr Dick and Mr F's aunt to Barnaby Rudge (see her Introduction to the novel); but such soft derangements would not suit the purposes of this novel, and the presentation of Barnaby is adapted to its subject, as are the wild, obsessed figures of Hugh, Lord George Gordon and Dennis the hangman. Dickens's habitual animation of objects is importantly remade for Barnaby, and even more morbidly for Dennis the hangman's imaginative activity when he talks evasively about the clothes he has inherited from the men he has hanged, and about seeing the condemned men's shoes and coat – without identifying the owners – walking or dancing down the street before they became his, in a way shockingly clear to the reader though unclear to his hearers.

There is little creative self-reference in the course of *The Old Curiosity Shop* but the first chapter contains Dickens's most theoretically suggestive portrait of the artist. The key word in title and story is of course 'curiosity', which almost becomes a synonym for imagination, largely because its many repetitions are first associated with the narrator. It is a word which Dickens often uses of himself and it turns up in other novels but presides over this one. It frequently recurs in the first three chapters, where it derives force from title, setting and the narrator, whose curiosity is his imagination. He was originally Master Humphrey, and Nell's story was first thought of as a short tale, but the original plan left interesting traces even after radical revision. The creative curiosity of the old man is related to his 'infirmity' as he mysteriously introduces it in one of Dickens's arresting beginnings:

Night is generally my time for walking ...
    I have fallen insensibly into this habit, both because it favours my infirmity and because it offers me greater opportunity of speculating on the characters and occupations of those who fill the streets ... a glimpse of passing faces caught by the light of a street lamp or a shop

window is often better for my purposes than their full revelation in the daylight ... (Ch. 1)

The original Humphrey goes on to 'confess' that he is an 'old, deformed man' who has been a melancholy timid crippled child. What Dickens does in both narrators is to pathologize, using a light touch, his own creative habits – walking, at night, in the streets, observing the passing people. The restlessness derives from his own restlessness which is often mentioned in his letters, and of course his own wounded pride and insecurity when he was sent to work as a child. His own love of night walking in the city is adapted for the infirm man's shy need to escape scrutiny but also generalized as an artist's creative preference for the stimulating suggestion, famously demonstrated by Henry James's choice of the 'germ' or 'donnée' and avoidance of a total history. Humphrey speaks of being 'wounded', anticipating Edmund Wilson's influential essay 'The Two Scrooges' in *The Wound and the Bow*. Using the prototype of Philoctetes long before Wilson did, George Eliot entertains the idea in *The Mill on the Floss* where Philip Wakem, her artist with a physical infirmity, makes the symbol more evident by quoting Sophocles. But Dickens got there first, without reading Greek or knowing the myth.

Humphrey tells us that one result of his childhood sorrow is a particular interest in 'the inanimate objects' that 'people' his chamber, and the key example is his old clock, which he loves and feels loved by as if it were alive, whose time-beat is like a human pulse, and which is the repository of his observations and inventions, an essential item in the setting and symbolism of the serial papers which were never completed in this seat of imagination. When *Master Humphrey's Clock* was dropped because of falling sales, the clock was taken over by the symbol and setting of what had originally been a story within the story. The antiques and junk in the Curiosity Shop become subjects and objects of the narrator's meditation, as he takes over Humphrey's function and aspects of his identity. Without so much pathology now, though keeping the infirmity and isolation, the character reflects Dickens's own inter-animation of the object world that began in the *Sketches*, though here it is generalized as a common rather than peculiar habit. The narrator explains how he is struck by seeing Nell in the curiosity shop and inspired to imagine her story: first he sees her as she was, then he reflects curiously, and establishes 'the curiosity-dealer's warehouse' as the seat of imagination:

I sat down in my easy-chair ... and ... pictured to myself the child in
her bed ... so slight and fairy-like a creature passing the long dull
nights in such an uncongenial place ...

We are so much in the habit of allowing impressions to be made
upon us by external objects, which should be produced by reflection
alone, but which, without such visual aids often escape us; that I am
not sure I should have been so thoroughly possessed by this one
subject, but for the heaps of fantastic things I had seen huddled
together in the curiosity-dealer's warehouse. These, crowding upon
my mind ... brought her condition palpably before me. I had her
image, without any effort of imagination, surrounded and beset by
everything that was foreign to its nature ... If these helps to my fancy
had all been wanting, and I had been forced to imagine her in a
common chamber ... it is very probable that I should have been less
impressed ... (Ch. 1)

As well as the inanimate objects there are details of the creative state that
relate clearly to Dickens's imaginative habits – the images crowding in on
the mind, that effortless seeing he described to Lewes, the 'helps to his
fancy' in Monmouth Street. As the narrator is characterized as creator in
lavish detail before being awkwardly faded out, and features of the novel
itself remarked and emphasized, Dickens's discussion of his creativity is
extended. The inspiration of creation, the act of creation, the result of
creation and the individual habits of the creator, are all brought into the
work of art.

In addition, there are two narrative details at the end which give extra
emphasis to narrative convolution and art. There is a kind of epilogue in
which we are told that 'the single gentleman' repeats the journey of Nell
and her grandfather, which he has learnt from Nell's 'narrative'. His
recapitulation of places and people emphasizes art and insists on reality,
like many rounding-off conclusions in Shakespeare, where characters go
off hoping to hear the whole story from a character, like Prospero or
Horatio, who is in a position to tell it:

... it was his chief delight to travel in the steps of the old man and the
child (so far as he could trace them from her last narrative), to halt
where they had halted, sympathize where they suffered, and rejoice
where they had been made glad. Those who had been kind to them,
did not escape his search. The sisters at the school ... (Chapter the
Last)

And there are the novel's last words, 'like a tale that is told!', joining the sense of reality with the admission of narrative art.

The Chimes is *A Christmas Carol*'s successor and in some ways a weaker imitation, the causal interplay between alternative endings absent, and its alternative unhappy ending made more particular and more plausible than the brief happy one to which we return. There is a good reason for this: the tragic ending emphasizes the damage done by heartless politicians and magistrates and darkens an unusually strong topical satire. What is missing here is what was impressive in the *Carol*, an imaginative centre. But both the *Carol* and *The Chimes* are fictions which highlight the author's imagination, reflexive in a high degree. *Pickwick Papers* created a compound structure which proliferates stories and highlights the narrative imagination, and what Dickens is doing in his two best Christmas fantasies is to incorporate with a finished story the process of revision and change which all artists experience and which he often records and discusses. In Dickens's case we have also many well known examples of his twists and turns of intention, like his decision well on into the novel, at Forster's suggestion, to make Little Nell die, and his more radical change of mind about the end of *Great Expectations*. Critics and editors have argued about this revision so much that the discarded ending in which Pip and Estella stay separate is often printed along with the happy-ever-after Dickens finally chose, to offer a text with a choice of endings, in a provisionality and openness like that of Sterne's unfinished self-deferring *Tristram Shandy*, the self-conscious provisionality of Diderot's *Jacques le Fataliste*, B. S. Johnson's modernist loose-leaf novel in a box and current choose-your-route-and-plot stories for children.

The Chimes has one of the most interesting reflexive endings in Dickens. Trotty's fear, like Scrooge's, is staged as a dream, but because it is not a surreal one the story as a whole resembles what we call magic realism, with hints of fantasy in a realistic action, not the separated elements of A *Carol*. At the end, however, Dickens gives some analysis of the dreaming state, as he does with Gabriel Varden and John Jasper, and also draws attention in grandiose language and iambic flow, to its wildness and dismemberments:

> Monsters uncouth and wild arise in premature, imperfect resurrection; the several, different parts and shapes of different things are joined and mixed by chance; and when, and how, and by what wonderful degrees, each separates from each, and every sense and object of the mind resumes its usual form and lives again, no man ... can tell. (Third Quarter)

We fade out in an intensely emotional passage which undermines the naturalistic description of dreaming:

> Had Trotty dreamed? Or, are his joys and sorrows, and the actors in them, but a dream; himself a dream; the teller of this tale a dreamer, waking but now? If it be so, O Listener, dear to him in all his visions, try to bear in mind the stern realities from which these shadows come . . . (Fourth Quarter)

Here Dickens questions his own use of the dream as genre and an analogy for his art, and his tender conclusion is reminiscent of Thackeray's complex ending – to a complex novel – in which the narrator, presented as the author of *Vanity Fair*, bids an elegiac farewell to his reader and his fiction. In *A Christmas Carol* the author's presence is generally reserved, apart from an occasional teasing remark at the beginning, like 'Mind! I don't mean to say that I know, of my own knowledge, what there is particularly dead about a door-nail' (Stave One). In this second Christmas fantasy, however, Dickens compounds the fantasist and the reader, when he admits his fantasy and – most significantly as an end to this topical story – corrects the admission of dreaming to insist on social realities and his own passionate political motivation. *The Chimes* is not one of his best stories but the author's presence at the end is finely sensitive to all aspects of the story and expresses in a new mode his pity for miseries of the poor and his hatred of the heartless governors. The characters in *The Chimes* are not vivid or particularized but like Jo in *Bleak House* they are seen as realities as well as fictions, plural rather than singular, and they are taken beyond the frame of art in one of Dickens's most interesting and reflexive endings.

Notes

[1] I have discussed George Eliot's creative pens in *George Eliot: A Critic's Biography*, Ch. 6.

Chapter 4

The Artist as Narrator in *Doctor Marigold*, *David Copperfield*, *Bleak House* and *Great Expectations*

Like his structural miscellanies, Dickens's frame narrators were inspired by *The Arabian Nights*, and like Scheherezade, they are given motive and a history. They do not usually reflect his needs and motives as thoroughly as Master Humphrey but there is a lively range of them, including Tibbs, an early example who started as a 'melancholy specimen of the story-teller' whose wife was always interrupting him but was comically promoted to narrate 'Scenes and Characters' for Bell's *Life in London*; the Uncommercial Traveller, a reporter rather like his author; and benign Mrs Lirriper, tamest of talkative women. One of the most talented is Doctor Marigold, 'Cheap Jack', editor and author whose periodical *Doctor Marigold's Prescriptions* is like *All the Year Round*, the weekly where it appeared, a 'general miscellaneous lot', with work by others and his own story written for a deaf and dumb protégée, Sophy, an abused child adopted after the death of his own abused child. Variously creative, he compares a cheapjack's eloquence, formulaic and improvised, with that of 'dear jacks' like politicians. Variously reflexive, he takes 'a bit of imagination' from other authors and after getting an idea for his 'new-made express' volume, rejoices: 'It pleased me, that I thought as I did; and as I was never a man to let a thought sleep (you must wake up all the family of thoughts you've got and burn their night-caps, or you won't do in the Cheap Jack line) I set to work ...' Finding the right title he uses Joe Gargery's image, 'How did I hammer that hot iron into shape?' (Ch. 1), is interested in selling his work by cheapening, and emphasizes the spoken word so important for Dickens: 'I was aware that I couldn't do myself justice. A man can't write his eye (at least *I* don't know how to) nor yet can a man write his voice, nor the rate of his talk, nor the quickness of his action, nor his general spicy way. But he can write his turns of speech ...' (Ch. 1).

Dickens's uncharacterized and anonymous narrators are generally reticent, but given to rare interventions like the discussion of 'streaky bacon' in *Oliver Twist*. In *A Christmas Carol* the narrator makes an

unexpected move. 'He' – there is no gender – has addressed the reader
once or twice before the story has got started but speaks in the first
person when Scrooge is visited by the first Ghost:

> The curtains of his bed were drawn aside, I tell you, by a hand. Not the
> curtains at his feet, nor the curtains at his back, but those to which his
> face was addressed. The curtains of his bed were drawn aside; and
> Scrooge, starting up into a half-recumbent attitude, found himself
> face to face with the unearthly visitor who drew them: as close to it as I
> am to you, and I am standing in the spirit at your elbow. (Stave Two)

One moment we are with a man starting up as a spirit draws his bed-
curtains, the next the narrator is with us 'in the spirit', the 'I' suddenly
appearing with no notice – except for 'I tell you'. The physicality of 'at
your elbow', and the double meaning of 'spirit' are surely not accidental
or casual, in a ghost story. It seems to be a one-off intimate joke, a little
Beckettian, that presents the narrator as a kind of spirit, which of course
in a way he is. The words 'close as I am to you' seem to play on that close
relationship that Dickens had with his reader. Like the spirits in the
story, he may make us jump or look round nervously but he is a benevolent spirit, and a guide, there for our good, in the spirit of the story.

As well as re-imagining himself in various roles as narrator, Dickens
invents a variety of talking and telling characters within the novels, from
the virtuoso Sam Weller to less stylish narrators who tell key stories at key
moments: Sol Gills tells Walter a sea-story about the famous Madeira,
Polly Richards tells the mourning Florence a fable of death and rebirth,
Amy Dorrit tells the story of the Princess, Lizzie Hexam tells Jenny Wren
about a rich lady in love with Wrayburn. Action is suspended for their
telling but it skilfully contributes to the action. And Dickens created
three story-tellers with large narrative responsibility: David Copperfield,
Esther Summerson and Philip Pirrip or Pip.

David Copperfield is Dickens's most literary novel, the only one whose
hero is a professional author. Its narrative is introspective, with events
which track a novelist's progress, beginning with his early learning and
reading, moving on to his story-telling and novel-writing, and in the early
sections drawing on the unfinished memoir Dickens gave to Forster, who
drew on it for his biography of his friend. David is a hero of art, the hero
as author, and the story of his career is clearly present but not insistent.
After he begins authorship with 'trifling pieces' in magazines and
graduates to fiction, he says his 'written memory' (Ch. 48), the partly
autobiographical novel purporting to be wholly autobiographical, is not

primarily concerned with his books, and makes the point again, much later, 'referring to my own fictions only when their course should incidentally connect itself with the progress of my story' and not entering 'on the aspirations, the delights, anxieties and triumphs, of my art. If the books I have written be of any worth, they will supply the rest' (Ch. 61). This lacuna in David's story is occupied by his author's real books including the one we are reading. David's novels are not Dickens's but it seems pedantic and literal-minded of Q. D. Leavis to insist on this (in *Dickens the Novelist*). Dickens's relationship with his readers was so close and familiar that when he says David's novels will supply the rest, in other words, can speak for themselves, it is a knowing allusion, a kind of special *occupatio*, and some readers are bound to see fiction go transparent at this point, to let the real novels show through – especially as we are told virtually nothing about the fictitious fictions.

Not many *Künstlerromane* do include specimens of art, for obvious reasons: Thackeray's *Pendennis* says little about its hero's works, though *Henry Esmond*, whose hero is many things as well as an author, does. Some writers solve the problem by translating literature into another genre, like Thomas Mann in *Doctor Faustus* and Lawrence in *Sons and Lovers*. Joyce's *A Portrait of the Artist as a Young Man* includes the poet's poetry and uses a free indirect prose style which grows increasingly rich and experimental as the artist reads, imitates and begins to create language, but it is the exception proving the rule.

Like Joyce, though less boldly, Dickens shows the child's imaginative language. David's first stirrings are those of the wondering child, sensuous and primitively animistic as seeing the 'red light' of dawn he asks, 'Is the sundial glad, I wonder, that it can tell the time again?' Although his childhood sufferings, growing up, affections, marriages and career, form the main trunk of the novel, his story branches out into other lives where he participates as a spectator, his story one amongst many in the multiple novel which includes the story of Emily, the Peggottys, the Steerforths and Rosa Dartle, the story of Agnes, Mr Wickfield, the Heeps and Micawbers – though the Micawbers like David wander from story to story – the briefer stories of the Strong marriage and Betsy Trotwood, and the even briefer glimpses of Barkis, Traddles and Martha. In the smaller branches Dickens shows there is 'a tale in everything' without telling every tale in full or at length. Everyone has a story. The story of David Copperfield is the centre of 'the web' he has spun, the large but never loose narrative with no 'unravelled end' (Ch. 63).

David's creative development is followed in the trajectory of his inner and outer life. The chief narrator's story is one strong thread interwoven with others, but the web is formed by his spreading friendships and sympathy. Thackeray thought Dickens might owe something to *Pendennis* but the creative development of Arthur Pendennis the novelist is not followed through the novel like David's in *David Copperfield*, which is the story of many lives told by one character able to observe and enter imaginatively into them all. He is not detached like Master Humphrey or confined in point of view like Esther or always at the centre of his story like Pip. The portrait of himself as the artist is made part of an otherwise typically Victorian novel of multiple action. It is as if *Middlemarch* included one story based on the life of Marian Evans, fictionalized as a writer of fiction in whose history all other characters were involved. That part of David's personal story which describes a novelist's career is a strong thread in the pattern, his creative motivation and urge part of the story: David uses the word 'wound' (Ch. 58) and he is the artist suffering the 'secret agony' of Charles Dickens. The relation between suffering and creativity is only once directly mentioned, by Agnes, and what is emphasized is the beginning and the development of imagination.

The novelist's growth, energy and power are made specific, like his author's in spirit if not always in fact. David's writing develops from his story-telling and that comes out of his reading. As a boy he works at reading and then at story-telling, and ordinary phrases light up with special meaning: neglected and lonely he reads 'for dear life', and in the school dormitory his romantic dreamy side is encouraged by so much 'story-telling in the dark'. He is learning his trade in the traditional way by the imitation of good models. He learns interactively, locating fictional characters in his own house and garden, using them to survive, make sense of experience and distance himself from its pains. He compares himself with his heroes who never lose dignity as he does and he consoles himself by identifying with his favourite characters and associating the Murdstones with the bad ones. The novels keep his 'fancy alive'. He re-tells their stories first to his schoolfriends, then to his rough workmates and the Orfling. When he runs away to find his aunt the stories keep up his spirits and he has adventures on the road like the young men in Fielding and Smollett, though he is 'a child's Tom Jones'.

Fiction is not the only source of sustaining imagery: it blends with memory and imagination to make the life-narrative. Another strand is a 'fanciful picture' of his mother, which gives him the nerve to start on his journey and helps to sustain him on the road to Dover: it is based not on direct memory but on the story she told him, about her 'fancy' that Betsy gently touched her hair: 'I seemed to be sustained and led on by my fanciful picture ... It always kept me company. It was there, among the hops, when I lay down to sleep; it was with me on my waking in the morning; it went before me all day' (Ch. 13). He explains, in the forward-and-backward-looking narrative, that later he came to associate the story of his mother's fancy with 'the sunny street' of Canterbury – it is an involuntary memory, long before Proust. When he arrived at the destination the story 'relieved the solitary aspect of the scene with hope' but 'when I stood with my ragged shoes, and my dusty, sunburnt, half-clothed figure, in the place so long desired, it seemed to vanish like a dream, and to leave me helpless and dispirited' (Ch. 13). The boy finds this 'strange'; the reader understands that dreams can't see you through everything.

David believes that a good memory has its source in close keen observation, and the novel often draws attention to acts of seeing and the ability to infer inside from ouside, story from scene. Like Humphrey, David is impressed by inanimate objects, particularly by what Madame Merle, in James's *Portrait of a Lady*, calls the envelope of 'expressive' things that surrounds us and cannot be distinguished from the 'self'. For David himself there are sacred objects like the crocodile book, the St Paul's Cathedral workbox, the lump of wax for Peggotty's thread, his father's novels. And he infers other people's life-stories from the things around them. One object which is brought into uncomfortably close focus, without being described, is Captain Hopkins's dirty comb, which David thinks it would be better not to borrow, as he stands on the threshold of his prison room and reads the life:

> I divined (God knows how) that though the two girls with the shock heads of hair were Captain Hopkins's children, the dirty lady was not married to Captain Hopkins. My timid station on his threshold was not occupied more than a couple of minutes at most; but I came down again with all this in my knowledge, as surely as the knife and fork were in my hand. (Ch. 11)

There is a sense in which the novel is about itself, most subtly. As David the spectator is frequently stationed on a threshold as he is here – another seat of imagination – looking and listening, the scene is made effective and the creative action quietly self-analysed. There is another framed and frozen scene where the same Captain Hopkins (originally Captain Porter) reads Micawber's (first John Dickens's) petition at a meeting where David (originally Dickens) is allowed to observe 'from a corner' as prisoners crowd in to sign. Immediately afterwards David formally discusses the relation between observation, story-telling, memory and fancy:

> As I walked to and fro daily between Southwark and Blackfriars, and lounged about at meal-times in obscure streets, the stones of which may, for anything I know, be worn at this moment by my childish feet, I wonder how many of these people were wanting in the crowd that used to come filing before me in review again, to the echo of Captain Hopkins's voice! When my thoughts go back, now, to that slow agony of my youth, I wonder how much of the histories I invented for such people hangs like a mist of fancy over well-remembered facts! When I treat the old ground, I do not wonder that I seem to see and pity, going on before me, an innocent romantic boy, making his imaginative world out of such strange experiences and sordid things! (Ch. 11)

'I wonder how many of these people were wanting' is obscure here but its meaning is made clear by Forster's version in the biography, under a running title, 'Captain Porter's Petition':

> Whatever was comical in this scene, and whatever was pathetic, I sincerely believe I perceived in my corner. I made out my little character and story for every man who put his name to that sheet of paper ... Their different peculiarities of dress, of face, of gait, of manner, were written indelibly on my memory ... When I looked, with my mind's eye, into the Fleet prison during Mr Pickwick's incarceration, I wonder whether half a dozen men were wanting from the Marshalsea crowd that came filing in again, to the sound of Captain Porter's voice! (Forster, Bk 1, Ch. 2)

Forster is writing factually and using Dickens's factual description of a source for *Pickwick Papers*, and the comparison shows Dickens not remembering but working with the text and transcribing his memoir rather carelessly and too selectively in the intricate process of adapting his self-portrait of the artist, for a fiction purporting to be fact.

Another observation-scene is linked with the petition-scene as it is placed in Traddles' Camden Town lodging and here too a listing of miscellaneous contents is expressive of the inhabitant and the observer on the threshold, as the novelist-as-narrator-as-novelist makes explicit:

> It was his only room, I saw; for there was a sofa-bedstead in it, and his blacking-brushes and blacking were among his books – on the top

shelf, behind a dictionary. His table was covered with papers, and he was hard at work in an old coat. I looked at nothing, that I know of, but I saw everything, even to the prospect of a church upon his china inkstand, as I sat down – and this, too, was a faculty confirmed in me in the old Micawber times. Various ingenious arrangements he had made ... (Ch. 27)

This draws attention to the 'faculty' of effortless imaginative inference before David's career starts, but later on when he is writing his first work of fiction, there is another observation and self-observation of a more subtle and complicated process and response. David is walking past the Steerforth house in Highgate on one of his solitary walks, thinking of the book he is writing, and notices its drawn blinds and the blank look of the one unshaded window:

> I do not remember that I ever saw a light in all the house. If I had been a casual passer-by, I should have probably supposed that some childless person lay dead in it. If I had happily possessed no knowledge of the place, and had seen it often in that changeless state, I should have pleased my fancy with many ingenious speculations, I dare say.
>
> As it was, I thought as little of it as I might. But my mind could not go by it and leave it, as my body did; and it usually wakened a long train of meditation. Coming before me, on this particular evening that I mention, mingled with the childish recollections and later fancies, the ghosts of half-formed hopes, the broken shadows of disappointments dimly seen and understood, the blending of experience and imagination, incidental to the occupation with which my thoughts had been busy, it was more than commonly suggestive. I fell into a brown study as I walked on ... (Ch. 46)

The narrator is not free to interpret and infer the life inside the house from its façade, because he already knows its history and its inhabitants, but his comment goes beyond obvious thoughts of the tragic past and present to remind us of his habitual response to inanimate objects, his imaginative tendency. As he reflects here on Steerforth's story he also hints at his own personal life, in a suggestive style which mixes the matter-of-fact with the poetic: the imagery of ghosts and shadows is right for his dim sense of personal disappointment. But the 'brown study' – its original tinge of 'brown' melancholy brought out – is a conscious and reflexive recognition of that artistic layering 'of experience and imagination' we saw on the Dover road when he joined memories of his

mother's memory and story with the inspiration of the picaresque
novels. In the scene inside the Highgate house David plays a spectator
role after Rosa Dartle summons him to hear Littimer's cold callous story
about Steerforth and Emily, but his meditation outside registers the
identity of an artist, the persistent self felt throughout the novel, if at
times subdued to other people's stories, still kept as an undercurrent.

We feel this creative undercurrent in another way when Peggotty
relates Emily's version of the same story, without sentimentality and so
vividly that *his* listener (David) is impressed and we are impressed by his
impression. Dickens avoids a direct encounter between David and Emily
after the elopement – on one occasion most implausibly, when he pas-
sively listens outside as Rosa abuses Emily. We can speculate on the
reasons for such evasion, which must include the immense problem of
imagining the emotion of such conversation and the smaller question of
rendering Emily's improved language in direct speech or in David's
impression. Her language is cleverly avoided as it is mediated through
Peggotty's story about her story – the travels with Steerforth, the decline
of love, her illness and escape:

> He saw everything he related. It passed before him, as he spoke, so
> vividly, that, in the intensity of his earnestness, he presented what he
> described, to me, with greater distinctness than I can express. I can
> hardly believe, writing now long afterwards, but that I was actually
> present in these scenes; they are impressed upon me with such an
> astonishing air of fidelity. (Ch. 51)

David's response punctuates the telling, the way in which he listens and
appreciates the long narrative unobtrusively reflecting his creative
knowledge and experience: what he responds to in Peggotty's 'seen'
narrative has been strikingly brought out for his own memory when he
records the wine warehouse in Blackfriars, a site recreated incisively and
bitterly, visual imprint registering the pain:

> Its panelled rooms, discolored with the dirt and smoke of a hundred
> years, I dare say; its decaying floors and staircase; the squeaking and
> scuffling of the old grey rats down in the cellars; and the dirt and
> rotteness of the place; are things, not of many years ago, in my mind,
> but of the present instant. (Ch. 11)

Here too, like the mention of the books he leaves to speak for themselves, is a moment when David's experience is identified, because identical, with the author's.

The scenes and stories of layered interpretation are backed up by many brief passing responses to expression, voice or gesture, like David's sharp reading of Heep's face at the dénouement in Wickfield's office or of Ham's premonitory seaward gaze, responses muted as they are noted, presenting the novelist as he relates the stories of others, and at a deep imaginative level – a special feature of this first-person narrative by a novelist inside the novel manipulated by a novelist outside.

Comment on David's novels by other characters is rare. There is a scattering of readers' responses in lighter vein, once or twice a knowing joke at the fictional writer, and probably the real one too, like Mr Omer's awed praise of the 'separate and indiwidual wollumes' of Copperfield's 'lovely work' and its 'expressions', with his protest, 'As to feeling sleepy! Not at all!' (Ch. 51), or Dr Chillip's professional response, which reminds us of Dickens's exhausted writing and readings: 'There must be great excitement here, sir,' he says, tapping his forehead, assuming David must find writing 'a trying occupation', and 'this action of the brain now, sir? Don't you find it fatigue you?' (Ch. 59). Intelligent Betsy Trotwood also observes the sheer hard work and application but goes a little further in shrewd comment: 'I never thought, when I used to read books, what work it was to write them', then in response to his admission that writing 'has its own charms': 'Ah! I see! ... Ambition, love of approbation, sympathy, and much more, I suppose?' (Ch. 62). Beneath all these dialogues is the quietly teasing subtext of Dickens and his novels.

But the novelist's career is romanticized as well as realized, and not always understated. Bereaved of wife and two dear friends David turns to Nature in the Swiss Alps, seeks 'the human interest ... lately shrunk from', to work on a story 'growing, not remotely' from his own experience, then after finishing it falls 'to work, in my old ardent way ... on a new fancy, which took strong possession of me. As I advanced in the execution of this task, I felt it more and more, and roused my utmost energies to do it well' (Ch. 58).

Dora is only a penholder and makes brief vague comment on Doady's success and fame but Agnes's response is intense: she knows about the wound and the bow, writing to tell David after the deaths of Dora, Steerforth and Ham that new sorrow will be a strength like the old. Agnes is alert to David's moral impulse, predicting that suffering will help him teach others. He 'saw her listening face; moved her to smiles or tears; and heard her cordial voice so earnest on the shadowy events of that imaginative world in which I lived' (Ch. 62) and when at the very end he writes 'far into the night' with her 'dear presence' bearing him company it is clear that she is his best reader and his Muse. The presence of the novelist's imagination, which has been so reticently but firmly indicated and followed, loses particularity as the novel ends.

Esther Summerson is the next strongly individualized and sustained narrator. She is not a professional novelist, but formally acknowledges her narrative function in the third chapter of *Bleak House*, 'Progress', beginning but not yet called 'Esther's Narrative'. Here she mentions writing her 'portion of these pages' with reluctance and difficulty. (We eventually learn that she is writing seven years after her happy ending.) Her retrospects are introverted stories of everyday life in neat, undecorated prose but sometimes adroit and elegant, partaking of her author's skill in metaphor, wit and balance.

As narrator Esther is also motivated by childhood suffering, loneliness and lovelessness, with the added injury of illegitimacy. David uses the word 'wound' to describe his suffering (*DC*, Ch. 58) and she uses it to describe the response to her godmother's cruel story: 'perhaps I might still feel such a wound, if such a wound could be received more than once, with the quickness of that birthday' (Ch. 3). Lonely David read his dead father's novels and lonely Esther confides her bitter birthday and resolution to do good and win love, to her doll. She tells her doll the story of her day, and buries her confidante, in a rite of passage, when she goes to school. She picks up fairy-stories somehow, because she tells 'Red Riding-Hood' and other nursery-tales to the Jellyby children. She shares David's creative gifts of observation and memory, drawing attention to her own 'noticing way' but qualifying it, 'not a quick way, O no! – a silent way', adding that it is quickened by love (Ch. 3). The sympathy Dickens left to be inferred in *David Copperfield* is too conspicuous as it is disclaimed by Esther but her outgoing imagination is important, and its connection with her telling not emphasized but left to be inferred.

Like David she reads inside from outside but her spectator-scenes are less clearly self-expressive, and early on when she and Ada Clare are companions, she sometimes uses a first-person plural, 'We saw'.[1] Her response is usually sharp and individual and she quotes other people's narratives with sympathy, wonder or astonishment. She closely observes people or things, to call them strange: on first meeting John Jarndyce, she thinks him or what she 'could see of him was very strange' (Ch. 3), and on her first visit to Kenge and Carboy's office she feels 'Everything was so strange – the stranger from its being night in the day-time' (Ch.

3). She is surprised because the sick Jo 'was strangely unconcerned about himself', commenting, 'if I may say so strange a thing' and later reads in his reaction to 'the comfort and brightness' of Bleak House 'an indifference that scarcely could be called wonder' (Ch. 31). In these sensitive passages she is aware of the attempt to express what cannot easily be expressed. Once she says with overstated understated modesty: 'It seems so curious to me to be obliged to write all this about myself! As if this narrative were a narrative of my life! But my little body will soon fall into the background now' (Ch. 3). (The 'curious' harks back to Master Humphrey.) At the close of 'Esther's Narrative', where self-reference clusters, she says a formal modest farewell to the reader, carefully addressing both sexes, speaking for character and author like a Shakespearean epilogue: 'The few words that I have to add to what I have written, are soon penned; then I, and the unknown friend to whom I write, will part for ever. Not without much dear remembrance on my side. Not without some, I hope, on his or hers' (Ch. 67).

She is not only the good housekeeper, literally and metonymically, but a story-teller who relates events on behalf of her author, though she is not given sole responsibility. Her image was more congenial to Dickens than us – an angel in the house, Dame Durden and Little Old Woman. Her disadvantages as narrator-heroine are modest self-reported praise and self-deprecation, but apart from these, Esther's is subtle story-telling, and it is a pity that such a bold idea as making a woman tell so much of the story should be at all undermined by the author's delight in domestic virtue. However, he does not confine her sensitive register to the domestic sphere but takes her into the public world of Chancery, making her the most outspoken and socially subversive of his three sustained narrators. Her voice is quiet and demure, and her charity-begins-at-home critique of the Jellyby and Pardiggle good works is an echo of her author at his most conservative and sexist, but she has outbursts of anger and contempt for the law, false philanthropy and love of money. Her judgement is fair, she articulates class sympathy and compassion, and it is she who insists that poverty cannot afford the order and cleanliness she exemplifies, like Dickens in real life: the mess and muddle of the Jellyby house is criticized but not the brickmakers' wretched dwellings.

Of course her narrative is contrasted with the compassionate, angry voice of the androgynous and truly omniscient first narrator, whose ironic, amused, confident, and forensic direct speech is that of a public orator or an angry pitying god. Hillis Miller believes the impersonal narrator has a wholly negative vision, in contrast to the benevolence of

Esther's, but the voice values virtue, and while often aggressive, has passions rooted in caring. It is a god's eye view at the beginning, moving from close-up to aerial view, from muddy Holborn to Essex marshes and Kentish heights. There is the tone of impersonal fiat in the first chapter, 'one might imagine' and 'On such an afternoon, if ever, the Lord High Chancellor ought to be sitting here – as here he is ...'. The voice is more impersonal than the prevailing narrative in Thackeray and George Eliot, whose generalizing voices are reserved but always personal.

This impersonal voice is freed from the past tense, in the first paragraphs entirely substantive and verbless. The relationship between the two narrators is a paradigm of two modes of diegetic summary, first-person and truly omniscient author. The relationship is made strange by the contrast of impersonal and personal, and by Esther's awareness of a partner in 'my portion of these pages' (Ch. 3) and the other's, 'While Esther sleeps, and while Esther wakes ...' (Ch. 7). There is at times an unusually direct appeal to readers, including lords, ladies, reverends and 'Your Majesty' after Jo dies. The social indignation is Dickens's but the narrator's lack of gender, history and personal identity anticipate T. S. Eliot's ideal of impersonality just as the bi-vocal narrative anticipates Joyce.

For the third novel where first-person narrative is individualized, Dickens imagines Pip, who tells the story of *Great Expectations* as an unprofessional narrator. He is the last of Dickens's full-length impersonations or characterizations of the story-teller, and like the Impersonal Narrator, who has the sweep and grandeur of a great generalizer, Esther, with her noticing ways, David Copperfield with his powers of observation and memory, Pip is an imaginary and an imaginative narrator. His imagination is always active, speaking for his author and for himself as an individual character.

Like David and Esther, Pip is a neglected and solitary child, badly parented by his guardian-sister but loved by his surrogate father. For Pip, Dickens has set aside explicit reference to creative motivation, and unlike David and Esther, he shows no awareness of being a writer or having a reader and draws no overt attention to his wound or his bow. However, his imagination is always present, amusingly self-excited, and like David's, given to personification and projection, from the first chapter when in the second paragraph, we are told of his 'first fancies', about his dead parents, stimulated and shaped by the forms and words of their graves. After he has stolen food for his convict the world of objects and nature is violently animated by his guilty conscience: 'The gates and dykes and banks came bursting at me through the mist' and

'The cattle came upon me with like suddenness, staring out of their eyes, and steaming out of their nostrils' (Bk 1, Ch. 3). Our attention is also constantly drawn to Pip's inventiveness by repetitions of 'fancy', 'fancied' or 'fancies', which occur between 30 and 40 times in the novel, occasionally referring to someone else, like Miss Havisham and Magwitch. On a few occasions the word 'imagine' is used as a synonym, and most of the time the fancying or imagining is shown without being named.

There are fancies that do not fit neatly into the main pattern, but keep the idea going, as they did in *Barnaby Rudge*. When Pip is nursed by Joe in London, he has a benign 'fancy' that he 'was little Pip again' (Bk 3, Ch. 18). There is a grim example when Wopsle, who is performing on stage, sees Compeyson behind Pip in the audience, and 'had a ridiculous fancy that he must be with you, Mr Pip, till I saw that you were quite unconscious of him, sitting behind you there, like a ghost' – the word 'ghost' is well chosen, a ghost from the past, frightening in reality (Bk 3, Ch. 8). And there is the fantasy in which Pip anticipates Miss Havisham's violent death in a hallucination of her hanging body: 'A strange thing happened in my fancy' – which opens a crack in the solid phenomenal world (Bk 1, Ch. 8).

Pip's guilty images sometimes appear in dreams: 'If I slept at all that night, it was only to imagine myself drifting down the river on a strong spring-tide, to the Hulks; a ghostly pirate calling out to me through a speaking-trumpet ... that I had better come ashore and be hanged there at once, and not put it off' (Bk 1, Ch. 2). Later on he imagines the convict 'fancying' a suspicious noise, and as he watches his relations and the soldiers while they imagine taking the convicts, 'in lively anticipation', he animates the forge fire and the pale afternoon as antithetical images for their aggressive zeal and his compassion:

> ... while they all stood clustering about the forge, enjoying themselves so much ... the bellows seemed to roar for the fugitives, the fire to flare for them, the smoke to hurry away in pursuit of them ... the pale afternoon outside, almost seemed in my pitying young fancy to have turned pale on their account, poor wretches. (Bk 1, Ch. 5)

This is one of Pip's many poetically inventive projections, like his anxious fancies after Magwitch's return, and after the message, 'DON'T GO HOME', his hotel room is full of 'night-fancies' that animate 'night-noises': 'those extraordinary voices with which silence teems', and the walls have a 'staringly wide-awake pattern' of a perforated candle-holder (Bk 3, Ch. 6). The ominous play of imagination goes back to the old clothes and shoes in *Sketches by Boz*.

Pip's dominant fancy is of course his great expectation about Miss Havisham, ironically perceived as actual: 'My dream was out; my wild fancy was surpassed by sober reality; Miss Havisham was going to make my fortune on a large scale' (Bk 1, Ch. 18). This fancy encourages and includes his hopes of Estella, who appears to him in the smithy fire and the darkness:

> ... when I was pulling the bellows for Joe, and we were singing Old Clem ... the thought how we used to sing it at Miss Havisham's ... would seem to show me Estella's face in the fire ... I would look towards those panels of black night ... and would fancy I saw her just drawing her face away, and would believe that she had come at last. (Bk 1, Ch. 14)

He tells Estella, in another of the lyrical passages that seem different from expressions of love in the other novels, 'You have been the embodiment of every graceful fancy that my mind has ever become acquainted with' (Bk 3, Ch. 5). He fantasizes about giving her up. 'I thought it would be very good for me if I could get her out of my head, with all the rest of those remembrances and fancies...' (Bk 1, Ch. 17) and settling for homely second-best Biddy. Indulging that dangerous patronizing fancy much later, he listens for 'the clink of Joe's hammer', fancies he hears it, and finds it 'but a fancy' (Bk 3, Ch. 19). It is part of his egocentric fancy that everything has stayed unchanged but the forge is silent because it is the blacksmith's wedding day. In the end, displacing his own expectations and at last properly imagining for others, he says he has 'fancied' the lives of Joe and Biddy when he was far away. In most of these personal fancies there is one strand of invention and one of perception. Invention is excited by deprivation, desire, fear, guilt, pity and shame, perception by desire, love, affection, and attention to the identity of people or things, which begins in the first chapter.

What is the narrative function of Pip's much-emphasized fancy in the novel in which he is hero and chief story-teller? We are constantly in the company of his fancy; it is the medium of narration. The title's 'Expectations' implies foresight, and Pip's fancy co-operates with Miss Havisham's, active like hers on behalf of self, as he constructs the story. Both make the mistake of using other people instrumentally, as characters in their story, Miss Havisham shaping Estella for her story of revenge, and shaping Pip's fanciful expectations of them both, in a circling narrative. All the while Magwitch's imagination is spinning his story, the making of his gentleman, in a ironic blend of gratitude and materialist dream in which he plans to reward Pip's natural young compassion with class-promotion and money.

There are scenes where the constructions of egoistic fancy are shattered. Magwitch reveals that Pip has been a character in his story, that he too has an active fancy and tells his own story in one of Dickens's great formal narrations. With Magwitch, Miss Havisham, Biddy and Joe, the first-person narrator's unreliability is shown with strong emphasis, as Pip's constructive imagination creates the form and language of the novel. Dickens uses this first-person narrative to show not only the powers of creative imagination but also its flaws and failure, though the optimistic tendency of Victorian *Bildungsroman* converts failure to triumph. But the failure has been shown. The tragic alternative conclusion which Dickens was persuaded to change was more in keeping with the imaginative failure than the happy ending, but the dangers of imagination are clear, and the narration is as reliable as it is self-revealing.

Notes

[1] Like David, she tells her story by telling other people's, but there is an apparent exception to the general rule that the stories within her story are told by her in personal speech. One episode in her narrative, 'Enlightened' (Ch. 51), begins 'When Mr Woodcourt arrived in London ...' and goes on to describe his meeting with Vholes and Richard in the third person, without reference to Esther's 'I', except when it is abruptly interrupted in her voice to say that Woodcourt 'told me that he could never forget the haggardness' of Richard's face and 'telling me generally of his first visit to Symond's Inn' but she does not specify time or place of his telling, and we seem to have an unassimilated narrative within hers, told from Woodcourt's point of view.

Chapter 5

Talkative Men and Women in *Pickwick Papers,*
Nicholas Nickleby, Martin Chuzzlewit and
Little Dorrit

Dickens is one of the few writers who can be called a language-changer, and though his basic style quickly assumed individual features, it is the unusual languages he invents for eccentric characters that show him at his most innovative and influential. He found material for comedy and satire in lawless people, outside the systems of normal educated English, which he knew thoroughly. Their brilliant idiolects were paradigms of creative language, liberated and self-generative, inspirations for more reflexive and experimental writers. Some of Dickens's best law-breakers are women, ridiculed but also privileged, outside academies and creative in gossip, who belong to a long misogynist tradition, including classical writers (like Callimachus, Semonides and Euripides) and most importantly Erasmus, who is not a feminist but whose heroine Moria, or Folly, cleverly and proudly flouts the man-made rhetoric books.[1] She ends her wonderful first-person treatise, *In Praise of Folly*, without the expected 'pseudo-encomium' which tidied up loose ends and summed up moral, joking, 'you must remember it's Folly and a woman who's been speaking' but quickly qualifying her irony with a Greek proverb, 'Often a fool speaks a word in season'. Like Chaucer's Wife of Bath before her, who also has a free-flowing narrative style though controlled by verse, Moria reminds us of gender, and her insistence also reminds us that she is a man's invention. She almost certainly influenced Shakespeare's clowns and jesters, 'wise enough to play the Fool'. His best lawless speakers are not the wise fools but Mistress Quickly and Juliet's Nurse, doubly advantaged as lower class as well as women, and Dickens's talkative women are in a direct line of descent from them.

But before Dickens found the talkative woman, he imagined his first fast free original talker in Jingle, a man whose 'rapid and disjointed communication' and 'system of stenography' (Ch. 7) draws on many sources – Dickens's own shorthand, cheap-jack street-talk and music-hall patter.[2] He is brilliantly invented for his novel, given appropriate character, light and shade, moral life, several false histories and a true one – in his mercenary elopement with Miss Rachel, sly foiling of Sam Weller and Pickwick, with happy reunion and forgiveness in prison. His language rattles on with gusto as he fires off anecdotes without wasting a word, in a telegraphese that uses dashes for punctuation and eliminates articles, conjunctions and pronouns: 'nothing like beefsteak for a bruise, sir; cold lamp-post very good, but lamp-post inconvenient – damned odd standing in the open street half-an-hour, with your eye against a lamp-post' (Ch. 2). It is a con-man's quick speech: his brazen boasts and tall tales take in the gullible Pickwick Club, and are a constant source of fun and irony: 'fired a musket, – fired with an idea – rushed into wine-shop – wrote it down – back again – whiz, bang – another idea, – wine shop again – pen and ink – back again ...' (Ch. 2). He is good at snappy endings as in his anecdote – one of 'hundreds' – about Ponto the pointer who refuses to pass the sign, 'Gamekeeper has order to shoot all dogs found in this inclosure' (Ch. 2). He is a star and a soloist, in this miscellany which combines hundreds of stories of varying tone, length, moral, social point and style.

Jingle's inventive subversion of periodic style made him a model for Leopold Bloom's stream of consciousness, and they are both salesmen, the unscrupulous extrovert and the benign introvert. They both resemble Joyce's illustrious model, talkative Ulysses, specialist in survival yarns, fake autobiographies and sad reminiscence of the Trojan war, maker of olive-brand to blind the Cyclops, olive-rooted marriage bed and wooden horse, in deed and word the most creative character in literature. Like ad-canvasser Bloom, down-at-heel Jingle is no epic hero but an accomplished plotter who cannot stop talking. Homer is less sentimental than Dickens and Ulysses goes on lying even when he is home in Ithaca but Jingle finally tells the truth, though he has his own kind of incorrigibility as he goes on even when half-starved, living 'on a pair of boots – whole fortnight. Silk umbrella – ivory handle – week ...'. The style is the man and in prison its brevity, bravado and irony come in handy: 'Can't step far – no danger of ever over-walking yourself here – spike park – grounds pretty – romantic, but not extensive – open for public inspection – family always in town – housekeeper desperately careful – very' (Ch. 42).

Jingle's rivals in narrative include the Bagman, another specialist in tall tales, the medical students who relish dissection-table anecdotes at meals, the Fat Boy who wants to make our flesh creep, and of course Sam Weller, deadpan teller of potted grim jokes, like 'There's nothin' so refreshin' as sleep, sir, as the servant-girl said afore she drank the egg-cupful o' laudanum' (Ch. 16), and the long comic stories already mentioned, about the man made into sausages and the doctor-defier who died eating crumpets. Sam came as a brilliant afterthought when sales were flagging, and is given his own Cockney version of those wheels which take fire from their motion in Coleridge's *Biographia Literaria* (Ch. 11): 'I goes on like an old barrow with a greased vheel' (*PP*, Ch. 6). These storytellers use gallows humour to dare poverty, drink, drugs, death, marriage, medicine and law. There are the formal inset stories told by the dismal man, the clergyman and Pickwick, to darken the high-spirited joking, farce and comedy of humours. *Pickwick Papers* is as richly plural as the 'Papers' of its title promises, a large loose monster whose multiplied tellings, like the stories of *The Arabian Nights* or plays within an Elizabethan play, vary narrative in a generic talkativeness.

But most of Dickens's talkative people are women, their invention no doubt encouraged by the success of Scheherazade as well as Shakespeare's garrulous women. His appreciation of Juliet's Nurse is nicely confirmed by the joke against critics in *Nicholas Nickleby* where he introduces his talking woman: Mr Curdle anticipates L. C. Knights' 'How Many Children Had Lady Macbeth?' by asking if the Nurse's husband really was 'a merry man' or whether it was 'merely his widow's affectionate partiality that induced her so to report him' (Ch. 24). Like the Wife of Bath, the Nurse and Mistress Quickly, Dickens's talkative women are widows past their first youth, but unlike Chaucer's and Shakespeare's in being vain, egocentric and too old for love – at least from their author's point of view. They are brilliant narrators but their creation is compromised by sexism and agism as the author invents their charmlessness. In a sense it doesn't matter because we trust the tale not the artist, and as Kate and Nicholas deplore their mother's refusal to grow old we are on her side because she is an entertainer and they are bores. Dickens makes Mrs Nickleby unsympathetic when she pushes Kate at Sir Mulberry Hawk with hopes of high-life marriage but her rich flow begins Dickens's most anarchic re-invention of language and narrative, and she is so creative that she undermines the misogynistic representation. She is sometimes traced back to Dickens's mother and he told a story about being asked by the real Mrs Nickleby if there ever was such a woman as the fictional one; but the writer of 'Our Monthly Gossip' in *Lippincott's Magazine* pointed out that the real Elizabeth Dickens was a clever mimic, with 'an extraordinary sense of the ludicrous' and a vein of pathos and the likeness was 'simply the exaggeration of some slight peculiarities' (quoted by Slater in *Dickens and Women*).

Mrs Nickleby may have taken Dickens by surprise as she grew. Her art develops under our eyes, from a brisk summary of weeping widow's complaints as she deplores the past 'with bitter recollections common to most married ladies' to voluminous direct speech. She flourishes self-pity and reminiscent habit to become a performance artist, her talk taking off, scatter-brained, rambling, absent-minded, digressive, enclosed and uninterruptable. She is a greedy soliloquizer, snatching the subject, seizing any excuse or cue. Her monologues are reminiscent and eagerly associative. The word 'milliner' calls up black oilskin-lined wicker-baskets, erased by 'visions of large houses at the West end, neat private carriages, and a banker's book, all of which images succeeded each other with ... rapidity' but the list is a stream of consciousness Dickens had met in Sterne as well as Shakespeare:

> I recollect when your poor papa and I came to town after we were married, that a young lady brought me home a chip cottage-bonnet, with white and green trimming and green persian lining, in her own carriage, which drove up to the door full gallop; – at least, I am not certain whether it was her own carriage or a hackney chariot, but I remember very well that the horse dropped down dead as he was turning round, and that your poor papa said he hadn't had any corn for a fortnight. (Ch. 10)

This random flow, inappropriate illustration, digression and excess circumstantiality are compounded by an arbitrary and unfeeling tone. The novel is punctuated by these monologues in which social particulars get more bizarre, style more illogical, and the outlook more optimistic, usually in contradiction to what is happening. Mrs Nickleby's strong point is failing to see a point, as in her anecdote of the cure for a common cold, 'used for the first time ... the day after Christmas' and working by April, and her 'curious' post-Stratford dream of 'a black gentleman, at full length, in plaster-of-Paris, with a lay-down collar tied with two tassels, leaning against a post and thinking' (Ch. 27). Forgettings and fumblings are aspects of this talkativeness that never stops to think: 'I forget, by the bye, whether that Miss Browndock was the same lady that got the ten thousand pounds prize in the lottery, but I think she was; indeed, now I come to think of it, I am sure she was' (Ch. 17) and 'I don't remember whether it was the Old Boar or the George the Third, but it was one of the two' (Ch. 18) and 'what was her name again? I know it began with a B, and ended with a G, but whether it was Waters or – no, it couldn't have been that, either' (Ch. 21). Her rhetorical questions and answers, blunders and corrections, both echo and exaggerate actual speech-habit, as she sways between total relevance and massive irrelevance. Her discourse has more variety than unity but shows a kind of structure, and at times even relevance, as when she innocently and loquaciously replies to Lord Frederick Verisopht's inquiry about Kate, on whose virtue he has designs: ' "She is quite well, I'm obliged to you, my lord ... Quite well. She wasn't well for some days after that day she dined here, and I can't help thinking, that she caught cold in that hackney-coach ... I think it was a hackney-coach", said Mrs Nickleby reflecting' (Ch. 26). Kate complains that she is driven by 'torrents' of recollection and her stories do not bear on the subject under discussion, but she can return to make an end, like Miss Bates in *Emma*: 'Having pretty well run herself out by this time, Mrs Nickleby stopped as suddenly as she had started off, and repeated that Kate was quite well ...' (Ch. 26).

Dickens composes a farewell speech for her which at last shows some feeling, for her listeners and the dead Smike, but without losing nonsense or non sequitur so in no risk of sentimental lapse: 'I have lost the best, the most zealous, and most attentive creature that has ever been a companion to me in my life – putting you, my dear Nicholas, and Kate, and your poor papa, and that well-behaved nurse who ran away with the linen and the twelve small forks, out of the question, of course' (Ch. 61).

The significantly named Miss Knag, unmarried but of course middle-aged and unattractive, is a rival: 'Mrs Nickleby stopped to breathe; and Miss Knag, finding that the discourse was turning upon family greatness, lost no time in striking in, with a small reminiscence on her own account ...' (Ch. 18). Her nonsense and speed are all her own, needing a narrative filler, 'hem': 'I had an uncle ... who lived in Cheltenham, and had a most excellent business as a tobacconist – hem – who had such small feet, that they were no bigger than those which are usually joined to wooden legs' (Ch. 17). Mrs Nickleby's fillers are common ones, 'by the bye', 'Oh dear me!' and 'at all events' but the next talkative woman, Mrs Gamp, more inventively supplies, 'as Mrs Harris says'.

Gamp develops the mixture of joke and reflexive narrative. Mrs Nickleby's sentences are usually punctuated and correct in grammar and lexis but Mrs Gamp is inventive in every way. She continues the household themes of children, illness and accident but with a professional and pathological slant. Her stories are told in a curt style and are unified and polished as suits her self-promotion: she cajoles customers, leers hopefully at young women, flatters old ones and extends her ego with Mrs Harris. She knows the tricks of charm, aggression, humility and modesty – like an ingratiating way of buttonholing interlocutors and addressing them by name. Many of her anecdotes discredit women as well as men, though they never turn against Self – the novel's theme – or Mrs Harris. She surpasses Mrs Nickleby's mild misandry in a way which harks back to the gender-awareness of Chaucer and Erasmus, though hers is a mere grain of suggestion as she reflects that the noisy dirty steamship (at times disliked by her author too) could bring on miscarriage: 'Ugh ... one might easy know you was a man's invention' (Ch. 40). Because her narration combines the unreliabilities of exaggeration, boast, flattery, lie and advertisement, the male author can laugh up his sleeve at her misandry but he seems less aware of the deconstructive power of this kind of gender-reference than Chaucer or Erasmus.

Her stories have a serial theme in her husband, who sends their son 'to sell his wooden leg for any money it 'ud fetch as matches in the rough, and bring it home in liquor' (Ch. 25), is laid-out in Guy's Hospital 'with a penny-piece on each eye, and his wooden leg under his left arm' (Ch. 19), and finished off as his widow sells his remains 'for the benefit of science'. She is deservingly praised by Mr Mould the undertaker – whom she flatters – for observation, reflection and mind, and though used to mock women she is a dangerous force, not quelled till Dickens uses her for his peripeteia and she is optimistically dismissed to drink less and nurse better – and not really then.

Her strong point is style, and you can't imagine Joyce's word-play without her model. Her errors are more poetic than Malaprop's, and compounded in portmanteau-puns, like 'Ingeins' which blends 'engine' and 'ingenious' (Ch. 40), 'wale of life' (Ch. 40) which improves the Christian lachrymose 'vale', 'Led a Martha to the Stakes' (Ch. 26), 'Lord Mayor and Uncommon Counsellors' (Ch. 29), 'witness for the persecution' (Ch. 40), and 'proticipate' (Ch. 40). Her revision of common wisdom is subtle and hilarious: 'we never knows wot's hidden in each other's breasts, and if we had glass winders there, we'd need to keep the shutters up' (Ch. 29) and 'Rich folks may ride on camels, but it an't so easy for 'em to see out of a needle's eye' (Ch. 25), an intertextual stroke which makes sense as well as nonsense out of Gospel wit. She neatly converts adjectives to verbs: 'Whether I sicks or whether I monthlies', wittily compares an infant's legs to Canterbury Brawn, combines malapropism with oxymoron in 'airy stones', and metonymy with personification in 'damp door-steps settled on their lungs' and the wooden leg 'gone likeways home to its account, which in its constancy of walkin into wine vaults, and never comin out again till fetched by force, was quite as weak as flesh' (Ch. 40). It is subversive and breathtakingly original language.

She invents a fictitious character in her familiar spirit and alter ego Mrs Harris, who also demonstrates the eloquence of an absence. Her pity and sorrow are factitious but her creative verve is the real thing and it is understandable that Dickens tried to prolong her unreconstructed vivacity in a sketch about a theatre production which never came off: 'I am informed as there is Ladies in this party, and that half a dozen of 'em if not more, is in various stages of a interesting state. Mrs Harris, you and me well knows what Ingeins often does'. She is aware of her 'beograffer', like Sancho Panza in the second part of *Don Quixote*, and recalls her predecessor in garrulous misandry, 'Dougladge' Jerrold's Mrs Curdle, for whom she feels sisterly sympathy, 'that sweet saint, Mrs C' (Forster, Bk 6, Ch. 1).

Flora Finching inherits Mrs Nickleby's inconsequentiality but with greater freedom in syntax. Hers is the real stream of consciousness, unstoppable and almost without formal stops, rhythmical and grammatical inspiration – perhaps along with Nora Barnacle – for Molly Bloom's unpunctuated flow:

> ... pray don't answer, I don't know where I'm running to, oh do tell me something about the Chinese ladies whether their eyes are really so long and narrow always putting me in mind of mother-of-pearl fish at cards and do they really wear tails down their backs and plaited too or is it only the men, and when they pull their hair so very tight off their foreheads don't they hurt themselves, and why do they stick little bells all over their bridges and temples and hats and things or don't they really do it! (*Little Dorrit*, Bk 1, Ch. 13)

Flora mixes dead metaphors: 'if he hadn't been cut short while I was a new broom' (Bk 1, Ch. 24) and her summary of Mr F's seven proposals is triumphant zeugma 'once in a hackney coach once in a boat once in a pew once on a donkey at Tunbridge Wells and the rest on his knees' (Bk 1, Ch. 24). Her disordered fluid prose can blur vehicle and tenor to turn everyday things surreal: 'with your Mama's parasol between them seated on two chairs like mad bulls' (Bk 1, Ch. 13). She has no time for prepositional clues, so confuses relationship: 'a coat-of-arms of course and wild beasts on their hind legs' (Bk 2, Ch. 9) and her conversational fillers are familiar but more oddly placed than Mrs Nickleby's and Miss Knag's: 'the what's-his-name horizon of et cetera' (Bk 2, Ch. 9). She likes ordered disjunction, as befits a 'moral mermaid' (Bk 1, Ch. 13) and it is through dualities that her prose combines poetic wildness, freedom, dislocation – and coherence. Like Mrs Nickleby she can make a large loop between beginning and ending; like her author she doesn't always know her destination but gets there in the end. Like Miss Bates who knows she is rather a talker she can say 'I don't know where I'm running to' (Bk 1, Ch. 13). Like Mrs Gamp she creates character, and her Mr F is tersely drawn from the life:

> ... don't mind me or wait for me because I always carry in this tray myself to Mr F's Aunt who breakfasts in bed and a charming old lady too and very clever, Portrait of Mr F behind the door and very like though too much forehead and as to a pillar with a marble pavement and balustrades and a mountain I never saw him near it nor likely, in the wine trade, excellent man but not at all in that way. (Bk 1, Ch. 24)

Her pictures of Italy rival her author's in speed and kaleidoscopic flicker, while keeping her benevolent and appreciative tone: 'In Italy is she really ... with the grapes and figs growing everywhere and lava necklaces and bracelets too that land of poetry with burning mountains picturesque beyond belief' (Bk 2, Ch. 9). Her style occasionally seems too clever and sharp, too much her master's voice, as when she says Mrs Clennam 'ought to be the mother of the man in the iron mask' and compares her to 'Fate in a go-cart' (Bk 1, Ch. 24).

Dickens puts into the talkative women his creative experience of letting go, in an extreme and isolated form, eliminating the revisionary and ordering process which Coleridge recognized as the educated man's 'Method' and power of 'surview' and importantly identified as a feature of class as well as gender (*Essays on the Principles of Method* 4, *Collected Works*, 1). In the Nurse and Mistress Quickly Coleridge saw the immethodical mind methodized, as they relate events 'in the same order and with the same accompaniments, however accidental or impertinent, in which they had first occurred to the narrator' (*Biographia Literaria*, Ch. 13). The disadvantage is praised by Coleridge and demonstrated by Dickens as a triumph of art. Insofar as it had an actual social basis in a gendered love of gossip and domestic conversation, it is what the novelist Constance Holme in her fine working-class novel *The Trumpet in the Dust* showed in gossiping women characters and shrewdly described as 'almost the only form of artistic expression open to most of the poor' (Pt 2, Ch. 1).[3] In other classes, many societies and various times, women's talkativeness is an obvious compensation for home-enclosure and public silence, while the etymology of 'gossip' recalls the ritual of celebration and goodwill. Like Moria, the talkative women of Dickens create strong linguistic subversions, and though like Shakespeare's women they are subordinate in his action, like them they dominate the scene when they appear. They tire their fictitious listeners, Lady Capulet or Kate Nickleby, but amuse the reader, reflect the writer at his most free, wild and relaxed, and change the language of literature. The creative informality of language celebrated by woman novelists like Virginia Woolf and Dorothy Richardson, and more radically politicized by later feminists as *écriture féminine* – which I shall discuss in my last chapter – takes more from Dickens than from Erasmus and Shakespeare as it adapts for its purposes a man's stereotype of woman's intuition and her domestic chat and gossip.

Notes

[1] In this chapter I have drawn on my article 'The Talkative Woman in Shakespeare, Dickens and George Eliot' in *Problems for Feminist Criticism*, ed. Sally Minogue, London and New York: Routledge, 1990.

[2] Earle Rosco Davis has traced Jingle's music-hall origins in *The Flint and the Flame: The Artistry of Charles Dickens*, London: Gollancz, 1964.

[3] I discuss good and bad gossip, Constance Holme, Dickens and other relevant authors in *Tellers and Listeners: The Narrative Imagination*, London: Athlone, 1975.

Chapter 6

Imaginative Extremes, Negations and Norms

In Dickens's images of imagination, the extremes, negations and norms are drawn from his reflections on his own mind. In 'Night Walks' which I discussed in Chapter 2, the Uncommercial Traveller wrote of his 'night fancy' outside Bethlehem Hospital 'Are not the sane and the insane equal at night as the same lie dreaming?' and went on to explain:

> Are not all of us outside this hospital, who dream, more or less in the condition of those inside it, every night of their lives? Are we not nightly persuaded, as they daily are, that we associate preposterously with kings and queens, emperors and empresses, and notabilities of all sorts? Do we not nightly jumble events and personages and times and places, as these do daily?... Said an afflicted man to me, when I was last in a hospital like this, 'Sir, I can frequently fly.' I was half ashamed to reflect that so could I – by night. Said a woman to me on the same occasion, 'Queen Victoria frequently comes to dine with me, and her Majesty and I dine off peaches and maccaroni in our nightgowns, and his Royal Highness the Prince Consort does us the honour to make a third on horseback in a Field-Marshal's uniform.' Could I refrain from reddening ... when I remembered the amazing royal parties I had myself given (at night) ... I wonder that the great master who knew everything, when he called Sleep the death of each day's life, did not call Dreams the insanity of each day's sanity. ('The Uncommercial Traveller', *Journalism* 4)

One of the most interesting dreams in Dickens is dreamt by Jarvis Lorry as he travels by night on the Dover Road in *A Tale of Two Cities*. It is composed in a half-sleep in the jolting coach, and combines his daily routine at Tellson's bank, the message 'Recalled to Life', and the worry of his mission. His disturbed mind is a screen on which Dickens can also project the image of Manette, the Bastille prisoner, as a figment of imagination and an image of what is to come:

But, though the bank was almost always with him, and though the
coach (in a confused way, like the presence of pain under an opiate)
was always with him, there was another current of impression that
never ceased to run, all through the night. He was on his way to dig
some one out of a grave. (Bk I, Ch. 3)

There follows a spectre-like dream image of the prisoner he is going to
meet, and the half-dream alternates between an anxious but rational
forecast of a likely interview and hallucinatory surreal grave-digging
and decomposition. The experience is marked by fitful sleep, dream-
sensations of physical touch, and one of the novel's repeated images, the
shadow, cast here by the dark night outside and the dark fantasy inside:

After such imaginary discourse, the passenger in his fancy would dig,
and dig, dig – now, with a spade, now with a great key, now with his
hands – to dig this wretched creature out. Got out at last, with earth
hanging about his face and hair, he would suddenly fall away to dust.
The passenger would then start to himself, and lower the window, to
get the reality of mist and rain on his cheek.

Yet even when his eyes were opened on the mist and rain, on the
moving patch of light from the lamps, and the hedge at the roadside
retreating by jerks, the night shadows outside the coach would fall into
the train of the night shadows within. (Bk 1, Ch. 3)

Lorry's 'jumble' of 'events and personages and times and places',
interestingly linked to pathology by the opiate comparison, serves the
novelist's purposes in tense anticipation and preparation, a foreboding
prospective movement which is to become habitual in the story and a
sounding of its resurrection theme, placed within the consciousness of
an imaginative character who disclaims imagination. It all presents the
dreaming mind which Dickens loves to dwell on.

It is not only dreams that are the insanity of ordinary life: Esther, Paul
Dombey and Pip are creative characters who experience those states of
delirium, hallucination and fantasy which are parts of ordinary life.
When Esther has smallpox and suffers from high fever her delirium has
a surreal setting and sensation:

I laboured up colossal staircases, ever striving to reach the top, and
ever turned, as I have seen a worm in a garden path, by some
obstruction, and labouring again. I knew perfectly at intervals, and I
think vaguely at most times, that I was in my bed ... I would find

myself complaining 'O more of these everlasting stairs, Charley,'–
more and more – piled up to the sky …

… Dare I hint at that worse time when … there was a flaming
necklace or ring or starry circle of some kind, of which *I* was one of the
beads! And when my only prayer was to be taken off from the rest …
(Ch. 35)

Dickens shows Esther in a state where she feels extreme fatigue and loses
her bearings but is intermittently conscious of her surroundings: the
action is abnormally slowed-down, and the imagery exotic and strange in
proportion and space – like Piranesi's *Carceri d'Invenzione (Imaginary
Prisons)* where staircases and shifts of scale loom large, and which
Dickens may have known or read about in De Quincey, who also discusses dreams and delirium, or, for a modern comparison, like the sets
and scenes designed by Salvador Dali for Hitchcock's film *Spellbound.*
Esther gets worse, displaced in time as well as space, destabilized, unable
to identify object and substance – is it necklace or circle, flaming or
starry? Her wild poetry is not romantic but internalizes horror, and her
reminiscence is troubled, obscure and reluctant.

Paul Dombey's imagery of wild waves and beckoning arms begins in
nostalgia and glamour, but when he is dying, though he has some
residual consciousness of place and people, his imagination torments
him: 'His only trouble was, the swift and rapid river. He felt forced,
sometimes, to try to stop it – to stem it with his childish hands – or choke
its way with sand' and asks, 'Why will it never stop, Floy?' (Ch. 16).
Dickens is good at describing the deranged imagination in normal
characters, who are the more fully realized for being shown in their
extraordinary lapses of reasoning.

One of the most original narratives is indirectly or parodically, connected with Pip's great expectations, and is quite different from his main
fantasies, with their dangerous plausibility. This is the set of bizarre lies
he tells when he comes home from his first visit to the Satis House which
nourishes so many dissatisfactions. The fascinating thing about this is its
resistance to interpretation: it is arbitrary and zany, a free-floating fancy
wrung out of the imaginative desperate child by the interrogation of the
adult world, which is driven by curiosity, class-jealousy and family
authority, and wonderfully rebuffed as the child pushes fantasy beyond
belief and forces his interlocutors to believe him. They ask how he got
on, and want a better answer than a child's common vague 'pretty well',
so they press him, 'What was she a'doing of?' and the gorgeous lies
follow:

> She was sitting ... in a black velvet coach ... And Miss Estella ...
> handed her in cake and wine at the coach-window, on a gold plate.
> And we all had cake and wine on gold plates. And I got up behind the
> coach to eat mine, because she told me to. (Bk 1, Ch. 9)

Here invention is urged on by the listeners, and the result is a kind of
lateral thinking: the fantasy of the immense dogs who fought for veal
cutlets out of a silver basket, the coach in Miss Havisham's room, and the
game in which Estella waved a blue flag, Pip waved a red one and Miss
Havisham waved one sprinkled with little gold stars and they fight with
swords, is initiated by prompting from the outside: 'Swords! ... Where
did you get swords from?' The fantasist makes some probability checks,
'But there weren't any horses to it', and his lies have a groundwork of
fact, 'there was no daylight in the room, but it was all lighted up with
candles'. As Wordsworth demonstrates in his 'Anecdote for Fathers' and
as we know from experience of the questioning adult and taciturn child,
if we ask a silly question we get a silly answer. If we insist on a story we
may get lies. And there is a good excuse for Pip, who has been shocked
by his new experience of sex, wealth and class and cannot tell anyone all
that has happened, because he is ashamed, and because he hasn't taken
it all in. When Joe asks 'What possessed you?' he gives the obscure true
answer: 'I don't know what possessed me ... but I wish you hadn't taught
me to call Knaves at cards, Jacks, and I wish my boots weren't so thick nor
my hands so coarse.' 'What possessed you?': like Dickens, David and
Esther, Pip is wounded, and injured pride is the cause of his drawing –
not so much the bow of Philoctetes as the long bow. 'What possessed
you?': creativity has many sources and behind Pip's brilliant lies there is a
child's shy self-respecting reticence, the difficulty of putting experience
into story, and, just a little, at least on the author's part, the fun of
teasing the inquisitive or gullible and the exhilaration of self-generative
art, the wheels taking fire from the rapidity of their motion. Homer
knew the connection between being a fine story-teller and a good liar,
and though Dickens is too conventionally moral to develop Pip's lying
skill, it shows his imagination.

Dickens shows the twists and turns of so-called normal minds, but of
course he is also good at imagining pathologically deranged states of
imagination, without privileging them, and some of his characters are
what the Victorians called mad. Permanently disturbed characters like
Smike and Mr Dick are made half-aware of their pathology, feeling pain,
anxiety and discomfort. Betsy Trotwood's insistence on Dick's sanity,
which she encourages by never treating him as a pathological case, is a

shrewd caring therapy and is backed by the author when Dick brings
about a reconciliation for the Strongs. But Dick's free delight and touch
of poetry as he flies his kite of inspiration or contrives wonderful toys for
the schoolboys, are offset by his puzzled pained obsession with King
Charles's head. The 'madman' who courts Mrs Nickleby with cucumbers
and marrows is done entirely from the outside but his surreal poetry is
true nonsense, anticipating Lewis Carroll and Edward Lear in its wild
style: 'jewels, lighthouses, fish-ponds, a whalery of my own in the North
Sea, and several oyster-beds of great profit in the Pacific Ocean'; and
'bring in the bottled lightning, a clean tumbler and a corkscrew' and 'all
is gas and gaiters' (Chs 41, 49). Dickens loves this kind of zany con-
glomeration, with meaning suspended but syntax and music preserved,
the jumble illustrated by Coleridge in Thomas Otway's language for
mania, 'Lutes, laurels, seas of milk and ships of amber' from *Venice
Preserv'd*, (quoted and discussed in the *Biographia Literaria*, Ch. 4), but his
cucumber man, though enjoyable, is certainly not romanticized as he
plays his small comic part in a misogynist farce.

Barnaby Rudge is Dickens's most sustained study in madness, his
character not played for laughs and offering vision, freedom and play, all
of which he judges a privilege and proudly introduces to the cold
rationalist John Chester, and in the presence of the unimaginative John
Willett, by praising the 'hurry and mystery' in a clothes-line:

Look down there ... do you mark how they whisper in each other's
ears; then dance and leap, to make believe they are in sport? Do you
see how they stop for a moment when they think there is no one
looking, and mutter among themselves again; and then how they roll
and gambol, delighted with the mischief they've been plotting? Look
at 'em now. See how they whirl and plunge. And now they stop again,
and whisper, cautiously together – little thinking, mind, how often I
have lain upon the grass and watched them. I say – what is it that they
plot and hatch?...

... Clothes! ... Ha ha! Why, how much better to be silly, than as wise
as you! You don't see shadowy people there, like those that live in
sleep – not you. Nor eyes in the knotted panes of glass, nor swift ghosts
when it blows hard, nor do you hear voices in the air, nor see men
stalking in the sky – not you! I lead a merrier life than you, with all
your cleverness. You're the dull men. We're the bright ones. (Ch. 10)

Wordsworth's Idiot Boy, to whom Barnaby is sometimes compared, is
much less articulate and has nothing of Barnaby's pride in madness or

his role as wild artist – because Barnaby draws on his author's own imagination and imaginative awareness. As Chester protests that the dancers are only clothes and Barnaby pities his dullness, we remember the old clothes in Monmouth Street, Master Humphrey changing curiosities into dramatis personae and David Copperfield looking at the sundial. Barnaby loves night and restless movement, creative hurry and rush, and looking into the fire: 'I don't like bed. I like to lie before the fire, watching the prospects in the burning coals – the rivers, hills, and dells, in the deep, red sunset, and the wild faces' (Ch. 17). His imaginative vivacity is not heartless: when he boasts of fantasy to the blind man he is not too mad to love and pity his mother:

> I am often out before the sun ... and am often there when the bright moon is peeping through the boughs, and looking down upon the other moon that lives in the water. As I walk along, I try to find, among the grass and moss, some of that small money for which she works so hard and used to shed so many tears. (Ch. 46)

In her introduction to the Oxford Illustrated edition Kathleen Tillotson judges Barnaby a melodramatic failure, lacking psychological truth, but I find him a true and convincing portrait of imagination, an unsentimental image of self-delighting though exhausting energy. He is not wholly romanticized: his naivety is inspired, 'the other moon', but the spirited poetry is not soft and some of his visions are terrible: he fears blood, which he dare not name, 'Is it in the room as I have seen it in my dreams, dashing the ceiling and the walls with red?' (Ch. 17). Dickens is not privileging fantasy but not disowning it either, not only passing on his own habits and inspirations and admitting the joy of letting go, but knowing that fear and rage can rouse imagination and showing uncontrolled creativity as dangerous.

The critique of fantasy is important in the novel: Barnaby is an image and an example of the wildness, delusion and damage of revolution. His susceptibility, terrors and obsessions – especially his fixations on blood and gold – and Mrs Rudge's maternal anguish at her child's 'darkened intellect' (Ch. 25) are personal and particular and contribute subtly to the moral drama of the Gordon Riots. And Barnaby does not function alone but with the supporting cases of Hugh, Dennis the hangman and Lord George Gordon, all unhappy qualifications of 'bright' madness.

Dickens's language is on Barnaby's side and he uses his controlled art to imagine Barnaby's congenial wildness, just as Yeats – who writes about being driven 'wild' by imagination – imagines his congenial Crazy Jane and pits her subversive energy against religion and conventional morality. Dickens draws on his own creativity and though he is on the side of rationality in politics and psychology, he takes a delight in manic Barnaby and names the novel, with all its ambivalence, after him. Barnaby is a revolutionary figure arguing the value of madness, but Dickens cleverly manages to make the political significance emerge slowly and first articulates the praise of folly and fantasy in a poetry which never hints at the politics of madness, and prepares for reconciliation in the end.

And in case bright Barnaby should engage too much sympathy and gloating sadist Dennis too little, Dickens creates a range of imaginative action, putting beside the extremes of madness the habitual lapses of reason; for example, the heroic locksmith Gabriel Vardon is seen driving home in a 'dog sleep':

> A man may be very sober ... and yet feel a strong tendency to mingle up present circumstances with others which have no manner of connection with them; to confound all consideration of persons, things, times, and places; and to jumble his disjointed thoughts together in a kind of mental kaleidoscope, producing combinations as unexpected as they are transitory. This was Gabriel Vardon's state, as, nodding in his dog sleep ... he got over the ground unconsciously ... he awoke out of a dream about picking a lock in the stomach of the Great Mogul, and even when he did wake, mixed up the turnpike man with his mother-in-law who had been dead twenty years. (Ch. 3)

Barnaby Rudge teems with such references to the everyday working of imagination and fancy, and almost every character answers to them positively or negatively. The Preface emphasizes 'fancy', insisting on the novel's origin in truth not 'the Author's fancy' and telling us that Dickens's pet raven, the model for Barnaby's bird, had an imagination: 'he would perch outside my window and drive imaginary horses with great skill'. The word 'fancy' appears in its range of meanings. John Chester speaks of his son's fancy and his fanciful attraction to Emma, and Hugh wonders if anyone has a fancy for his dog. Haredale speaks of Solomon's 'foolish fancy ... bred in his fears and superstition' (Ch. 34), and Chester calls Dennis the hangman's refusal to reveal his trade 'A strange fancy' (Ch. 40). At the end of the novel a dream from which Haredale wakes in horror is ascribed to a 'condition' of the 'mind ... favourable to the growth of disordered fancies ...' (Ch. 81). Sim Tappertit the revolutionary apprentice-leader feeds on various 'fancies' – 'which fancies, like the liver of Prometheus, grew as they were fed upon'

(Ch. 4). Joe Willet's 'wonderful visions' are followed in one of the brisk walks that inspired Dickens: 'He walked along ... big with great thoughts of going for a soldier and dying in some foreign country where it was very hot and sandy, and leaving God knows what unheard-of wealth in prize-money to Dolly, who would be very much affected ...'. The narrator draws attention to the way Joe's emotions are dynamic but centred, 'sometimes sanguine, and sometimes melancholy' but with one 'main point and centre' (Ch. 31).

Another variant is John Willet's lack of imagination, which extends to his misunderstanding and appropriation of the word: he sees it only in its absence, does not see it when it is there, and demonstrates it by lacking it. He offers his catch-phrase after Barnaby defends 'the bright ones' and Chester calls him strange: and John says 'He wants imagination ... I've tried to instil it into him ... but ... he an't made for it ...' (Ch. 10). He diagnoses Hugh's repression, 'That chap ... though he has all his faculties about him, somewheres or other, bottled up and corked down, has no more imagination than Barnaby has' and develops his theory, explaining that Hugh never had his faculties 'drawed out' (Ch. 11). Later when Haredale says Hugh has an evil eye John repeats automatically, 'There's no imagination in his eye' (Ch. 34). He recommends the top of the Monument as a temptation-free place with 'no drink – no young women – nothing but imagination' (Ch. 13). Shocked into imaginative action after rioters sack the Maypole Inn, he says 'the old dumb Maypole' outside gave him ideas of suicide and his friend Solomon is appalled by 'this mournful effort of ... imagination' (Ch. 56). The narrator makes a rather feeble joke when he describes Willet's 'double chin', 'such ... as the liveliest imagination could never in its boldest flights have conjured up' (Ch. 72).

Dickens enjoyed the comic disclaimer of imagination so much that he went on using it. Meagles in *Little Dorrit* keeps saying he and his wife are 'practical' when he is describing their generosity and sympathy, and his trick is irritating because it seems too affected and mock-modest but also because he is really not very imaginative so we may agree with him.

As we have seen, Jarvis Lorry In *A Tale of Two Cities* is shown dreaming in the Dover coach, and his imagination is vivid, tender and sympathetic, though he disclaims it, most emphatically and ironically in the Dover scene where he tells Lucie about her father, insisting that he is a mere man of business. He is matched by Miss Pross, a blunt, plain down-to-earth speaker who is sharply perceptive but prides herself on a grasp of reality, asserting the not wholly perverse 'Never imagine anything'. The narrator draws attention to her description of the traumatized Manette's

compulsive repetition of his former exercise in the restricted space of a
prison cell:

> 'Sometimes, he gets up in the dead of the night, and will be heard, by
> us overhead there, walking up and down, walking up and down, in his
> room. Ladybird has learnt to know then that his mind is walking up
> and down, walking up and down, in his old prison. She hurries to him,
> and they go on together, walking up and down, walking up and down,
> until he is composed ... In silence they go walking up and down
> together, walking up and down together ...'
> ... Notwithstanding Miss Pross's denial of her own imagination,
> there was a perception of the pain of being monotonously haunted by
> one sad idea, in her repetition of the phrase, walking up and down,
> which testified to her possessing such a thing. (Bk 2, Ch. 6)

Except perhaps in Lorry's dream, and in the Bastille letter, we never
enter Manette's mind, the most disturbed in this novel, shown intermittently fixated on the past and prison, and ironically responsible for
his son-in-law's death sentence when his letter is produced by Defarge
and the past bursts into the present. What Dickens does for his disturbance, and at the same time for Pross's sensitive observation, which
he discriminates by having her disclaim imagination, is to provide a
critical comment on her – so on his own – rhetorical miming of the
obsessed repetitive behaviour. (Of course another novelist would leave
her language to speak for itself but Dickens had to make sure readers got
the point.) He loved repetitions but he has Pross use other figures too,
like the terse diagnostic metaphor 'his mind is walking' and the tender
variant 'walking up and down together' as she observes therapy in progress. It is interesting that in this scene she is talking to Lorry, already
established as congenial in empathetic imagination and modesty. It is a
creative conversation even though one character does most of the
talking.

The imaginations of Lorry and Pross are shown with more solidity of
psychic specification than that of Lucie Manette, who shares Little
Dorrit's self-aware fanciful bent but is shown in a more stylized and
superficial fashion. There is a corner in the Manettes' Soho house which
is full of echoes, and Lucie fancies she can hear footsteps coming from
the future, but Sydney Carton and the narrator take her fancy over, to
make it more ominous but less particular. Though it may have been
intended to give Lucie an individual interiority, it ceases to do this as it is
absorbed and generalized in the novel's prolepsis and pattern.

The unfinished *Mystery of Edwin Drood* begins with a chapter called 'Dawn', set in a squalid East End opium den where someone is recovering consciousness after drugged sleep. All we know at the beginning is that we are inside a mind:

> An ancient English Cathedral Town? How can the ancient English Cathedral town be here? The well-known massive gray square tower of the old Cathedral? How can that be here! There is no spike of rusty iron in the air, between the eye and it, from any point of the real prospect. What is the spike that intervenes, and who has set it up? Maybe, it is set up by the Sultan's orders for the impaling of a horde of Turkish robbers, one by one. It is so, for cymbals clash, and the Sultan goes by to his palace in long procession. Ten thousand scimitars flash in the sunlight, and thrice ten thousand dancing-girls strew flowers. Then, follow white elephants caparisoned in countless gorgeous colours, and infinite in number and attendants. Still, the Cathedral tower rises in the background, where it cannot be, and still no writhing figure is on the grim spike. Stay! Is the spike so low a thing as the rusty spike on the top of a post of an old bedstead that has tumbled all awry? Some vague period of drowsy laughter must be devoted to the consideration of this possibility.
>
> Shaking from head to foot, the man whose scattered consciousness has thus fantastically pieced itself together, at length rises ... (Ch. 1)

It is one of many present-tense passages in a novel which alternates past with present narrative, and here its free indirect style can be impersonal and put us inside the mind's movement as 'scattered consciousness fantastically pieced itself together', tracing a rational questioning of the senses, an attempt to reconcile fancy and reality and sustain the dream by reconstruction and submission – and of course all these psychological details are actual features of dreaming. The disturbed mental state is made especially immediate and substantial by being unassigned to a person: we are not told it is the action of John Jasper's mind but gradually infer this during the second chapter. The Eastern exoticism and the image of impalement may owe something to De Quincey's description of his more horrifying and violent opium dreams, or Dickens may have been informed by friends – Wilkie Collins perhaps – who took opium, but John Jasper's slow recovery to reality and reason is not in De Quincey, and it is in Dickens's other more 'ordinary' dream scenarios, like Vardon's. And to put John Jasper besides De Quincey is to recognize the incorrigible comic element present even in Dickensian pathology.

For most of the unfinished novel's 23 chapters – half the intended length – Jasper's consciousness is kept from us, screened by cryptic and deceptive dialogue and brief hints, until we enter his mind again in the last chapter 'The Dawn Again', which parallels the first, 'Dawn'. He returns to the Princess Puffer's den, and only at this stage do we learn definitely that the Cathedral-tower-Turkish-robber fantasy was not an opium dream but the aftermath of one; we infer the actual dream, the deep dream, from Jasper's slow bit-by-bit enigmatic questioning of Puffer, one of the best things in the novel.

He asks: 'Suppose you had something in your mind; something you were going to do', and 'But had not quite determined to do', and 'Might or might not do' and at last, 'Should you do it in your fancy, when you were lying here doing this?' The old expert replies 'Over and over again' and he responds 'I did it over and over again. I have done it hundreds of thousands of times in this room.' When she ironically asks if 'it' was pleasant to do, he says, 'with a savage air, and a spring or start at her', that it '*was* pleasant to do'. He goes on 'I did it millions and billions of times. I did it so often, and through such vast expanses of time, that when it was really done, it seemed not worth the doing, it was done so soon'; she observes, 'That's the journey you have been away upon?' and he replies 'That's the journey.' The dream of a murder which in this strange intimacy is never called murder, is placed by flashback just before the kind of exotic fantasy which forms part of the fragmented half-waking dream at the start: 'I always made the journey first, before the changes of colors and the great landscapes and glittering processions began. They couldn't begin till it was off my mind. I had no room till then for anything else.' Jasper uses 'the journey' as a euphemism for his murderous fantasy though Princess Puffer uses it literally, and it leads to an introduction of another euphemism, the 'fellow-traveller' – an important covert reference to the victim Edwin Drood. Jasper says that when he experienced something 'real' it was inferior to what he imagined, goes on to say he is having a vision he finds 'too short' and wants to prolong, and in cryptic back-reference says, 'No struggle, no consciousness of peril, no entreaty', and finally, 'what a poor, mean, miserable thing it is'. The dissatisfaction with the reality is a substitute for guilt, a perverse dissociation which looks ahead to that never-written last prison-narrative Dickens told Forster about. The reliance on suggestion and implication is a new thing in Dickens, and of course functional in the thriller, which turns – or would have turned – not on 'Who did it?' but on the process of detection and discovery, and on the murderer's inner life before and after he did it.[2]

Between these two widely spaced episodes, the only scenes in the opium den and the only scenes where we have access to Jasper's inner life, he occasionally says revealing things, such as, 'What is the matter?' and 'Who did it?' which Crisparkle hears him cry out as he springs 'from the couch in a delirious state between sleeping and waking' (Ch. 10). But the reader can read the neutral loaded 'something', 'it', a 'journey', and 'fellow-traveller', as sinister details in the detective story, the murderer's psychology, and the phatic communion of two degraded characters who have only opium in common.

John Jasper is seen through Rosa Bud's thoughts and feelings. After the disappearance of Edwin Drood the first mention of any suspicion against him is placed in her consciousness, a doubtful fantasy based on her fear of his passionate deceitful nature, and what he has told her, 'my love is mad ... I might have swept even him from your side when you favored him', which weighs both for and against him (Ch. 19). Rosa thinks he would be unlikely to say this if guilty but the narrator hints, 'what could she know of the criminal intellect?' (Ch. 20). These are nuances in the character and the detection story, as Rosa considers the case against Jasper in 'excited memory and imagination' where 'half-formed, wholly unexpressed suspicion tossed ... now heaving itself up, and now sinking into the deep; now gaining palpability, and now losing it' (Ch. 20). As she remembers, imagines, and questions her imagination, her inner action marks a stage in the plot, and takes its place in the novel's psychological scale and spectrum.

Another character to whose inner life we have access, of an indirect kind, is Mr Grewgious, Rosa's guardian, the most imaginative of those characters who disclaim imagination, an old bachelor with a soft heart, calling himself 'Angular' but disproving the disclaimer in 'A Picture and a Ring', where he uses the word 'picture' as metaphor and imbues the ring with life and power. The scene begins in a long comic action, and the fun of the flying waiter and the immoveable waiter makes a marked contrast to the ominous conclusion. Grewgious proposes a toast to his ungrateful literary clerk Bazzard, apologizing for not speaking 'imaginatively, but I have no imagination', then after a toast to the absent Rosa says, 'I am a particularly Angular man, and yet I fancy (if I may use the word, not having a morsel of fancy) that I could draw a picture of a true lover's state of mind'. He may be wrong in 'many particulars' because he has 'neither soft sympathies nor soft experiences' and hints at Edwin's lack of ardour and respect by speaking of the ideal lover 'permeated' by the beloved. In spite of 'never getting within ten thousand miles' of poetry and making heavy weather of bird imagery and ornithology he is allowed an eloquent conclusion: 'my picture does represent the true lover ... as living at once a doubled life and a halved life' which leaves Edwin turning 'red' and then 'white, as certain points of this picture came into the light'.

Grewgious proves his imagination by his story of the ring, which was to be – or almost certainly would have been if the novel had been finished and the missing body found – a clue to the victim's identity. After looking in the fire and finding inspiration there like so many other Dickens characters, Grewgious decides to give Edwin the ring, as he has been charged to do by his dead friend. His actions are elaborated with ritual effect: he feels in his pocket for his keys, looks for the right key with a candle, goes to the bureau, touches a spring which opens a secret drawer, and his hand trembles as he holds an 'ordinary ring-case' but speaks before taking the ring out. (The solemn slow procedure is only rivalled by the Bloomsbury shopkeeper's ceremonious display of his golden bowl to Charlotte Stant and Amerigo in Henry James.) Grewgious formally introduces the object, tells its history and his own:

> 'Mr Edwin, this rose of diamonds and rubies delicately set in gold, was a ring belonging to Miss Rosa's mother. It was removed from her dead hand, in my presence, with such distracted grief as I hope it may never be my lot to contemplate again. Hard man as I am, I am not hard enough for that. See how bright these stones shine!' opening the case. 'And yet the eyes that were so much brighter, and that so often looked upon them with a light and a proud heart, have been ashes among ashes, and dust among dust, some years! If I had any imagination (which it is needless to say I have not), I might imagine that the lasting beauty of these stones was almost cruel.' (Ch. 11)

He hands it over with solemn words and charges Edwin to give it back if anything should be 'even slightly wrong' between him and Rosa, or if they have 'any secret consciousness' that they are committing themselves to 'this step' because long accustomed 'to look forward to it'. Edwin looks troubled and there is 'some indecision ... in the action of his hand' as he takes the case and places 'it in his breast'. Bazzard the clerk has been conveniently asleep and conveniently wakes, the ring is taken out again and shown to him so that he may witness 'the transaction'. When they have gone Grewgious is disturbed, and the scene is made strange as he wonders, 'Her ring. Will it come back to me?' and, 'My mind hangs about her ring very uneasily tonight.'

If we expected the ring to be a sentimental souvenir we are wrong:

Grewgious regards it with more than nostalgia. He is not eager to hand it over because he does not find that Edwin fits his 'picture' of the lover. Like all the best objects in fiction, the ring has more than one function: it is a sacred object which says a great deal about Grewgious, which persuades Edwin to withdraw from his semi-engagement to Rosa, and which was to have been crucial in the final discovery and detection. It is entrusted to Edwin as a betrothal present he never gives – he is shaken into sincerity by Grewgious's true poetry, his picture and the ring – and only Grewgious, Bazzard and the reader know it was in Edwin's pocket. The murderer does not know: he throws away Edwin's gold shirt-pin and gold watch and they are picked up in the river, but the gold ring would have been found intact, on the body in the quick-lime, which John Jasper knows – because Durdles has told him in a grisly chant – is 'quick enough to eat your boots. With a little handy stirring, quick enough to eat your bones' (Ch. 12). Edwin would have been identified by Grewgious, Angular man and prime plot-mover, perhaps with Bazzard as witness. In 'The Picture and the Ring' the emphasis is on the love token Grewgious takes from a secret drawer to open his secret life, and so Dickens cleverly deflects attention from the crime story, goes on with his intricate plot and deepens his mystery, and his characters.

Dickens's fascinated and fascinating ways with inanimate objects, which can become animate in his text – as they do in 'Meditations in Monmouth Street' and *The Old Curiosity Shop* – are shown most cunningly, as the ring becomes ominous, almost magical, like Desdemona's handkerchief. Like that famous property, the ring is a talisman, imprinted by love, loss and trust, and re-solemnized as it is handed over with the warning. Like *Othello*, this novel is a human story of crime and punishment, without supernatural presences but with uncanny stirrings. After all, the novel's title is *The Mystery of Edwin Drood*.

The novel's taxonomy of imagination includes tiny instances like the horrid boy Deputy's 'delicious fancy' that the dead 'are hurt' when he stones their 'tall headstones … sufficiently like themselves, on their beat in the dark' (Ch. 23) and Datchery's wonderful literal-metaphorical image, 'The ghost of a cry' (Ch. 12), but the drama of creativity is made active in the extremes of imagination, sane and destructive, virtuous and vicious, shown by Grewgious and John Jasper.

Notes

[1] Other critics compare Dickens and Piranesi, for instance Jeremy Trembling: *Dickens, Violence and the Modern State: Dreams of the Scaffold.*

[2] There have been many attempts to finish the novel, including many conclusions which have absolutely no foundation in the text, but I am making the obvious inferences, only from the published text, Kate Dickens's testimony and Forster's report in 'Last Book' (Bk 11, Ch. 2). For further detail see the Clarendon edition.

Chapter 7

Subversions and Oppositions

Readers of *Paradise Lost* have sometimes felt that the Devil is so articulate and alluring that he undermines the Divine power and presence. To descend a little from Milton's Sublime, we find Dickens also creating powerful subversions, presences that accompany his portraits and proposals of morality, to counter, criticize or undermine them. He may have learnt about imaginative subversion and the parodic principle from Cervantes, one of his boyhood authors, whose Sancho Panza is an ancestor of Sam Weller and like him in his relationship to master and patron, though Sam is more deferential and when he turns up like Sancho, for a sequel, less amusing and profoundly disturbing in his awareness of fiction. Politically speaking, Sancho and Sam are masters' men who do not ultimately subvert their masters' position but they are also wonderfully comic rebels who prevent us taking the benevolent Pickwick and the mad Don Quixote too solemnly. They valuably undermine and yet tolerate the heroic stance.

Chuckster is a layabout and notary's clerk in *The Old Curiosity Shop*, invariably linked with honest Kit, a poor servant largely defined by his fidelity and deference to social superiors, Nelly and her grandfather and the highly idealized Garland family. Kit's virtues are offset and criticized by the cynical Chuckster who laughs loudly when Kit promises to come back to work off his shilling, when he wishes 'he might be blessed if he could make out whether Kit was "precious raw" or "precious deep"' (Ch. 20), is negligent when minding the pony as Kit's deputy, calls Kit 'snob' or 'Snobby', and keeps up his critique until the end of the novel when he dwindles into the home friend of Dick Swiveller and the Marchioness. He is everything conscientious Kit is not: negligent and casual in demeanour and dress, an extravagant and flowery speaker, on one occasion engaging in a brisk Shakespeare duet with Dick Swiveller, fellow member of the Divine Apollos. Like some other comic characters in Dickens he is supernumerary to the action, which would be unaffected if he were omitted, but because Kit's loyal service comes close to servility Chuckster is like a gargoyle whose jeering presence brings us irreverent relief. I used to think he undermined Kit but if he does this from time to time he also licenses Kit's class deference and the work ethic. Since these values have become less popular, we may think of Chuckster as the product of Dickens's unconscious and predictive tact. Perhaps this is why Chesterton thought he was the best thing in Dickens. He is a loose cannon, the joker in the pack, running wild.

In *Martin Chuzzlewit* there is a more radical and uncontrolled undermining of serious action and sentiment, and a lot that needs undermining. Martin's requited love and Tom Pinch's unrequited love for Mary Graham are presented in a high-flown style and tone. Pinch longs hopelessly and selflessly for Mary, in deadly earnest: 'Thou art by her side'. In the last chapter the comic lover Moddle flees the altar and writes his betrothed Charity Pecksniff a farewell from a schooner at Gravesend: 'I love another. She is Another's. Everything appears to be somebody else's. Nothing in the world is mine ...' (Ch. 54) and 'The burden – 300 tons per register – forgive me, if in my distraction I allude to the ship – on my mind – has been truly dreadful' (Ch. 54). A little later in the same chapter, we find prematurely grey-haired Tom playing the organ: 'In the soft strain which ever and again comes stealing back upon the ear, the memory of thine old love may find a voice perhaps.' Tom gazes at his lost beloved's child, 'in the romp and dance; who, wondering sometimes to see thee look so thoughtful, runs to climb up on thy knee, and put her cheek to thine'. Comic satire is a dangerous and destabilizing neighbour to sentiment, as Jonathan Swift discovered when his *Tale of a Tub* offended the Church of England by a parody of religious extremes which put readers in an irreverent frame of mind. When Mary Garth in *Middlemarch* tries to explain that bad curates make her think less of the Church, Mr Farebrother agrees, 'setting men's minds to the tune of contempt', and this is what Chuckster and Moddle do in their different styles.

In *David Copperfield* there is another dangerous relation, connective and divisive, between the serious-comic treatment of David's love for Dora and the straight-faced solemnity of his love for Agnes, which like Tom Pinch's romance, is a story unfortunately insulated from comedy. In this novel as in *Martin Chuzzlewit* Dickens is not always controlling his total structure of mode and tone.

He uses comic metaphor and hyperbole to mime time's variable pace for the narrator, increasing emotional distance as David looks back on love and courtship:

If I may so express it, I was steeped in Dora. I was not merely over head and ears in love with her, but I was saturated through and through. Enough love might have been wrung from me, metaphorically speaking, to drown anybody in; and yet there would have remained enough within me, and all over me, to pervade my entire existence ...

... I, the moonstruck slave of Dora, perambulated round and round the house and garden for two hours, looking through crevices in the palings, getting my chin by dint of violent exertion, above the rusty nails on the top, blowing kisses at the lights in the windows, and romantically calling on the night at intervals, to shield my Dora – I don't exactly know what from, I suppose from fire. Perhaps from mice, to which she had a great aversion. (Ch. 33)

Deep down, Dickens knew that even though we dismiss early loves as immature, they had their grave moments – if they did not they would be less life-shaping. The telling of this love-story needs and finds a serious register as well as a comic one:

It seemed such an extraordinary thing to have Dora always there. It was so unaccountable not to be obliged to go out to see her, not to have any occasion to be tormenting myself about her, not to have to write to her, not to be scheming and devising opportunities of being alone with her. Sometimes of an evening, when I looked up from my writing, and saw her seated opposite, I would lean back in my chair, and think how queer it was that there we were, nobody's business any more – all the romance of our engagement put away upon a shelf to rust – no one to please but one another – one another to please, for life. (Ch. 44)

This may have been intended to sound slighly ominous but it strikes a true note in its recognition of a young couple's adjustment to shared solitude, an affective episode not unlike Anna and Will Brangwen's honeymoon in *The Rainbow* or Gabriel Oak's famous vision of the daitiness of love in *Far From the Madding Crowd*, 'When I look up, there you will be, and when you look up, there I will be.' Though the whole story of this love and marriage is far from comic, it has the advantage over the story of David's always-felt-but-suppressed love for Agnes in being narrated in more than one mode. The level tone and plain language of David's recognition of married commitment are noticeably absent from his reported happy-ever-after, which is ecstatic, unspecific and the worse for not keeping in touch with ordinary life. It is Dora who brings reality with her.

Reality is present in the comic narrative of domestic chaos and misadventure but also in the rare moments when Dickens's love-story is told in a way neither romantic nor comic, and the first sober recognition of the dailiness and the isolation of marriage is one, a bridge between the fun of the courtship-story – where Dora has touches of Maria Beadnell – and the fictitious domestic story, which has serious emotional scenes, like the post-wedding recognition just quoted and the more intense passage where Dora suggestively dismisses David's effusive and thoughtless 'better to be naturally Dora than anything in the world' with her realistic and mature recognition, intelligible to the reader but not her listener, 'In the world! Ah, Doady! it's a large place!' (Ch. 48).

There is another example of dangerous neighbourhood in *Our Mutual Friend* where Bella Wilfer's coy playful way with her father is inadvertently parodied by the wheedling tone and little-me-ish manner of old would-be-young Tippins. One woman is young and attractive and the other scrawny and repulsive, but when the tender and satiric styles are so similar, the tender style – and it is very tender – is called into question. If Sir Andrew Aguecheek's clowning contributes a little to our reception of Orsino's love-melancholy, it is only a little, and we can feel both for Orsino and for Andrew's 'I was adored once too': Shakespeare never insulated comic deflation from romantic intensity, Dickens could blend affective tones wonderfully, like a combination of minor and major key for soloist and orchestra in a concerto, as he does for the workhouse death of Oliver's mother – 'Let me see the child, and die', in the company of comic attendant, 'Think what it is to be a mother ... do' (*OT*, Ch. 1), or the vision of Paul in the company of visionless Toots, but he can be blind to the subversive effect of exposing high sentiment to the comic spirit.

There are a few morally extreme characters who are strongly condemned in Dickens's narrative but have a destabilizing effect on our reading. Every now and then a villainous character expresses a response which the novelist seems not to expect, though he may have known better unconsciously. Such characters unsteady or divert the course of the novel in which they are cast as immoral by inadvertently undermining the moral argument or sympathy. They are more prominent and more serious Chucksters.

In *Finnegans Wake* Joyce perceptively re-named Dickens's story *The Old Cupiosity Shop*, scenting the lubricious suggestion in the image of Nell, concupiscence in the white bed of childhood, and knew that in transposing desire to Quilp Dickens has his family values and erotic gratification too. Quilp sleeps in Nell's bed, 'coiling into it', smacks his lips when she kisses her grandfather, asks her to be his 'number two' or his 'second' and leers, 'Such a fresh, blooming, modest little bud ... such a chubby, rosy, cosy, little Nell!' (Ch. 9). It is a dangerous and no doubt unconscious displacement but the author actually admits his monster's sexual drive and fascination – which I found puzzling when I read the novel as a child – saying through Mrs Quilp, a reliable witness: 'Quilp has such a way with him when he likes, that the best-looking woman here couldn't refuse him if I was dead ... and he chose to make love to her' (Ch. 4). By the time we come to those long-drawn-out last scenes Nell is no longer rosy and chubby: Dickens loved meeting the hundreds of readers at home and abroad who wept for 'the child' and some of whom, in that time of high child mortality, found personal solace in the weeping, but Quilp subverts the purity of her presentation. In *The Violent Effigy* John Carey says Dickens found it a relief to create Quilp while imaging chaste childhood but the relief is deeply compromising: the author-judge punishes Quilp as he uses him to indulge his own transgressive gaze. Quilp has more vitality than his author can handle and no doubt this is why Dickens's super-ego killed him off somewhat abruptly, leaving the young heroine exposed to less erotic dangers. In a fascinating interview Dickens had with Dostoyevsky, he apparently told his great Russian admirer that both his pure simple characters like Nell and his villains were himself; the good were what he would like to be and the evil derived from his worse self.[1]

Uriah Heep is another character made physically and morally repulsive but he turns out to be an effective political mouthpiece, a character with a grasp of social realities who can articulate them so reliably and specifically as to enlighten David Copperfield. David first sees Heep as a disgusting character whose candour he suspects, later identifies him as a self-seeking greedy hypocrite, and finally recognizes a black villain who drops the 'umble' mask, 'I can't allow people in my way' (Ch. 42). But Uriah sees and utters a deep social truth, laying false humility at the door of his politically muddled and benevolent education. His is much more than an indictment of a charity school and extends to society at large, raising the political and moral problem of sentimental Victorian attitudes to poverty.(Dickens himself was ambivalent, attacking patronage and excessively doctrinal education in Ragged Schools, but participating himself in the management of Angela Burdett-Coutts's Urania House, for the reclamation and education of ex-prisoners, in which he showed humane sympathy but also some patronizing attitudes, as was perhaps inevitable.)

Uriah reveals his feeling for Agnes, David tells him furiously that she is as far above him as the moon, and he replies by suggesting that David has always thought him 'too umble'. David does not answer him directly but says evasively he is 'not fond of professions of humility ... or professions of anything else', and provokes Uriah's apologia:

> But how little you think of the rightful umbleness of a person in my station, Master Copperfield! Father and me was both brought up at a foundation school for boys; and mother, she was likewise brought up at a public, sort of charitable, establishment. They taught us all a deal of umbleness – not much else that I know of, from morning to night. We was to be umble to this person, and umble to that, and to pull off our caps here, and to make bows there; and always to know our place, and abase ourselves before our betters. And we had such a lot of betters! (Ch. 39)

He tells David how he and his father got monitor-medals and his father became a sexton, by being umble, and concludes,' "Be umble", says father, "and you'll do!" And really, it ain't done bad!' (Ch. 39).

After this diagnostic defence of umbleness Dickens lets David grasp the social significance of Uriah's style and his conditioning: 'It was the first time it had ever occurred to me, that this detestable cant of false humility might have originated out of the Heep family. I had seen the harvest, but had never thought of the seed.' (Perhaps it was the first time it had occurred to Dickens too.) David goes on, 'I had never doubted his meanness, his craft and malice; but I fully comprehended now, for the first time, what a base, unrelenting, and revengeful spirit must have been engendered by this early, and this long, suppression' (Ch. 39).

In the dénouement where Uriah is unmasked by Micawber, and turns on David, 'I have always hated you', David replies 'As I think I told you once before ... it is you who have been, in your greed and cunning, against all the world. It may be profitable to you to reflect, in future, that there never were greed and cunning in the world yet, that did not do too much, and overreach themselves. It is as certain as death' and Uriah counters:

> Or as certain as they used to teach at school (the same school where I picked up so much umbleness), from nine o'clock to eleven, that labour was a curse; and from eleven o'clock to one, that it was a blessing and a cheerfulness, and a dignity, and I don't know what all,

eh? ... You preach, about as consistent as they did. Won't umbleness go down? (Ch. 52)

Uriah gets the worst of the great recognition scene but not of the social argument. David continues to think of Uriah as a creature of another species and certainly never sees him as in any way like the poor 'outcast' he himself once was – and in the wine warehouse, David, perhaps like Dickens in the blacking factory, was in many ways insulated by his own class-image. But Uriah's sharp eye sees, and his thin skin feels, their resemblance, which is why his spiteful remarks about David's early poverty and street-life, which he discovers from Micawber, are jealous, hurtful and very much to the point. (It is also of course why David is wary when Micawber turns up in Canterbury.) Uriah's social insight is admitted and dropped, and the cynical villain is last seen making the politics of umbleness pay in a model prison run by gullible authority. It is true that David is not Dickens, but there is no attempt to place David's enlightenment, and its lack of consequence passes without comment.

Neither David nor Dickens is an explicit critic of hypocritical Victorian charity and Christian benevolence, like Sir Henry Wotton in *The Picture of Dorian Gray*, who makes a politician look at him 'keenly' when he wittily says that charitable works in the East End try to solve the 'problem of slavery' by 'amusing the slaves' (Ch. 3). In *A Woman of No Importance* the line is repeated by Lord Illingworth, another cynical philosopher/dandy elegantly posing as poseur. Dickens was less radical than the good socialist Oscar Wilde and any sympathy he felt for Uriah's social critique was not followed through. In Uriah he may be voicing insight without fully realizing what he was doing, as if the deep truth could only be told – and so intelligently and passionately – by a cynical villain who speaks from experience and in his humble way analyses, judges and manipulates social fact just as well as Stendhal's Julien Sorel.

David's recognition of social cause and his refusal to feel sympathy are not reconciled, nor do I suggest that the reconciliation is easy, in any society: seeing the origin of crime does not make us love the criminal. But neither Dickens nor David articulates that problem. And since Dickens seems to identify with his autobiographical projection, in a *Bildungsroman* where hero moves from immaturity and error to maturity and improved understanding, it is awkward that he lets Uriah win the social argument so brilliantly. Did he put more into Uriah than he first intended? We know that Dickens's characters opened out and surprised him: is Uriah an illustration of the cliché about characters running away with their author? Did Dickens think he had so discredited his dishonest power-drunk villain in the dénouement that he inadvertently let him gain the credit of social diagnosis? David accepts the explanation but the moment passes without further development, as if it were not anything Dickens wanted to dwell on and examine. The submission to the unconscious mind has snags as well as advantages and Uriah is a mixed blessing.

Dickens was fully and passionately aware of social environment and influence. This is clear in explicit comments like those the Ghosts make in *A Christmas Carol*, in 'fractionalized' characters like Wemmick and Jaggers, symbolic figures like the children Want and Ignorance and the permutations of character and destiny in *The Chimes*. The awareness is very powerfully expressed in a well-known, long and unusual passage of authorial generalization in Chapter 47, 'The Thunderbolt', in *Dombey and Son*:

> Hear the magistrate or judge admonish the unnatural outcasts of society; unnatural in brutal habits, unnatural in want of decency, unnatural in losing and confounding all distinctions between good and evil; unnatural in ignorance, in vice, in recklessness, in contumacy, in mind, in looks, in everything. But follow the good clergyman or doctor ... down into their dens ... Look round upon the world of odious sights ... Breathe the polluted air ...

Perhaps serial publication made it easier for one hand not to know what the other was doing, as seems to be the case in these unconscious subversions, comic and tragic. But they are a deep and important feature of Dickens's creativity, because they come from this novelist's double impulse, to present the brutalized and the obnoxious creature, and to recognize the origin of what is brutal and obnoxious – the Uriah who is detested by David, but also eventually understood by him, and still detested.

The novelist does not always understand his own creature. As D. H. Lawrence said, we must trust the tale and not the artist. *Little Dorrit* gives us an example. Tattycoram is a foundling affectionately named after her patron Thomas Coram by kind Mr and Mrs Meagles. Deprecated by the morally reliable and sympathetic Arthur Clennam, as Heep was by David, the fascinating and problematic Miss Wade steps in to confound the reader and persuade Tattycoram to bite the hands that feed her – and took her into their home as maid to their daughter Pet, a beloved child whose twin has died and who becomes the unfortunate wife of Henry Gowan. The Meagles are generous characters, but with the decline of the upstairs–downstairs norm of Dickens's day, they strike the modern reader as insensitive and patronizing, as Miss Wade and the temporarily reconstructed Tattycoram feel and say. As Beryl Gray points out in her telling comparison of Tattycoram and George Eliot's Caterina Sarti, in 'Mr Gilfil's Love Story',[2] there is a gap between Meagles's account of the parent-like decision to pity a foundling and Tattycoram's position as servant. Meagles briefly regrets the 'jingling nickname' but not its stamp of low origin, and since Thomas Coram was one of Dickens's heroes, it is unlikely that he was aware of any stigma or reductiveness. When Tattycoram accuses her employers of behaving like employers she is criticized by Arthur Clennam and no doubt by the average Victorian reader who followed the author and found her unreasonable. But we see the point when Tattycoram objects, and cringe with her as her benevolent employer warns her to count to 25 and control her temper. Miss Wade's inset story, 'Diary of a Self Tormentor', is the neurotic confession of a neurosis but in her bonding with Tattycoram, and in Tattycoram's subversive rage, the response is likely to go against the grain of the novel's expectations. The two women are not villains like Uriah, but like Uriah, they articulate a critique of class inequality and injustice which is ahead of its time. Like Uriah they are placed in an ambivalent relation to morally sympathetic characters who have come to represent a dated moral norm. And like Uriah they may tap a deep subversive doubt in Dickens, who admired and supported the Foundling hospital, making one of his finest speeches about it, but often voiced his distaste for the name and nature of patronage. Tattycoram is brought back to the Meagles family and gratitude but at least the novel finds space – and for Miss Wade's story, an emphatic separate space – for this point of view, even though it seems to subvert the moral coherence of the fiction.

Dickens's response to class is in any case uneven: his account of the entirely unpatronizing Dick Swiveller and his clever Marchioness is a gratifying Cinderella story, and his compassion for Jo and the brickmakers is movingly particularized. He was not the only didactic novelist of his time to be inconsistent on the subject: George Eliot saw tragedy in Caterina Sarti's problematic social position, and created a fine working-class heroine in Eppie, but she wrote a heartless essay, 'Servants' Logic', where an amused class-superiority is more unpleasant than anything in Dickens.[3] Thackeray delights the liberal reader as he stages his man-to-man confrontation of Morgan the manservant and Major Pendennis the master, but is not so egalitarian as to make Morgan sympathetic or finally triumphant, and though Henry Esmond is critical of power and privilege in Queen Anne's England, his estate in Virginia has 'happy negroes' on the last page. In life these three humane novelists relied on good domestic service and simply accept the servant–employer – even the slave–master – divide. In spite – or because – of such assumptions they reveal uncomfortable social truths inadvertently and unconsciously, and if at the cost of a break in coherence, the deep message is still welcome. Dickens met Uriahs when he admired the work of Ragged Schools but disliked ineptly doctrinal instruction; he talked to Tattycorams when he helped run Urania House and felt the difficulty of combining full imaginative tolerance with orderly domestic routine.

If the scientist's imagination has to test itself by negation, trying to disprove its hypotheses, there may be the same obligation for the artist – especially the moral artist – and Dickens, sometimes consciously as with Uriah, sometimes unconsciously as with Miss Wade, sometimes harmoniously as with Chuckster, sometimes discordantly as with Tattycoram, puts into his work a creative opposition, to question or subvert the expressed value or moral assumption, to test and try the system and argue against the story.

Notes

[1] Stephanie Harvey, 'Dickens's Villains, A Confession and a Suggestion', *The Dickensian*, no. 458, Vol. 98, Pt 3, Winter 2002.

[2] 'Nobody's Daughters: Dickens's Tattycoram and George Eliot's Caterina Sarti', *The George Eliot Review*, no. 32, 2001.

[3] 'Servants' Logic', *Pall Mall Gazette*, 17 March 1865; Thomas Pinney, *Essays of George Eliot*, London: Routledge and Kegan Paul, 1968.

Chapter 8

Crises of Imagination in *Oliver Twist, A Christmas Carol, Dombey and Son, Bleak House, Hard Times* and *The Lazy Tour of Two Idle Apprentices*

I want to concentrate on a group of powerful passages in early, middle and late writing, in which Dickens imagines imaginative crisis. My examples are the brief respite in the guilt-haunted imagination of a murderer; the reform of a miserly businessman induced to remember his past and imagine his future; an imaginative attempt to communicate with her husband by a woman in a heartless marriage; a moment of companionable feeling for an outcast dying boy; an attempt by a scatterbrained woman to make sense of her little life as she is dying; and the observation of a disturbed patient looking at the floor.

Bill Sikes's murder of Nancy was a favourite subject for Dickens's reading-performances, and here he is taking shelter in a shed after his brutal crime, isolated and haunted by the dead face: 'Those widely staring eyes, so lustreless and so glassy, that he had better borne to see them than think upon them, appeared in the midst of the darkness: light in themselves, but giving light to nothing' (Ch. 48). He rushes out to escape, but the 'figure was behind him', returns to find the 'eyes were there' then at last he hears distant shouting, and dashes off to throw himself with energy and courage into fighting a fire. Dickens shows us a guilty imagination in very strong images, then grants imagination a brief rest and relief in company and action:

> There were people there – men and women – light, bustle. It was like new life to him ... flying from memory and himself, plunged into the thickest of the throng ... Hither and thither he dived that night; and now working at the pumps, and now hurrying through the smoke and flame, but never ceasing to engage himself wherever men and women were thickest ... This mad excitement over, there returned, with tenfold force, the dreadful consciousness of his crime. (Ch. 48)

'Flying from memory and himself': the inner drama of Sikes shows Dickens's early interest in our sense of identity, later shown in similar psychic discomfort but in the very different circumstances and minds of Jonas Chuzzlewit and Amy Dorrit. The fire-fighting episode is followed by Sikes's return to guilty memory, re-imagined in a turbulent action which does not stop until he accidentally hangs himself. The fire-fighting scene takes us from inside to outside: Dickens knew the effect of such antithesis, but the fire-fighting scene goes deeper than contrast, putting us in touch with something in Sikes which is larger than his criminality. It does not make us sympathize with his violence but without comment it makes us feel that he is a human being, a sharer in common humanity. Moreover, as we see into his mind we also see him, without any sentimentality whatsoever, as a social case, the product of his environment, a murderer made by his life in the streets. This insight does not depend entirely on this scene because Nancy articulates it when she explains to Brownlow and Rose Maylie why she can't tear herself away from the streets where her life has been 'squandered' (Ch. 40). Dickens's awareness of criminal conditioning is implied, if rather obscurely, in a preface to the third edition, where he explains that in Oliver he wanted to show 'the principle of Good surviving through every adverse circumstance', and goes on to suggest that men like Sikes 'would not give, by one look or action of a moment, the faintest indication of a better nature': 'Whether every gentle human feeling is dead within such bosoms, or the proper chord has rusted and is hard to find, I do not know ...'. The image of rust implies a process, and this idea is borne out by the scene of the fire, which gives us a glimpse of a residual human need beyond contingency. This is implicit, and any attempt to make it explicit would be in danger of sentimentalizing crime and the criminal. The scene achieves its effect in short compass and without emphasis, and its symbolism or sympathetic action is strong, the fire not only offering an outlet and relief but expressing the tumult, violence and destructiveness of Sikes himself. Dickens often too plainly prompts and primes our response, but on this occasion he realizes character and history through generalized action, in a startling and extrovert crowd scene.

The idea for *A Christmas Carol* arrived as a sudden inspiration in October 1843 and the story was written rapidly for publication in December. It is a fantasy and a fable, a morally and socially didactic tale with two endings, one in a dream and one in reality – though the reality of fiction. He closes with a happy ending but not until he has taken what Thomas Hardy called a full look at the worst. Scrooge wakes up from a nightmare but is left with its aftermath. The need for continuity of affect and memory which Wordsworth insisted on in *The Prelude* is urged by the therapeutic fable in which Scrooge's ghosts teach him that to isolate the self from past and future is to be isolated from society, and vice versa. For Scrooge as well as the reader the unhappy ending is not separated from the happy one but shadows its particulars as a possibility. Scrooge is the heartless man to whom Providence offers a second chance through his dreaming, an imaginative cure for his defects of imagination. Dickens skilfully designs the three acts and stages of past, present and future, in order to redeem the old sinner in the nick of time. This is done partly by uncovering the childhood deprivation which has made Scrooge what he is at the wide-awake start of the novel, in a pre-Freudian analysis, and appealing to an imaginative nostalgia which opens the springs of love. The dreams also make Scrooge look outside self, mythologizing and enlarging the social horrors to which he has turned a blind eye, making him 'know' what he has callously said he does not know, poverty and neglect, and by going back to what Dickens, when describing Nancy, called 'original nature' (*OT*, Ch. 40). Scrooge is moved by terror and self-interest, by a nightmare future in which he sees his unmourned death and burial. Dickens creates a complex cure and conversion, using the power of literary fantasy to show the power of dream-narrative: as Yeats said in the quotation he invented for an epigraph to *Responsibilities*, 'In dreams begins responsibility'.

No wonder Dickens's fable was a best-seller and is still immensely popular. It uses the Christmas spirit and spirits with an existential dimension, not imposing Christian doctrine. Close to Dickens in humour and dark sensibility, Scrooge has a double catharsis, comic as well as tragic. The eloquent carol, 'God bless you merry gentlemen, may nothing you dismay', which the boy sings to unreceptive Scrooge, is mirror and microcosm of the fable in which the Christmas hero is enabled to feel real joy and dismay by dreaming joy and dismay. Scrooge is also purged of pity and fear by pity and fear, but he is less a tragic than a comic hero. He is like Lorry, Pross and Grewgious, who disclaim imagination: when he tries to deny the existence of ghosts with a pun about 'grave' and 'gravy', and begs Marley's ghost, in the full flight of other-worldly eloquence, not to 'be flowery', he keeps up his spirits and shows his fear. Marley says those who don't imagine, whose spirit does not go out beyond self or the counting-house, must be healed by dreaming. Though the narrator observes that Scrooge has no fancy, the whole story is his dream, a fiction rooted in his repressed memory of pain and happiness, and his deep nightmare of fear and pity. He emerges with integrity, a creature in touch with his past and his future, a properly conscious creature of time.

My next example involves a momentary release from passion, which is both like and unlike that of Sikes: to compare him with Edith Dombey is to appreciate Dickens's range. In 'Domestic Relations', Chapter 40 of *Dombey and Son*, there is a brief and startling lull – for Edith and the reader – in the war between the Dombeys. It is the more marked for being narrated in a different mode from other episodes in their high marital drama, which are stagey in language and presentation. In this scene the emotion is lowered in an action and dialogue both realistic and ordinary. Edith Dombey seems to me at her most modern, in mind, attitude and even language, as she tries to reason with Dombey, in a prose which is not lofty and body language which is not melodramatic. The scene shows a profound fresh psychology and morality.

As in the Sikes episode, contrast works powerfully. The scenery and props expect a conflict and confrontation, the setting highly expressive, a boudoir where expensive clothes and jewels are flung around in deliberated carelessness and disarray, with both characters fully aware of the significance. Edith has arranged a woman's room, clothes, accessories and jewels like a text to be read by her husband, and he knows how to read it. But she decides to stage a different drama – or rather, to tell a different story. The subdued manner as well as the matter of the conversation – in which she does all the talking – remind one of a modern novel or play.

After her resistance to Dombey's domination Edith makes an unexpected move, conciliatory in content and cool, almost friendly in temper; she suggests a modus vivendi. Though she does not know it, it is doomed to fail because she has not realized the strength of Dombey's pride or his hostility to his daughter, and makes the fatal error of proposing Florence as a motive for compromise. She introduces her proposal with a clear recognition of its exceptional purpose and its strangeness, a recognition which emphasizes her control and rationality: ' "... consider that there is no common meaning in the appeal I am going to make to you. Yes, for I am going;" she said it as in prompt reply to something in his face; "to appeal to you" ', and Dombey sits down 'to hear the appeal'. Her reading of his response, and her repetition 'I am going', are followed by further preliminaries and qualifications, in an almost Jamesian notation of effort, pride and reluctance: 'If you can believe that I am of such a nature now ... as would make what I now say almost incredible to myself, and to any man who had become my husband, but, above all, said to you, you may, perhaps, attach the greater weight to it.' She moves on, 'I feel no tenderness towards you ... I know as well that you feel none towards me. But we are linked together ... We both must die; we are both connected with the dead already, each by a little child. Let us forbear.'

Then follows the most surprising part of this surprising speech. Once again there is a formal prefatory remark registering her grave, deliberated and difficult delivery. The description of her facial language is more precise and realistically purposive than it usually is and in nearly every sentence those Dickensian iambic pentameters which often signal facile emotion sound rather good:

'There is no wealth,' she went on, turning paler as she watched him, while her eyes grew yet more lustrous in their earnestness, 'that could buy these words of me, and the meaning that belongs to them. Once cast away as idle breath, no wealth and power could bring them back. I mean them; I have weighed them; and I will be true to what I undertake. If you will promise to forbear on your part, I will promise to forbear on mine. We are a most unhappy pair, in whom, from different causes, every sentiment that blesses marriage, or justifies it, is rooted out; but in the course of time, some friendship, or some fitness for each other, may arise between us. I will try to hope so, if you will make the endeavour too; and I will look forward to a better and a happier use of age than I have made of youth or prime.'

Throughout she had spoken in a low plain voice, that neither rose nor fell ... (Ch. 40)

This cool reasonable proposal of a working relationship in a terrible – an almost impossible – marriage, and the admission of her motive for the marriage, are what make her speech so unVictorian and so unDickensian. It is plain and truth-telling eloquence. It is not only psychologically realistic but astonishing in its quiet language and in the emotional and intelligent control Edith is imagined as exercising, in what she says and how she says it. She is reasonable, as she proposes attempting a reasonable course, quiet as she suggests quieting the storms of their incompatibility, almost friendly as she imagines the possibility of something like friendliness, and the coherence of style and matter make her proposition truly imaginative and subtly self-illustrative.

There is the additional nuance that Dickens is not only deepening character and preparing action in his novel but imagining an adjustment and relationship which belong to a fiction and an experience as far removed as possible from anything else we know in his habitual life and art. It is one of the most original and realistic insights in his novels and expressed in the eloquence of reason, plain speaking and truthfulness. Its failure to affect Dombey – as Edith wishes and dares to hope – is eloquent too. Like the talkative comic orators, she moves the reader, though not the character within the fiction, and as an example of Dickens's range of language – his imaginative eloquence – her speech in this scene is a profound and rare success.

Dombey refuses reason and revision; hostilities are resumed; the boudoir and its scattered dresses and jewellery are the set and props for the high drama they seemed to be expecting.

For Edith's character this is a deepening and particularizing episode, and all of a piece with the remarkable – and radically feminist – insight, with which Dickens makes her imagine, organize and carry out the elopement with Carker, in which with inspired political economy she humiliates both her sexual oppressors, appearing to cuckold the husband who has bought her and expects her submission, and fooling the seducer who wants to possess her, and expects her submission, bringing scorn on them both in their own eyes and the eyes of the world, while enjoying the extra gratification of using them as they tried to use her. Of course this revenge is not admirable but it is not presented with crude triumphalism as it apes the traditional male and military triumph which cries woe to the vanquished.

A contrasting crisis from *Dombey and Son* is concerned with a very different characters and dramatized in a very different mode. It is a dialogue between the wet nurse Polly Richards and the young Florence Dombey, one of many Dickensian narratives which are structurally and psychologically functional in their individual novels and also implicit models of creativity. When Polly Richards comes to nurse Paul after his mother's death she meets Florence who is mourning her mother, and responds to her distressed questioning with a tender story perfectly suited to a child's comfort and comprehension. The story is told in response to urgent need, and Florence's questions play a large part in shaping the narrative, an inspired improvisation quite different from Little Dorrit's story to Maggy, where the listener's suggestions are used but the story is motivated by the teller's needs. This story is a genuine collaboration, the first question 'What have they done with my mother?' provoking the theme of burial; the little girl's shuddering response 'no, not the cold ground' to Polly's answer 'in the earth' is spontaneously emended and for positive emphasis, 'No, the warm ground', from which view the ideas and images of flowers and growth flow naturally, in a spontaneous traditional elegy of rebirth, with dignifying mythological undertones. It could so easily have been sanctimonious religion but it is poetry. The creative implications are clear: Dickens emphasizes emotional inspiration, an unpremeditated response to otherness and a collaborative energy. The affective drive and the impromptu composition are found in many of Dickens's internal narratives but the warm easy collaboration is less common. Indeed, Dickens is keen on the opposite, stories told to unresponsive listeners, Louisa's desperate rhetorical code which her father cannot begin to decipher, and Edith's thwarted imaginative attempt to propose a new start and a new life, stories that fall on deaf ears, for a time or forever.

The next example is different again, though like Polly's narrative it shows Dickens's capacity – not wholly consistent – to handle a religious subject with imaginative delicacy, here in the sensitive area of an educated adult introducing Christian belief and ritual to an illiterate child. Polly needed no education to help Florence, and Florence was quick to respond. Jo, the poverty-stricken crossing-sweeper in *Bleak House*, is dying and has the Lord's Prayer read to him by the doctor Allan Woodcourt, just after he starts up, with a wild look, crying 'It's time to go to that berrying ground, sir.' There have been other people present at the bedside, but Dickens carefully leaves Jo alone with Allan for an intimate ritual. To soothe the wild feeling and sweeten the image of a foul burying-ground rather than for pious reasons Allan at once offers the prayer. It is another creative collaboration; the listener trusts the teller:

'Jo, can you say what I say?'
'I'll say anythink as you say, sir, fur I knows it's good.'
'OUR FATHER.'
'Our Father! – yes, that's wery good, sir.'
'WHICH ART IN HEAVEN.'
'Art in Heaven – is the light a-comin, sir?'
'It is close at hand. HALLOWED BE THY NAME!'
'Hallowed be – thy –'
'The light is come upon the dark benighted way. Dead!' (Ch. 47)

Jo repeats words, and even comments approvingly, but not on the words 'Heaven', 'Hallowed', daily bread, trespasses or forgiveness – all in different ways cruelly irrelevant to him – only to the word 'Father'. This is the one subject, image and word in the prayer which he understands, though only in the kindness of surrogate fathers: fatherless, he has received fatherly affection from three men, Nemo (Captain Hawdon), Snagsby and Allan Woodcourt. Dickens was deeply interested in children's response to religion, writing his simple version of the Bible for children, and writing letters to his sons when they went – except Henry, all very young – into the world, to insist that his own emphasis was not on doctrine but on the New Testament Christ. He felt very strongly the futile irrelevance of contemporary Anglican emphasis on dogma in the education of poor children, having seen this at work when he visited Ragged Schools, about which he had mixed feelings, neither wishing them away – they were better than nothing – nor approving their usual methods of instruction. He had read the relevant Blue Books of the Crown Commissioners, 1842 and 1843, where the confusion and ignorance of poor children, who mixed up 'God' and 'Dog', was movingly registered (*Letters* 3, 459). Marx quotes some of the interview between the educated adult and the uneducated children in *Capital*, and Dickens makes his response to the public inquiry, in the affective form of fiction. We have only to think of 'wery good' being applied to any other item in the prayer to recognize that deliberately or intuitively Dickens chooses to let Jo remember what little he knew of human affection as he listens to the traditional words about Heavenly love.

The imaginative crisis is a nice bit of intertextuality too, defamiliarizing a well-worn text, so inviting Christian and other readers to take another and a closer look at the Lord's prayer in the light of Dickens's selection and Jo's comprehension.

It is characteristic of Dickens that he can turn from such closely imagined particulars of speech, feeling and mind to imagine the reader. He moves the action from Jo's death and demands our compassion for the real world in which author and readers live, and will not let us stay with the luxury of literary compassion which he has made us feel, and which we genuinely if too easily feel for imaginary characters, imaginary suffering and imaginary death. He insists that we leave the text and remember what we do not need to imagine, the real lost children 'dying thus around us every day'. He shocks the complacent reader and reminds us why and for whom he was writing. Modern readers – like some Victorians – have mixed feelings about the pleasure Dickens felt when readers or listeners responded with praise and tears to child-deaths in *The Old Curiosity Shop* and *Dombey*, and his creative art is not afraid to forget aesthetic detachment, lose distance and become frankly kinetic. The prayer-scene in *Bleak House* can reassure those who think Dickens a sentimentalist encouraging sentimental indulgence that he could imagine a child's death without a sentimental touch. It can explain and support his refusal to limit the affective appeal of art.

Mrs Gradgrind of *Hard Times* is one of Dickens's self-centred dotty women, like Mrs Nickleby but without her narrative flair and surge. For most of the novel we feel amusingly distanced from her but come closer in her death scene. (She was also sympathetic when she talked to her children about 'something ological' and wondered what on earth she can call her son-in-law.) When she lies dying, she is transformed yet still in character, her old silly vagueness made pathological by painful and disturbing death, but pointed by Dickens, as she loses identity but preserves it in new form. Louisa speaks to her, with a gentleness that speaks for her capacity to love, but this is not her scene:

> 'Are you in pain, dear mother?'
> 'I think there's a pain somewhere in the room ... but I couldn't positively say that I have got it.'
> After this strange speech, she lay silent for some time. Louisa, holding her hand, could feel no pulse; but kissing it, could see a slight thin thread of life in fluttering motion. (Bk 2, Ch. 9)

She tells Louisa she wants to say something, drifts in and out of consciousness, recalling her old complaint and the author's old joke, that whenever she tries to say something she never hears the last of it. Then she comes vaguely to the point, and dies while imagining she is writing a letter to tell her husband something important:

> 'But there is something, – not an Ology at all – that your father has missed, or forgotten, Louisa. I don't know what it is. I have often sat with Sissy near me, and thought about it. I shall never get its name now. Perhaps your father may. It makes me restless. I want to write to him, to find out for God's sake, what it is. Give me a pen, give me a pen.'
> Even the power of restlessness was gone, except for the poor head, which could just turn from side to side.
> She fancied, however, that her request had been complied with, and that the pen she could not have held was in her hand. It matters little what figures of wonderful no-meaning she began to trace upon her wrappers. The hand soon stopped in the midst of them; the light that had always been feeble and dim behind the weak transparency, went out ... (Ch. 9)

Here as in *Bleak House* Dickens is open to the charge of softening deathbed distress and idealizing the capacity for deathbed vision, but the scene of Mrs Gradgrind's dying and seeing, like Jo's, is unsentimental

because its psychology is so profound, coherent and particular. Even on
her deathbed Mrs Gradgrind is the comic character, her old silly self, her
fluttering vagueness kept but changed into dissociations of the dying
brain – 'I couldn't positively say' – her scattiness there but used in
grasping at something truly elusive – it has eluded her clever husband
and, according to Dickens in this novel, the Utilitarians too. As she tries
to 'trace upon her wrappers' what she is on the point of understanding,
we see the traditionally observed fumbling of dying fingers. The process
of life-denying transformations is seamless, the scene wonderfully individual, thematic, and even comic, as Dickens like Shakespeare gathers
together all the features of a character for the deathbed: Mrs Gradgrind
may seem far removed from Brutus, Juliet, Antony and Cleopatra but she
is with them in her farewell finite variety.

Bill Sikes, Edith, Jo, and Mrs Gradgrind are caught in creative
moments, taken beyond their usual selves and shown freshly and startlingly in a demanding crisis, but also in relationship to everything that
has gone before and is to follow. My last example is strictly speaking not
a crisis in this sense at all, but it is an intense moment in which Dickens –
in the figure of a narrator – identifies imaginatively with an alien, dull,
enfeebled state of mind and recognizes in its strangeness a common
humanity.

The episode appears in the last and fourth chapter of 'The Lazy Tour
of Two Idle Apprentices' (a collaboration with Wilkie Collins for
Household Words in 1857) just before a sensational inset story, 'The
Bride's Chamber', a self-styled *Diablerie* which has attracted attention
because the chief character wills his unwanted wife, called Ellen after a
real-life source, to will her own death. In the same section of Francis
Goodchild's story of his day there is the description of Doncaster races
with arch covert references to Ellen Ternan, which I mentioned in
Chapter 1. The anecdote I have in mind is in strong contrast to both
narratives. It is about mental illness and a piece of psychological writing
far more subtle than the better-known 'Bride's Chamber' and in a mood
very different from the rhapsody about the St Leger.[1]

It describes one of Dickens's frequent investigative visits to institutions, in this case what was called a lunatic asylum, but the patient
described has nothing in common with Dickens's creative mad people,
Barnaby, the cucumber man, Mr Dick and Miss Flite, with whose wild
energy he could vigorously identify. On this occasion Dickens, in the
person of Francis Goodchild, is attending closely to something outside
himself and most unlike himself. This was the year when Dickens met
Ellen Ternan, and the episode of Goodchild and the patient comes in a

section of 'The Lazy Tour' where he is very occupied with his own personal difficulties, feelings and situation. He has come back to the Inn, where his companion, Thomas Idle (Wilkie Collins) has been laid up with an injured ankle, in a cheerful mood but as he starts this story it is clear that he has been depressed by witnessing depression.

He tells his friend that the disturbed inmates he has seen are 'a society of people who have nothing in common but that they have lost the power of being humanly social with each other', and describes watching one of them:

> a poor little dark-chinned, meagre man, with a perplexed brow and a pensive face, stooping low over the matting on the floor, and picking out with his thumb and fore-finger the course of its fibres. The afternoon sun was slanting in at the large end-window, and there were cross patches of light and shade all down the vista, made by the unseen windows and the open doors of the little sleeping cells on either side. (*Journalism* 3)

The patient is advised by Goodchild's guide in the asylum to go and read, and he goes but only to come back almost at once, and the narrator describes his behaviour. As on so many occasions Dickens is standing on the threshold of somebody's life, taking it in. Here is close observation of close observation: the man is looking down at the floor, as he was when Goodchild first saw him;

> ... again poring over the matting, and tracking out its fibres with his thumb and fore-finger ... it came into my mind, that probably the course of those fibres as they plaited in and out, over and under, was the only course of things in the whole wide world that it was left to him to understand – that his darkening intellect had narrowed down to the small cleft of light which showed him, 'This piece was twisted in this way, went in here, passed under, came out there, was carried away here to the right where I now put my finger on it, and in this progress of events, the thing was made and came to be here.'

The last sentence is a restrained effort to think in the patient's language, and comes as a shock, like the speech of the dead mother in the Saint Bernard ice. There has been a pathological concentration which inspires imitation and – up to a tactful point – a projection. The patient is looking at the minute detail of thread in a pattern, and though Dickens / Goodchild sees him seeing it as a thing that has been made, he refrains from seeing it, as an artist might, as an example of craft or a metaphor of aesthetic shape. The artist could do this but not the patient, and the observer's gaze is 'narrowed down' with him and his gaze, willingly minimizing his attention as the patient is doing involuntarily. Then Goodchild steps back from his observation of the man's observation and the object observed, to reflect, generalize and identify, but with decent empathetic restraint:

> I thought how all of us, God help us!, in our different ways are poring over our bit of matting, blindly enough, and what confusions and mysteries we make ... I had a sadder fellow-feeling with the little dark-chinned man, by that time, and I came away.

You can see why Dickens detested patrons and condescension: the bit of matting is seen as an example but it is not elevated, not seen as abnormal, not patronized, only recognized as, and with, a 'fellow-feeling'. Everything is made simple, but the simplicity registers sincerity in a self-analysing act of imagination, respecting otherness and muting sympathy. And at this time of upheaval, doubt, and emotional change, Dickens was especially susceptible to confusions and mystery; perhaps this episode, like the more conspicuous and vibrant rhapsody at the races and the wife-killing story, has its connection with Dickens's real life.[2]

Sikes, Edith, Scrooge, Jo and Mrs Gradgrind are all exciting characters, and the creation of their imaginative impulse is exciting too. So of course are Dickens's mad people, in a way more excitingly – though never simplistically – privileged. But here in this exceptional scene Dickens feels for an unexciting and minimal act of mind, reduced by depression, and he describes it with fine decorum. There is no assertion of the narrator's feeling or character, only the simple act, the simple object and the simple sympathy. The anecdote is a model of scrupulous imaginative observation and record.

Notes

[1] Michael Slater describes the 'desolating image of earnestness' in this episode and its significance as an 'emblem of the human condition'. ('Responsibility and Earnestness', *An Intelligent Person's Guide to Dickens*).

[2] Harry Stone sees Dickens identifying his deep disturbance and dark side with the 'insane' man: I think Stone is melodramatizing the episode and making no distinction between Dickens's self-subduing empathy here and the violent projections in 'The Bride's Chamber' story (*The Night Side of Dickens*).

Chapter 9

Forecast and Fantasy in *Little Dorrit*

Little Dorrit is a deeply introspective novel which personalizes and analyses the backward and forward motion of inner life in many characters.[1]
In this presentation of memory and imagination Dickens concentrates
on acts of forecast and fantasy, both conscious and unconscious, as
micro-narratives in a subtle cellular structure composed of inner
anticipations and retrospects and also the confessions, confidences, lies,
truths, reports, gossip, miniature biographies and autobiographies that
are the stuff of social exchange. The novel's psychic life is rich but the
great reporter is as usual aware of the importance of observation, and his
sociological imagination is always at work, critical and moral in accurate
forecast or wild fantasy.

   To begin with the inner life. In the internal narratives of *Little Dorrit*
Dickens emphasizes fantasy. Like all good novelists he does two things at
the same time: he prefigures future action in what Henry James in the
Preface to *The Tragic Muse* called the art of preparations, and he also
imagines individual imaginations as his characters look ahead realistically or fancifully. At times the author's and the characters' forecasts
overlap, as they do in other novels, for instance when the narrator of *The
Mill on the Floss* says Tom and Maggie are dreaming as they imagine adult
life will be like childhood but are not altogether wrong. In Dickens, too,
the lifelines have subtle and unpredictable continuities and dis-
continuities. As we have seen in *A Tale of Two Cities*, Mr Lorry has a
nightmare about Manette which is a bizarre anticipation of something
that really happens. After Amy Dorrit is freed from prison and poverty
she has nightmares about wearing old prison clothes at a grand dinner,
and though she never does, her dread anticipates the banquet where her
father hallucinates that he is back in prison.

   It is not only the major characters in *Little Dorrit* who have wild fantasies which are or attempt forecasts: Mr and Mrs Meagles need what
Ibsen was to call the life-lie, when they make-believe that their dead
daughter is alive and growing up with her twin; Pancks the gypsy fortune-
teller-detective instructively forecasts some exciting events but not the

fall of investments; Mrs Plornish's painted thatched cottage in squalid
Bleeding-Heart Yard is not wholly fake; the blackmailer Blandois hor-
ridly hugs his doomed prospects; there is a link between Flintwich's
secrets and his wife Affery's unbelievable true dreams; John Chivery
composes heartrending permutations of his tombstone text. But the
most individualized and many-layered fantasies are those of the three
major characters, who are all what Henry James calls sensitive centres of
consciousness. Their narratives are cleverly made by them and for them,
in seats of imagination solidly realized as location, stimulus and symbol –
garrets, prisons, palaces, balconies, doorways, slums, streets and coaches.
Starting with sketches of streets and still life, moving into his curiosity
shop, Dickens continued to observe and invent the physical and psychic
conditions in which imagination likes to work – in privacy, crowds, quiet,
noise, ease, unrest, continuity and change.

In 'A Puzzle', he tracks Arthur Clennam's inner life in minute detail,
dipping in and out of his stream of consciousness. One narrative episode
shows what George Eliot in *Daniel Deronda*, referring to Gwenolen Har-
leth, ironically calls the 'constructive' imagination, and Dickens creates
its temptations and weaknesses: Arthur tells himself a story about Amy,
and a novelist's experience of revision is brought to bear when the
fantasy is disturbed by unpalatable news of the real world in Mrs Chivery's naive intense account of John Chivery's love for Amy. The
mother's story of the son's story clashes with Arthur's story, because she
knows Little Dorrit's past and her present which he has ignorantly
idealized, and possibilities in her future which he has never forecast. We
cut into his consciousness as he realizes that she is a girl born and bred
in prison, a friend of the turnkey's family and a child who played in the
prison yard, and he reluctantly recognizes the fiction he has made,
unable to 'feel positive' about it but justifying and hankering after its
imaginative selections:

> He had come to attach to Little Dorrit an interest so peculiar – an
> interest that removed her from, while it grew out of, the common and
> coarse things surrounding her – that he found it disappointing, dis-
> agreeable, almost painful, to suppose her in love with young Mr.
> Chivery in the back yard, or any such person. On the other hand, he
> reasoned with himself that she was just as good and just as true, in love
> with him, as not in love with him; and that to make a kind of
> domesticated fairy of her, on the penalty of isolation at heart from the
> only people she knew, would be a weakness of his own fancy, and not a
> kind one. Still, her youthful and ethereal appearance, her timid

manner, the charm of her sensitive voice and eyes, the very many respects in which she had interested him out of her own individuality, and the strong difference between herself and those about her, were not in unison, and were determined not to be in unison, with this newly-presented idea ... (Bk 1, Ch. 22)

Here Dickens uses the free indirect style which he uses more rarely than, say, Jane Austen or George Eliot, and it is just right here for Arthur's combination of indulgent feeling and self-criticism. Art is fantasy-driven, and uncontrolled fantasy is a temptation for the artist, so it is instructive and moving when we find self-critical checks and corrections like Arthur's. In 'Easter, 1916' Yeats succumbs to his self-lulling flow of music and image then reminds himself that he is not a mother singing a lullaby and his terrible subject is 'not sleep but death', strikingly focusing and then revising art's romantic unreal vision. Dickens is a more intuitive and less sophisticated dreamer than Yeats, and kept less critical and sophisticated company, but when Arthur tells himself that Amy is not 'a domesticated fairy' it is as sharp and strong a demystification as Yeats's self-correction. Arthur has to face the 'weakness of his own fancy'. His fiction, like his author's, has its weaknesses.

Later on Dickens finds a good image for Arthur's imaginative uncertainty in particular, and the way the mind works in general, placed in one of his own favourite creative habitats: 'The crowd in the street jostling the crowd in his mind, and the two crowds making a confusion' (Bk 1, Ch. 22). Clennam goes on being confused: he can't grasp Little Dorrit's eloquent confession of guilt about enjoying 'the river, and so much sky, and so many objects, and such change and motion', her view from the Iron Bridge which is the sacred secret penny seat of her imagination – while her father is 'in the same cramped place'. We see the sentimentalist and optimist still hanging on to his image of a domesticated fairy, hastening to comfort her and himself, 'you take with you the spirit and influence of such things, to cheer him', to which she sensibly responds, 'I am afraid you fancy too much, sir' (Bk 1, Ch. 22). He goes on fancying, as he feels and interprets her response to his touch: 'The Little Dorrit, trembling on his arm, was less in unison than ever with Mrs Chivery's theory, and yet was not irreconcilable with a new fancy which sprung up within him, that there might be some one else, in the hopeless – newer fancy still – in the hopeless unattainable distance' (Bk 1, Ch. 22).

The inner and outer events of this scene are recalled much later, towards the end of the second book, 'Riches', in a chapter called 'The

Pupil of the Marshalsea' where we see Clennam, a slow learner, at
another stage in his sentimental education, once again needing to be
prompted from the outside, when John Chivery reveals Amy's secret
which his affection has divined. Dickens praised a story he was rejecting
for *All the Year Round* (*Letters* 12, 695) for the way its action 'was psychologically tracked', and particularly in this novel, he shows his
awareness of psychological tracking. He delicately registers the continuum of Arthur's affective ebb and flow, and here he shows Arthur
energized and startled out of stasis and depression into fresh meditation,
dynamically back-tracking, questioning himself, then moving briskly
forward to enlightenment:

> Consider the improbability.
> But, it had a preponderating tendency, when considered, to become
> fainter. There was another and a curious enquiry of his own heart's
> that concurrently became stronger. In the reluctance he had felt to
> believe that she loved anyone; in his desire to set that question at rest;
> in a half-formed consciousness he had had, that there would be a kind
> of nobleness in his helping her love for any one; was there no sup-
> pressed something on his own side that he had hushed as it arose? (Bk
> 2, Ch. 27)

The lover's 'half-formed consciousness' and 'suppressed something' are
as subtle as the narrator's analysis of Maggie's feelings for Philip Wakem,
or Maggie Verver's unriddling of her husband's protectiveness, and this
inner drama is a new venture in Dickens's handling of introspection and
emotion. (Arthur's inner life is not always finely drawn: there is the
archness of his 'decision' not to fall in love with Pet Meagles.)

Towards the end of Book 1, Chapter 24, 'Fortune-telling', between
Arthur's two long meditations, Dickens places Little Dorrit's fantasy and
forecast. It is a conspicuous narrative inset, in the form of a fairy-tale but
naturalized as a story for Maggy, who has been promised it as a reward
for taking a message to Clennam when Amy can't face him. She has
taken to musing alone in her garret, looking out of the window, and the
imaginative transformations in her story are suggested as the bars on the
walls, clear in Phiz's illustration, lose their rust and turn to gold. It's all
according to tradition: Maggy is Umberto Eco's empirical reader who
identifies the story with her own and Amy is attentive to her like the
motherly girl she is, but like her author is not solely occupied with the
listener, and 'a rather sad smile' tells us she is composed enough to
please but is expressing, while disguising, her own deep feelings. Like

her author, she is improvising and does not know where the beginning will take her, so playing for time with a handy convention imagines a rich King with palaces which Maggy revises to hospitals with baked potatoes. Maggy assumes that the poor woman in a cottage is 'An old woman', because this is what you expect, but in this fairy-tale it is 'Quite a young one', because Amy is making her heroine like her in age, as well as size, needlework and poverty. After this correction she also has to drop her first discreet 'Some one' because when she mentions 'him' the avid listener pounces. 'Some one was a man then?' and she admits, 'yes, she believed so'. The tiny woman shows her secret, first as 'a shadow' then something 'bright to look at', and for Maggy it remains a secret. The one supernatural detail, it takes its place quietly in the shadow-play of a novel beginning in the shade of the Marseilles prison, and full of shadows. We first see Miss Wade in shadowed isolation, and the lover's bright shadow is replaced by the shadow of the Marshalsea, which Amy must keep secret when the family come into their fortune but which like all the other secrets in this novel, comes out in the end. There are shadows cast by the leaning tower of Pisa and by death, and shadow persists as the lovers pass along the London streets 'in sunshine and in shade ...' to meet the light and darkness of common life (Bk 2, Ch. 34).

Little Dorrit's fairy-tale is several in one, told to the listener in the novel, in the knowledge that Maggy, however alert to hints and clues, will not understand all the hints and clues that are understood by the reader, and devised by a novelist who had his secrets too and kept some of them. Though a fairy-tale, Little Dorrit's story has no happy ending (though one is proposed by Maggy at the end of the novel). It reflects its novel's themes of love and secrecy, but Dickens's central plot-secret has no king, princess or unhappy end. In Maggy Dickens smiles at his ideal reader's response as she praises, agrees, questions, and asks for more: Phiz shows Maggy gazing at Amy, who is gazing out of the window, looking away from conscious communication to see the story before her, as Dickens said he did. Unlike Clennam's, Little Dorrit's story is realistic, even pessimistic, a thoroughly imaginative piece in every sense, and Dickens's comparison of her inspiration to that of a poet is deeply meant, though he is not talking about her as a teller of tales:

> ... she was inspired to be something which was not what the rest were, and to be that something, different and laborious, for the sake of the rest. Inspired? Yes. Shall we speak of the inspiration of a poet or a priest, and not of the heart impelled by love and self-devotion to the lowliest work in the lowliest way of life! (Bk 1, Ch. 7)

Her fairy-tale is told again. She tells a lie to Clennam, 'I have no secret' and sharp blundering Maggy prompts, 'If you an't got no secret of your own ... tell him that about the Princess.' Amy leaves it to her, and she changes from listener to teller, reconstructing the story with a few changes, matter-of-factly translating the unnamed hiding-place into a cupboard (Bk 1, Ch. 32). But she has intuited a link between her friend's secretiveness and her story about a secret.

Long after the truthful fairy-tale Amy comes out as teller in a different style, more personal and historical but still dreamy, as she writes to Clennam from Italy, describing landscape, cities and buildings, drawing on her author's skill as an observant, ironic and flexible travel-writer while developing as a character. The letters fuse with the narrator's earlier account of her inner life, and both indirect and direct narrative remind us of Dickens's *Pictures from Italy*. Her confused and excited perceptions of travel and places, described or dramatized, present her character, mind and feelings – as Dickens's did too, but not so fully or consciously. The narrator's descriptions and her own travel-narratives draw on Dickens's descriptive writing at its best, with imagery particularized by mood, not always precisely dramatizing a point of view but stamped with personal mood and mind. They are vivid descriptions, paced, condensed and sharpened by dramatic function, more profound and particular than the best of *Pictures from Italy* and very different from the laboured literary banality of Dickens's high-flown vague nature descriptions in *The Old Curiosity Shop* and *Barnaby Rudge*. The letters in particular express Little Dorrit's modest ordinariness, her subdued affection for the friend she writes to, her past experience and her new surprise. If we compare the imitations of Wordsworth made for David Copperfield's inspirational Alps we see how differently Dickens is doing a creative mind and its conditions here: he uses landscape indirectly to make the outside world reflect the inner life, human and non-human nature co-substantiating each other, for better or worse, as Amy realizes:

> ... the more surprising the scenes, the more they resembled the unreality of her own inner life as she went through its vacant places all day long. The gorges of the Simplon, its enormous depths and thundering waterfalls, the wonderful road, the points of danger where a loose wheel or a faltering horse would have been destruction ... the opening of that beautiful land, as the rugged mountain-chasm widened and let them out from a gloomy and dark imprisonment – all a dream – only the old Marshalsea a reality. (Bk 2, Ch. 3)

It is her first foreign trip and Dickens not only draws on the dilapidated splendours and social contrasts he emphasized in his letters and *Pictures from Italy* but details of travelling, like the strangeness of waking up in unfamiliar hotel rooms, the fuss and bother of travel preparation, and journeys on unfamiliar roads:

> Little Dorrit would wake from a dream of her birth-place into a whole day's dream. The painted room in which she awoke, often a humbled state-chamber in a dilapidated palace, would begin it; with its wild red autumnal vine-leaves overhanging the glass, its orange trees on the cracked white terrace outside the window, a group of monks and peasants in the little street below, misery and magnificence wrestling with each other ... To this would succeed a labyrinth of bare passages and pillared galleries ...
>
> ... Among the day's unrealities would be, roads where the bright red vines were looped and garlanded together on trees for many miles ... white villages and towns on hill-sides, lovely without, but frightful in their dirt and poverty within ... beggars of all sorts everywhere ...
>
> ... squalid villages where there was not a hovel without a gap in its filthy walls ... where there seemed to be nothing to support life, nothing to eat, nothing to make, nothing to hope, nothing to do but die ...
>
> ... troops of idle soldiers leaning out of the state-windows, where their accoutrements hung drying on the marble architecture, and showing to the mind like hosts of rats who were (happily) eating away the props of the edifices that supported them ... (Bk 2, Ch. 3)

In the passages describing the journey there is insistent social comment in the collision and contrast of 'misery' and 'magnificence', accompanying and intensifying the psychic unrealities, all within the visual and sympathetic scope of Amy Dorrit but ironized in Dickens's style, and indeed making the social emphasis he also made in *Pictures from Italy* where he brings together the rich–poor contrasts of a rotten society, his impressions political but inseparable from personal details like his fastidious distaste for smells and filth. Here what he observed, enjoyed and judged is experienced again, imagined for his intelligent, observant and sensitive heroine, skilfully generalized from his knowledge on her behalf.

We see this in what he imagines for her and what he sets outside her point of view. The extraordinary scenes as the Dorrits arrive at the Saint Bernard Convent, which F. R. Leavis has finely appreciated, are not dramatized from her perspective, but are shown with a steady, ironic and tragic apprehension of the world that is larger and older than his young heroine's, creative though she is:

> Seen from those solitudes, and from the Pass of the Great Saint Bernard, which was one of them, the ascending Night came up the mountain like a rising water. When it at last rose to the walls of the convent of the Great Saint Bernard, it was as if that weather-beaten structure were another Ark, and floated away upon the shadowy waves …
>
> … At length, a light on the summit of the rocky staircase gleamed through the snow and mist …
>
> … silently assembled in a grated house … were the dead travellers found upon the mountain. The mother, storm-belated many winters ago, still standing in the corner with her baby at her breast; the man who had frozen with his arm raised to his mouth in fear or hunger, still pressing it with his dry lips after years and years. An awful company, mysteriously come together! A wild destiny for that mother to have foreseen, 'Surrounded by so many and such companions upon whom I never looked, and never shall look, I and my child will dwell together inseparable, on the Great Saint Bernard, outlasting generations who will come to see us, and will never know our name, or one word of our story but the end.'
>
> The living travellers thought little or nothing of the dead just then. (Bk 2, Ch. 1)

What the anonymous narrator sees is beyond the personal, in Nature and death, and Dickens most imaginatively used what he had seen himself: the snow, the mountains and the frozen human bodies. At this point, Dickens wants to go beyond all his living travellers, to put into his novel his own creative experience of the world which is larger than we are, which for different reasons none of his travelling characters can grasp. In *David Copperfield* he had romanticized the Alps and made them serve his writer-hero's purposes, but now he knows better and sets his story on the threshold both of the human and the inhuman. Being Dickens, he does so by imagining the mother's speech which takes us outside his novel, and outside fiction. He does not exalt or falsify the imagination of Little Dorrit, and the novel is not told from her perspective alone, though hers is wider and deeper than Clennam's, which is given more to recover and more scope to grow. (His imprisoned childhood has been loveless, her prison rich in love.)

The novel is called *Little Dorrit* and after this remarkable excursus it returns to her. For the carefully chosen locale of Venice, which Dickens said became a bit of his brain and made into a different experience for his heroine's imagination, the personal focus sharpens, but though he is using his memory and his old text, he adapts them for Amy. He was particularly moved by Venice, which he thought transcended expectation and imagination, describing his first visit there in *Pictures from Italy* as a dream, not a reality, in a fantastic description, blurred, accelerated, ecstatic, teasing. His dream is re-created for Amy's imagination: 'In this crowning unreality, where all the streets were paved with water ... Little Dorrit ... sat down to muse' (Bk 2, Ch. 3). In her balcony scene, the cultural information supplied by the narrator is beyond her scope but apt for her mental state, the ancient curious high balcony, like and unlike her old high attic in the prison. (The woman's outward gaze through a high window is repeated again in a bow-window overlooking the Corso in Rome, and is a trope that may have been reinforced for George Eliot by Dickens.) The experienced unrealities are unfamiliar works of art and nature, their exoticism repeated in each detail, from streets 'paved with water' and gondoliers seen from a palazzo, to the musing-place 'of massive stone darkened by ages, built in a wild fancy which came from the East to that collection of wild fancies' (Bk 2, Ch. 3).

Like the Swiss visit, the Venetian experience is first described by the narrator, whose sensibility is brought close to Dorrit's, and articulated again in her letters, which omit most, but not all, of the geographical, historic and architectural detail – not that this is extensive. Her style is simple but she does not simplify. She feels the defamiliarization the narrator chronicled, her old occupation gone and her reverie inspired by time and place. She feels strange for her own reasons but it is like the strangeness Dickens mentions in his own creative responses. She writes her beautiful love-letters and travel tales in a plain original way, aware of her inner experience and closely observing scene and landscape with an intelligent puzzled response. Dickens provides her critical version of social unreality when she wonders that the fashionable foreign world in which she feels displaced seems less real than prison and remarks that she hasn't a strong enough sense of herself to take in new sights. She perceives her own wonder clearly but is not at ease with it:

It is the same with all these new countries and wonderful sights. They are very beautiful, and they astonish me, but I am not collected enough – not familiar enough with myself, if you can quite understand what I mean – to have all the pleasure in them that I might have. (Bk 2, Ch. 4)

Simply, confidingly, truthfully and humorously, she tells Clennam the vivid story of her 'curious' hallucinations: 'What I knew before them, blends with them, too, so curiously. For instance, when we were among the mountains, I often felt ... as if the Marshalsea must be behind that great rock; or as if Mrs Clennam's room where I have worked so many days, and where I first saw you, must be just beyond that snow.' (We see why the frozen dead could not be seen from her point of view: unlike the other travellers she is imaginative enough, but 'not familiar enough with herself' for the necessary detachment.) She goes on, extending the defamiliarization, to see the London streets where she was 'shut out with Maggy', in Venice but expecting to see London people in a passing gondola, 'It would overcome me with joy to see them, but I don't think it would surprise me much ... In my fanciful times, I fancy that they might be anywhere' (Bk 2, Ch. 4).

We are taken to the verge of the irrational, as her blurred dreamy consciousness is motivated by a longing for home and alienation from the present. Here too, Dickens is adapting his own past impressions as well as inventing new and specific Little Dorrit feelings. In one of the narratives he wrote as the Uncommercial Traveller for *All the Year Round* there is a description of a similar feeling, though it is the geographical reverse of Amy's experience, because an English scene blurs into Swiss landscape when Dickens goes for one of his night walks:

> The day broke mistily ... and I could not disembarrass myself of the idea that I had to climb those heights and banks of cloud, and that there was an Alpine convent somewhere behind the sun, where I was going to breakfast ... when I was sufficiently awake to have a sense of pleasure in the prospect I still occasionally caught myself looking about for wooden arms to point the right track up the mountain, and wonder that there was no snow yet. (*Journalism* 4)

This is not only like Dorrit's imaginative blurring but also explained as a creative state between sleep and waking like Gabriel Vardon's, and Dickens even relates it to creative art, though only bad poetry, adding the detail that 'on this pedestrian occasion he imagined himself speaking a language he once spoke fluently and had forgotten'. (He learnt Italian and French but forgot the Italian.)

In Dorrit's second letter she is getting used to tourist life and acquiring guidebook facts so Dickens can risk naming a monument to image what she calls her 'curious' melancholy about ruins (Bk 2, Ch. 11). In Pisa she focuses on the shadow of the leaning tower, and she reflects on its age and uses a resonant phrase, 'soft and retired' (Bk 2, Ch. 11). She is relating the shadow to herself – 'soft and retired' – and to the shadow of the prison wall in their Marshalsea room, and feels that the ancient Pisa tower was strangely there long before her new life began and strangely there while she was growing up in prison. Though Dickens's accounts of Pisa and its tower on a grassy site are sharp and responsive in *Pictures from Italy*, his fictional version is more original and sensuously specific. He had to exclude the response to the Saint Bernard from Amy's experience but Dickens makes her see Pisa more sensitively than he did in the travel-book.

Another unreality, again recognized as unreal, is her recurring dream of being a little girl doing needlework, and of dining with a large company in the threadbare mourning dress she wore when she was eight, worried by extravagance, fear of shaming the family and 'disclosing what they wished to keep secret' (Bk 2, Ch. 11). A breaking of family taboo, realistic dream as well as a narrative prolepsis, it emphasizes the strength of Little Dorrit's social nurture and psychic health, as she rejects her family's dangerous wish-fulfilling attempts to break with the prison and the warm loving past, and choose the loveless world of wealth and privilege.

Dickens dramatizes sensations of fantasy as they make normal mental activity strange. Amy's self-admitted delusion and wonder, like Clennam's sense of mental crowdedness, are sharpened by an artist's experience but made plausible and individual and 'ordinary' for the novel. Her wonder and her consciousness of curious experience makes a modest version of creative pride which is wholly justified by her delicate fancies. When she uses the word 'wonderful' it is not banal but registers a response that she cannot define intellectually – and neither can Dickens. It is like Keats's sense of being 'teased' out of thought as he contemplates the Grecian urn, and Kant's Sublime, which daunts the mind's capacity and baffles our comprehension (*The Critique of Judgment*). The sense of wonder is also very Lawrentian, and one of the many valuable insights in Leavis's chapter on this novel is his insistence that Dickens is like Lawrence because Lawrence learnt from him: he emphasizes not the wonder, but the closely related sense that the truly creative person, like Tom Brangwen in *The Rainbow*, knows that he does not belong to himself.

Dickens's 'failure' to follow the sophisticated theoretical distinction between Fancy and Imagination has a special advantage in this epistolary narrative, where the word 'fancy' is used unself-consciously, amateur-ishly, in lower case, suitably modest for Little Dorrit's consciousness. In these letters, Dickens writes his love-story, makes his character – no domesticated fairy – psychically singular and alive.

Little Dorrit is deepened by variations of forecast and fantasy, shown in conscious and less conscious intelligence. Mr Dorrit's fantasy-work, which amounts to the whole of his dramatized inner life, is shallow compared with his daughter's. Hers is the most sensitive register of consciousness; *pace* Leavis, who sees in her the creative life of love and service but not art, I think she is the artist in the novel, her imagination fully articulated, especially in the letters which are her true texts, deep, wise, cautious and empathetic.

Her father's final flight of fantasy is like her's in questioning reality, and when it presides the reader's sense of reality is shaken. The link between the two minds is a vital contrast: when Little Dorrit is imagi-natively disturbed in Switzerland and Italy, she is always aware that her fancy is mere fancy while her father takes his fantasy-world so seriously that it really becomes hallucination. It is important that her sense of continuity is not suppressed, and her fear is always placed, controlled and communicated, demonstrating the function of the intelligent, analytic imagination which is her guide to survival in Anglo-Venetian nouveau-riche society and in the London streets at night, where she was once locked out of the prison and imagined a party for herself and Maggy. (As I said, she recalls this in Venice.) Like her descendents Maggie Tulliver and Isobel Archer, she knows and shows that the present cannot be severed from the past. The ethic she articulates and repre-sents, always insists, like Wordsworth's, George Eliot's and Proust's, on continuities of feeling, time and place. Scrooge had to learn that too, but in the simplicities of dream-fable.

Her father is her opposite then, failing in control and integrity during the prison days when he veered from self-deception to sentimental col-lapse, and in his time of wealth and privilege still committing the psy-chically destructive sin of cutting present from past. He denies his time in prison so is kept imprisoned: the prison imagery registers his repression just as it does Mrs Clennam's, if more literally. His breakdown is preceded or caused by his dangerous construction of a future with no foundation. His forecast is dramatized at a third-person remove and with strong irony because he can't admit that it is fantasy. Unlike Amy, he can't be responsible for his existential self or his own narrative, because he can't recognize either. Even his narrator has to make the fantasy

evasive and elusive, and does so brilliantly by the feat of extending and
elaborating the traditional image of a castle in Spain or in the clouds or
in the air, which he often uses, in his letters, in *David Copperfield* and as
the primary sad symbol in 'The Poor Relation's Story'.

Mr Dorrit's castle-building begins in Book 2, Chapter 18, 'A Castle in
the Air', and it is also the beginning of his end, a fine example of
Dickens's ability to do many things at once – make a general and local
pattern, join pathos and comedy, and make a deep psychological
observation. William Dorrit's creative forecast and fantasy begin on the
road in the privacy, relaxation, and motion of his coach journey through
France to Italy – again paralleling Dickens's own experience of travel but
made particular to the character. Dorrit has left the restrictions and
threats of memory behind him in London:

Having now quite recovered his equanimity, Mr Dorrit, in his snug
corner, fell to castle-building as he rode along. It was evident that he
had a very large castle in hand. All day long he was running towers up,
taking towers down, adding a wing here, putting on a battlement
there, looking to the walls, strengthening the defences, giving orna-
mental touches to the interior, making in all respects a superb castle
of it.

... As he strolled back to his hotel ... he carried his head high:
having plainly got up his castle, now, to a much loftier altitude than
the two square towers of Notre Dame.

Building away with all his might, but reserving the plans of his castle
exclusively for his own eye, Mr Dorrit posted away for Marseilles.
Building on, building on, busily, busily, from morning to night. Falling asleep, and leaving great blocks of building materials dangling in
the air ... (Bk 2, Ch. 18)

The construction detail mockingly develops and renews the proverbial
image, and it is tersely generalized in a bathetic joke when it is extended
to Dorrit's 'Courier in the rumble, smoking Young John's best cigars ...
perhaps as *he* built a castle or two, with stray pieces of Mr Dorrit's money'
(Bk 2, Ch. 18). The castle, so solid and so flimsy, is ironically compared
with real buildings, Notre Dame in Paris, the ancient monuments the
travellers see on the road, unnamed churches, humbler houses and
natural wonders. The mock grandeur and scope of comparison are
comic, as Dickens brilliantly elides time and place, inner and outer life:

Not a fortified town that they passed in all their journey was as strong, not a Cathedral summit was as high, as Mr Dorrit's castle. Neither the Saone nor the Rhone sped with the swiftness of that peerless buliding; nor was the Mediterranean deeper than its foundations; nor were the distant landscapes on the Cornice road, nor the hills and bay of Genoa the Superb, more beautiful. Mr Dorrit and his matchless castle were disembarked among the dirty white houses and dirtier felons of Civita Vecchia, and thence scrambled on to Rome as they could, through the filth that festered on the way. (Bk 2, Ch. 18)

In these fast castle-buildings Dickens registers the motion and speed of fantasy life,[2] its process and activity observed as the familiar psychic response to travelling: Dorrit's imagination is stimulated by solitude, passivity and motion on the journey from England through France to Italy. The fantasy can't start in England where he is surrounded by high society and haunted by the low, but needs distraction and hurry. In *Pictures from Italy* Dickens produces a similar effect of speed when he describes his haste from Italy to try out *The Chimes* on London friends. In the novel he devises a psycho-drama of travelling, a correlative for speed like camera-shake in a film. 'On the Road' hurtled Little Dorrit through unfamiliar and unnerving landscapes, merging places and people to record her confused and estranged impressions and he uses similar kaleidoscopic images for her father's very different journey.

Dorrit's mind 'could not be quite easy in that desolate place'. Even when he fears the postillions as 'cut-throat looking fellows' he still works 'at his castle in the intervals'. Outside Rome he is provided with a waste land:

And now, fragments of ruinous enclosure, yawning window-gap and crazy wall, deserted houses, leaking wells, broken water-tanks, spectral cypress-trees, patches of tangled vine, and the changing of the track to a long, irregular, disordered lane, where everything was crumbling away, from the unsightly buildings to the jolting road – now, these objects showed that they were nearing Rome. (Bk 2, Ch. 19)

Dorrit's perception is not entirely confined to fantasy; he can take the odd look at the world outside, not unreasonably fearing brigands, dreading a religious procession and priest as sinister threats, his para-noia reflecting and adapting the anti-Catholic feeling so marked in *Pictures from Italy*. The procession 'mechanically chanting by' is won-derfully ominous, an image of death internalized for Dorrit, 'made fanciful by the weariness of building and travelling', feeling menaced 'as the priest drifted past him, and the procession straggled away, taking its dead along with it' (Bk 2, Ch. 19). (Perhaps it inspired the Venetian funeral fantasy in the film *Don't Look Now.*)

At home, late and unwelcomed, his disintegration begins to show in repetitive, 'fitful' even 'unintelligible' speech, and what Amy marks as 'two under-currents ... pervading all his discourse and all his manner', a pull towards the past and another towards the new rich shoddy life. Dickens ends the episode by joining inside and outside, returning us to the dominant fantasy as Dorrit inspects and locks up his Paris purchases, 'dozing ... castle-building' and 'lost' before he creeps to bed as dawn touches 'the eastward rim of the desolate Campagna' (Bk 2, Ch. 19). He also reverts to the old self-protective prison-game about his brother's aging and poor health, displacing his own sick fatigue and aging until that illusion is in its turn displaced by the final fantasy at Mrs Merdle's great dinner, the return to past and prison. Again doing several things at once, Dickens tilts levels of reality, dramatizes consciousness, and goes on with his social critique. Like Amy's dream, but without her rational awareness, Dorrit's fantasy displaces the reality on which his hold has become increasingly feeble.

The interruption of Mrs Merdle's great farewell banquet by his hal-lucinations of prison is in a sense benign, and recalls Little Dorrit's true sense that the Marshalsea was a stronger presence than Italy. Dorrit's wandering mind dismisses his hostess and fellow-guests as he is displaced – idealistically and selectively, in a return which is sentimental in Dorrit but not in Dickens – to the warm loyal fellowship of prison (Bk 2, Ch. 19). Here long-dead Dick, 'best of all the turnkeys', who named him Governor of the Marshalsea and was Amy's godfather, comes to help him up 'the narrow stairs' he cannot climb alone. Only Dickens – and Shakespeare – can imagine like this.

The disrupted feast is the beginning of Dorrit's dying and also a deep social threat, Dickens's version of the banquet in *Macbeth*, though it does not compound horror but brings great moral relief. Dorrit's grand delusions and the phantasmagoria of high society need shattering. The dismissal of the extravagant dinner, the insincere hospitality, the pre-datory guests, the sinister servile servants, the shabby glamour, the whole louche set, makes a transformation scene and a small revolution: 'his poor maimed spirit, only remembering the place where it had broken its wings, cancelled the dream through which it had since groped, and knew of nothing beyond the Marshalsea' (Bk 2, Ch. 19).

As Amy watches she sees a greater shadow than that of the prison wall, and the slow process of dying continues in shifts of fantasy and reality, acknowledging uncertainty in life and death. Dorrit's end is Dickens's best piece of morbid drama: on the deathbed, Dickens twists his recurrent castle image to observe and register the change from life to death: 'the lines of the plan of the great Castle melted'. Those blurring lines of a 'great castle' must have influenced that great Dickensian Kafka as he imaged his *Castle*'s uncertainty, mutability, illusion, and inaccessible telos. (It is a less deliberated but more profound imitation than his 'imitation' of *David Copperfield* in *America*.) Like Dickens, Kafka knows that existential anxieties are also social and his Castle is governed by an inaccessible, puzzling and taunting hegemony very like the Circumlocution Office.

As often, the prevailing image belongs to a pattern but makes a local emphasis. The castle image leads to one climactic episode where it functions like Nell's green plants, the doctors' racing watches at Mrs Dombey's deathbed, Paul's wild waves and the cart Jo drags uphill in *Bleak House*. Dorrit's castle-building makes a local structure for his death-scene, its metaphor underlined by the twinned chapter titles, 'A Castle in the Air' and 'The Storming of the Castle in the Air'.

Death comes out of the castle-image more startlingly for the reader than in the other Dickensian death-scenes. The imagined and imaginary image melts, the body-features change, the prison imprint fades, age is obliterated, time comes to a stop. The scene is steadied by a sense of common experience, as memory, fantasy, body and mind all dissolve. Most of the castle-building has been treated comically and with critical matter-of-factness but when the 'great Castle' melts, the tone is solemn, the symbol changes, the castle turns active. The episode takes us to the verge of the supernatural but no farther: there is no hint of transcendence at the moment of death. (That comes a page later, when both brothers face their 'Father' in one of Dickens's rare numinous moments.)

> Quietly, quietly, all the lines of the plan of the great Castle melted, one after another. Quietly, quietly, the ruled and cross-ruled countenance on which they were traced, became fair and blank. Quietly, quietly, the reflected marks of the prison bars and of the zigzag iron on the wall-top, faded away. Quietly, quietly, the face subsided into a far younger likeness of her own than she had ever seen under the grey hair, and sank to rest. (Bk 2, Ch. 19)

The phrase 'the great Castle', set in the context of death, transforms and promotes the past images of Dorrit's fantasy, all those ridiculous epithets of elaboration and magnitude: 'very large', 'superb', 'high', 'deep', 'beautiful'. The image of a castle is cunningly modulated, changing while recalling the critical tones that placed it earlier and now make a last appearance to stand gravely for all fantastic forecasts and their dissolution.

Clennam, Little Dorrit, and Mr Dorrit present analyses of conscious and unconscious mind, affective and cognitive life, psychologically detailed and socially solid in a way that anticipates George Eliot and Henry James, neither of whom recognized Dickens's achievement as a psychologist – Leavis believed he surpassed them. But Dorothea's and Isabel's shortsighted–farsighted ideals are imagined by novelists who criticized Dickens but were saturated in his novels. They learnt from his bad dreams as well as his good ones. If George Eliot imagined becoming a demon and James dreamt vastation, Dickens can turn reality to nightmare. His fantasy is stranger than their's, in content and form, anticipating surrealism, the Absurd and modernist dislocations.

Dickens writes his own phantasmagoric and grotesque portrait of society, which is most real when most crazy. He brilliantly merges the sociological with the psychological imagination, criticizing society and inventing character, as he keeps the tension going, marks themes, makes character and experience more real for being strange and more strange for being real. Frail vessel and bearer of human affections, Little Nell grown up and grown healthy, Little Dorrit voices and metonymizes this social vision, showing Dickens as a conscious critic who assimilates didactic message to fictional medium, and an intuitive critic who draws on his own artist's imaginative experience to dramatize conscious and unconscious mind. He endows characters with his particular creative bent, and this heroine's imagination is the heart of his novel. Little Dorrit is ordinarily and humanly heroic as she accepts and articulates the dangerous elements in which we try to survive.

Notes

[1] Arthur Clennam. Little Dorrit, and Dickens's affinity with Blake, are discussed by F. R. Leavis in what is probably the best criticism of the novel: *Dickens the Novelist*, F. R. and Q. D. Leavis.

[2] Other novelists fascinated by the speed and flimsy materials of imaginative construction include Jane Austen, whose Emma indulges and criticizes her own day-dreams about Frank Churchill, George Eliot whose Rosamond

constructs a solid fantasy of house, clothes, furniture and wedding-visits after first meeting Lydgate, and Joyce whose Celtic twilight poet Chandler, in 'A Little Cloud' (*Dubliners*), quotes from reviews before ever writing a word.

Chapter 10

Creative Conversation in *Hard Times, Great Expectations* and *Our Mutual Friend*

Dickens is a master of dialogue, and uses it in many kinds of drama and narrative. Barnaby Rudge's defence of madness and Paul Dombey's description of his sea-vision are almost wholly spoken as monologue but they are made dialogic to accentuate an intuitive exchange or show imagination reaching or attempting to reach another mind. Sometimes Dickens uses dialogue to dramatize power, as when Rogue Riderhood in *Our Mutual Friend* slowly gains the ascendancy over Bradley Headstone in a sinister travesty of classroom question and answer. Sometimes dialogue animates narration, as in the scene in a Dover hotel where Jarvis Lorry tells Lucie Manette her father is alive, in a slow-moving conversation which is sensitive on both sides, each reaching out cautiously to the other. There are meetings of creative affinities where thought or fancy proceeds in dynamic collaboration, each speaker egging on the other in a dramatic model of what we call lateral thinking, mind energized by stimulus from outside, as when Jenny Wren shares a fairy-tale fantasy with Mr Riah, greeting him as 'godmother' and delighted when prompt on his cue he calls her 'Cinderella' (Bk 3, Ch. 2) and they play out a joyful *fantasie à deux* which develops over several chapters into an elaborate and serious role-game, with Fascination Fledgeby joining in and for a while spoiling the fun.

Hard Times is a novel rich in creative conversation. It is centrally and explicitly concerned with imagination, its absence, its repression, its changes and its growth, and the dialogue frequently turns on a contrast of minds. Its most famous exchange is the one in which Louisa Gradgrind tries to talk to her father, and a well-meaning communication ends in failure. It is not a disguised monologue because there are clearly two participants and they try to reach each other: Louisa struggles to use the language of emotion she has never learnt and appeals incoherently to Gradgrind who listens and is even vaguely troubled but can speak only in a language of fact and reason:

'You are not impulsive, you are not romantic, you are accustomed to view everything from the strong dispassionate ground of reason and calculation. From that ground alone, I know you will view and consider what I am going to communicate.'

He waited, as if he would have been glad that she said something. But she said never a word.

'Louisa, my dear, you are the subject of a proposal of marriage that has been made to me ...' (Bk 1, Ch. 15)

She is still silent, he repeats the last six words and she replies without emotion, 'I hear you, father' and asks questions he cannot answer, about feelings, about love: 'do you think I love Mr Bounderby?', 'do you ask me to love Mr Bounderby?' and 'does Mr Bounderby ask me to love him?' He recommends her to ask a different question, about facts, and refers to her age and Bounderby's with statistics about disparity of age in marriage, finally isolating two questions for her to ask, 'Does Mr Bounderby ask me to marry him?' and 'Shall I marry him?' It is he who sets in train her answer – or approach to an answer – through metaphor. Seeing her look out of the window, he asks, 'Are you consulting the chimneys of the Coketown works, Louisa?' and she takes his prompt, 'There seems to be nothing there but languid and monotonous smoke. Yet when the night comes, Fire bursts out, father!' Her feeling is registered in the movement of 'turning quickly', but he does not 'see the application of the remark', 'To do him justice ... not, at all.' The metaphor of stifled fire which expresses her repression and its dangers, is itself a repressed communication which fascinatingly links the social and political suppression of Coketown workers to repression of feeling in the individual.

After she accepts and is asked to name a day she repeats, 'What does it matter?' and 'her repetition of these words seemed to strike with some little discord on his ear'; once again the narrator signifies feeling in movement, Gradgrind moves his chair nearer, holds her hand and asks if she has 'entertained ... any other proposal?' When this possibility is disclaimed with an irony he cannot hear, he 'is quite moved' by his success, asks her to kiss him and calls her his favourite child.

His response and his own repression are indicated in his body language and other cues: he is by no means unobservant of her, and shows some capacity to imagine in the question about other proposals as well as in his initial question. Although Gradgrind cannot read the language of feeling and the code of metaphor, his prompting shows some intuition, and though Louisa cannot speak the language of emotion she can work with silence and metaphor. This is why her symbolic speech is presented as a spontaneous grasp at the imagery available just outside the room. Louisa's only speech at this stage is symbol and in choosing the Coketown chimneys but not interpreting them, she unconsciously – though not unconsciously on Dickens's part – brings out the significant social nuance and links the personal with the political.

When in the end she leaves Bounderby and there is a proper dialogue between father and daughter, it looks back to the earlier failure. Like Dombey, Gradgrind is a case of imaginative repression, as the first uncommunicative dialogue hints. There is no sudden transformation and no diagrammatic or simple contrast of mind. Father and child first have a complex conversation which is remembered and revised to make it clear – or clearer – that the symbolism of repressed feeling applies to Gradgrind as well as Louisa. Moreover, the drama of repressed and released affect now takes a new turn: once freed, the voice of feeling says some surprising things. In the earlier conversation Louisa could not even use the conventional vocabulary of love, but when she tries to tell her father her love-story which is not exactly a love-story, she can speak the strange truths of the heart, confessing without banality that she does not know if she loves Harthouse or not, sounding more like a character in Henry James or Virginia Woolf than Dickens. This second dialogue, in Chapter 12 of Book 2, shows the psychological respect her author develops for her, and helps to explain his decision not to give her the romantic happy ending he imagines for other heroines.

The single conversation between Sissy Jupe and Harthouse takes place between opposites but it is a dynamic rare and true 'conversation', an exchange and a change. Sissy's part is remarkable for its truthfulness, clarity, simplicity, and much more than this. She has been a reliable speaker from the start, the only schoolchild to value metaphor, the circus-child who understands fantasy and play, but can't persuade Machoakumchild and Gradgrind of their value. She puts her point, however, in rationally aesthetic terms when she defends flowery home decoration against literal-minded stupidity, on the grounds of beauty. Her conversation with Harthouse in Book 3, Chapter 2, 'Very Ridiculous', is a meeting of strangers which swiftly becomes a conversation of moral values. The speakers have not met before and the debate is the more emphatic for the lack of intimacy, eliciting and conceptualizing the quality of both characters, inviting us to recognize in what they say and how they say it, not just two individuals but truth pitted against falsehood, plain speaking against sophisticated rhetoric, candour against disguise. The exchange is reminiscent of Cordelia's defence of truth to Lear. Virtue rebukes but also influences vice, crucially if not permanently, and Harthouse admits Sissy's disinterested power in a way reminiscent of the recognition of William Dobbin's integrity by Becky Sharp, or the effect of Dorothea's generous candour on shallow self-centred Rosamond Vincy.

The conversation is between strangers, but strangers who get to know each other with amazing speed. It is composed of dialogue, inner monologue and narrative, its setting Harthouse's hotel – 'the stake to which he was tied' – where he waits after Louisa has failed to turn up for their planned elopement. Harthouse's point of view directs the narrative, and as he reads Sissy's face and demeanour he is impressed by a focus and self-indifference he finds unusual in a pretty woman meeting a man for the first time: 'She seems to have her mind entirely preoccupied with the occasion of her visit, and to have substituted that consideration for herself.' Straight away, his conventional response and expectation are confounded. Sissy gets to the point without preliminaries, 'I think ... you have already guessed whom I left just now' and when he mentions his anxiety she keeps to bare narrative 'I left her within an hour', ignoring his feeble 'Ah – ', going on, 'At her father's.' There follows a description of his lengthening face and increased perplexity: Dickens uses stage-directions and the unspoken inner speech that shadows all our dialogues – almost as subtly as Flaubert for the agricultural show in *Madame Bovary* or George Eliot for the archery meeting in *Daniel Deronda* – to emphasize Harthouse's silence and passivity. He tells himself he does not know where they 'are going', her manner and her matter confound him, and for the first time in the novel the gentleman and prospective member of parliament is not in control.

The narration of response is subtle, brief and to the point. Sissy blurts out her news without ceremony, in jerkily unlinked simple sentences and repetition that register sincerity and urgency:

> 'She hurried there last night. She arrived there in great agitation, and was insensible all through the night. I live at her father's, and was with her. You may be sure, Sir, that you will never see her again as long as you live.'
>
> Mr Harthouse drew a deep breath, and, if ever man found himself in the position of not knowing what to say, made the discovery beyond all question that he was so circumstanced ... (Bk 3, Ch. 2)

The balance of power is weighted on her side:

'Must believe? But if I can't – or if I should, by infirmity of nature, be obstinate – and won't –'

'It is still true. There is no hope.'

James Harthouse looked at her with an incredulous smile upon his lips, but her mind looked over and beyond him, and the smile was quite thrown away.

She proceeds to the next stage of her mission, her simple, spontaneous and unabashed reproach addressing his guarded unease: 'I have only the commission of my love for her, and her love for me' and ... 'I have no further trust, than that I know something of her character and her marriage. O Mr Harthouse, I think you had that trust too!' The appeal works unsentimentally, the narrator choosing a grotesque image to lament a spoiling of nature but also a rare deep response: Harthouse is 'touched in the cavity where his heart should have been – in that nest of addled eggs, where the birds of heaven would have lived if they had not been whistled away'. Though speaking in what Dickens calls 'his frivolous way' Harthouse speaks sincerely as he denies having deliberately taken advantage of her father being a machine, her brother a whelp, and her husband a bear, and for the first time examines himself: without 'evil intentions' he has 'glided' from one step to another 'with a smoothness so perfectly diabolical, that I had not the slightest idea the catalogue was half so long until I began to turn it over'.

He shows close attentiveness as a listener when he recalls her referring to a 'first object' and asks for the second, to be told baldly that he must go and never come back, making 'the only compensation' in his power, 'I do not say that it is much, or that it is enough; but it is something, and it is necessary'. He responds not by simply agreeing but by admitting guilt, in an impressive self-revision which he knows is brought about by Sissy's plain simple speaking, without polite forms: she has asserted no 'influence over him beyond her plain faith in the truth and right of what she said', not 'concealed the least doubt or irresolution, or ... harboured for the best purpose any reserve or pretence', not 'shown, or felt, the lightest trace of any sensitiveness to his ridicule or his astonishment'. Insincerity, conventionality and self-interest come up against bedrock integrity, the encounter perfectly imaged in a simile eloquent of her clarity, moral beauty and imperturbable strength: 'he could as easily have changed a clear sky by looking at it in surprise, as affect her'.

He ends with a gentleman's compliment and question, polite, urbane and graceful but with his usual flirtatious, frivolous, conventional and 'polished' irony rebuked out of existence. In the course of this unusual conversation he has rapidly grown sensitive to Sissy's qualities and his request is formal but completely sincere:

> You will permit me to say ... that I doubt if any other ambassador, or ambassadress, could have addressed me with the same success. I must not only regard myself as being in a very ridiculous position, but as being vanquished at all points. Will you allow me the privilege of remembering my enemy's name?

The plain speaker hesitates for a moment as she interprets his indirection 'enemy', and the return to 'ambassadress' in the next stage direction makes its own point:

> 'My name?' said the ambassadress.
>   'The only name I could possibly care to know, tonight.'
>   'Sissy Jupe.'
>   'Pardon my curiosity at parting. Related to the family?'
>   'I am only a poor girl,' returned Sissy, 'I was separated from my father – he was only a stroller ...'.

The affected flourish in his emendation of 'ambassador' to 'ambassadress' and his half-flippant 'enemy' are among many fine touches in this unsensational and delicate rendering, in direct and indirect speech, of a conversation where despite a great difference in language, mind speaks to mind and changes mind.

One of the most crucial scenes in *Great Expectations* is a conversation between Pip and Jaggers, with the clerk Wemmick present. Here one mind does not change another, but two minds communicate fully for the first time. The conversation is important for the plot because Pip forces Jaggers to admit that the murderess Molly is Estella's mother and it is a psychologically penetrating exchange in which the two men challenge and discover each other's character. As in the conversation of Sissy and Harthouse, style is subtly expressive, and Dickens is able to imply what is not as well as what is said. Pip has a bandaged arm after the fire at Satis House and his injury 'caused' the 'talk to be less dry and hard' (Bk 3, Ch. 12). Pip tells Jaggers he has asked Miss Havisham about Estella and discloses his guess about her mother's identity; Jaggers tries to turn the talk, 'What item was it you were at, Wemmick?' and Pip makes 'a passionate, almost an indignant appeal to him to be more frank and manly with me'. This begins an elegantly compressed passage of reported speech, a device of first-person narrative Dickens uses sparingly:

I reminded him of the false hopes into which I had lapsed, the length of time they had lasted, and the discovery I had made: and I hinted at the danger that weighed upon my spirits. I represented myself as being surely worthy of some little confidence from him, in return for the confidence I had just now imparted. I said that I did not blame him, or suspect him, or mistrust him, but I wanted assurance of the truth from him. And if he asked me why I wanted it and why I thought I had any right to it, I would tell him, little as he cared for such poor dreams, that I had loved Estella dearly and long ... (Bk 3, Ch. 12)

The syntax and diction are formal but the rhythms, repetitions and climax register an urgent rising appeal which has its effect, and there follows the high point of narrative and emotional discovery as Jaggers, so hard, so unconfiding and always so prudent, reveals – with some reserve – his humane side, the side which has now and then been hinted at. The language of his story-telling is punctuated with the forensic, provisional and guarded, 'Put the case'; he avoids names and refers to himself in the third person. The dry neutral language makes an ironic medium for the sympathy and generosity implied in his story, and there are telling pauses and repetitions:

Mr Jaggers nodded his head retrospectively two or three times, and actually drew a sigh. 'Pip' said he, 'we won't talk about "poor dreams;" you know more about such things than I, having much fresher experience of that kind ... add the case that you had loved her, Pip, and had made her the subject of those "poor dreams" which have, at one time or another, been in the heads of more men than you think likely ...' (Bk 3, Ch. 12)

Dickens makes Jaggers and Wemmick exemplify what the Marxist critic T. A. Jackson called 'fractionalised man', part reified and distorted by social role, and part affectively free and vital, and each part sealed off from the other (*Charles Dickens, The Progress of a Radical*). Though we have seen the two sides of Wemmick, in chambers and at home in Walworth, this is the first disclosure of the other side of Jaggers, strongly implicit in the last speech where he suggestively picks up Pip's words about 'poor dreams'. At last he comes into the open:

'Pip,' said Mr. Jaggers, laying his hand upon my arm, and smiling openly, 'this man must be the most cunning imposter in all London.'

'Not a bit of it' returned Wemmick, growing bolder and bolder. 'I
think you're another.' (Bk 3, Ch. 12)

Jenny Wren or the Dolls' Dressmaker, whose real name is Fanny
Cleaver, is a crippled child who handles her handicap, pain, drunken
father, poverty, need for revenge and hope of love, by creating powerful
fantasies, sweet and violent, benign and malicious. She says 'we Pro-
fessors' and is the artist in the novel, her trained craft of designing and
sewing dolls' dresses a good image for the novelist's art, involving the
making of human simulacra, study of people, inspiration, imitation,
invention and hard work. She is a good observer and listener and when
Lizzie Hexam uses fiction and indirection to tell the story of her love for
Wrayburn, Jenny receives it with intelligent sympathy. The story-telling
scene is in some ways like Amy Dorrit's story for Maggy, but though
Jenny begs Lizzie to look in the fire, 'the hollow down by the flare'
because she is 'a poor little thing' and wants the story, this is an
exchange between imaginative equals. Jenny proposes a particular subject, 'What would you think of him, Lizzie, if you were a lady?' 'I a lady?
... Such a fancy!' 'Yes. But say: just as a fancy, and for instance.' And
question and answer compose the story, in a magical incantation by the
fire:

> 'Shall she be rich?'
> 'She had better be, as he's poor.'
> 'She is very rich. Shall she be handsome?'
> 'Even you can be that, Lizzie, so she ought to be.'
> 'She is very handsome.' (Bk 2, Ch. 11)

Misery can turn Jenny into 'a quaint little shrew' but the heart of her
fantasy is a radiant vision, with angels in their slanting rows, humanized
as loving children, its power demonstrated when Wrayburn remembers it
as he lies badly injured, expecting to die, and summons her to dream
her dream in his sick room and for him. The scene as she sits and sews at
the foot of his bed is rooted in the earlier occasion when she told Lizzie
and Eugene the fantasy. The pink May and roses she smelt in that 'Not at
all flowery' neighbourhood and the angelic children who played light-as-
air games were her healing transformations, as Lizzie says, 'Pleasant
fancies to have, Jenny dear' and implies in a look at Eugene, 'given the
child in compensation for her losses' (Bk 2, Ch. 2). Jenny's sublimation
of pain is passed on to the wounded man, who had listened without
enthusiasm but remembered her rhapsody.

The deep psychology of affect and image preserves the vision from sentimentality, and the Biblical connection with Jacob's dream of angels passing up and down the ladder is left unstressed, deepening the mythological resonance. Moreover, the child's vision is described quite early in the novel, so it can have its intense moment and be treated allusively at the end, when the conversation between Jenny and Eugene is marked by silence and the leap of intuition. Good art stays in the memory: the healing creative communion is silent because she does not have to repeat the story of the flowers and angels, only be there in his room with her golden hair let down. We have seen Jenny's malice and aggression in her talk to her drunken father, her spiteful physical revenge on Fascination Fledgeby and her dislike of real children, so though she sees angels she is far from being an angelic presence like Paul's vision of his mother or Agnes pointing upward. Jenny Wren is Lizzie's friend, a creative maker, a dreamer of dreams, and a fey creature experienced in pain, strangely and suitably imagined by Dickens to sooth the injured man and to be most naturally invoked by his sick consciousness as a benign medium. In his *Charles Dickens* Steven Connor says Eugene's 'accession to full and responsible individuality' is marked with 'the fixing of his scattered wits on the single word "Wife"', in contrast to his earlier discourse, with its nonchalant but sterile delight in the plurality of meanings' – shown in his commentary on the word 'Reading' in Book 2, Chapter 10. But Wrayburn can communicate only through Jenny: their silent converse is impressive in itself and makes plausible the imaginative leap with which she intuits the word 'Wife' which he cannot articulate (Bk 4, Ch. 10). The exchange of intuition is no abrupt plot-convenience or solution – though it makes the happy ending – but a conversation completely assimilated to poetic pattern and character.

Chapter 11

Assertions of Style: Rhythm and Repetition in *A Tale of Two Cities* and *Our Mutual Friend*

Assertions of style show awareness of art, and though Dickens flaunted figurative language throughout his career, he does so more intensively in some novels than others. *A Tale of Two Cities* is a highly stylized work where figurative language is frequent and conspicuous, but we can only guess at possible reasons for this. As I have mentioned, George Eliot said she kept thinking the people in *Romola* ought to be speaking Italian, and obviously the same applied to the dialogues of Dickens's French characters; though he does not complain, perhaps because he was less of a linguist, he adopts a similar – and similarly tedious – technique of translating French phrase and idiom into English, which meant an unremitting attention to every word and phrase. In addition, he was working with Carlyle's *French Revolution*, and though his style is not at all like that of this source, Carlyle's highly individual prose might easily have encouraged extreme mannerism.

A favourite feature in the novel is repetition, which I have already mentioned as a figure approved by the narrator when Miss Pross mimes Manette's obsessional walking, in the presence of Mr Lorry whose dream in the stagecoach repeats the image of digging. But all through the book repetition sets up marked rhythms that are both local and sustained. Repetition imprints themes and more conspicuously than in *Little Dorrit* it helps to unify the novel and intensify crisis. Here too some chapter titles are set in pairs, and linked with other titles, images and themes in the text, like resurrection, shadows and footsteps.

Within the novel repetition begins famously in the first sentence, 'It was the best of times, it was the worst of times, it was the age of wisdom, it was the age of foolishness'; there are cunning shifts from 'age' to 'epoch' and 'season', then again to 'spring', 'summer' and 'winter'; and in the second paragraph there are neatly balanced and contrasted kings with large jaws and fair and plain queens of France and England. As the narrator notices signs of revolution in the fourth paragraph he calls Fate

'the Woodman' who marks trees to be cut down and made into boards
for the guillotine, and Death 'the Farmer', because he collects farm carts
or 'tumbrils', used for livestock, to be converted into guillotine trans-
port: these namings are repeated comparisons and personifications.
Later on the aristocracy is labelled and metonymized as 'Monseigneur',
and after the 'voices of vengeance' (Bk 2, Ch. 21) have been heard we
are told that one of the revolutionary woman, lieutenant to Madame
Defarge, 'had already earned the complimentary name of The Vengeance'
(Bk 2, Ch. 22) and from then on this is what she is called. 'Woodman'
and 'Farmer' are grim and homely nicknamings, 'Monseigneur' and
'Vengeance' significant class stereotypes, native to this revolution, fig-
uring the roots and the acclimatization of its Terror. But as well as
having a function of political emphasis, these figures are incremental
images which Dickens makes very much his own, artistically self-conscious flourishes of language-play, language-growth and generative form.

One of the striking internal stories is told by a workman who saw the
arrest, torture and execution of the Marquis's murderer, whose child was
casually run over by the aristocratic carriage. The mender of roads
comes to Paris and 'recounts' what he has seen to Jacques One, Two and
Three, and his terrible narrative is simple but far from naive, often
repeated to his neighbours, a practised art. There is a Dickensian
emphasis, like that in Peggotty's version of Emily's story, on the narrator's creative and absorbed seeing: 'The mender of roads looked *through*
rather than *at* the low ceiling, and pointed as if he saw the gallows
somewhere in the sky' (Bk 2, Ch. 15). The telling is slow and plain,
mostly in the present tense, placed by mime and gesture in country, class
and character but given gravity, formality and intensity by clusters of
repetition like those in the main narrative. The teller is 'Jacques Five'
but there is a ritualistic and dignifying repetition of his work title, 'the
mender of roads', and of 'the village', 'all the village ... all the village', of
'whisper', and at the end a repetition of the conspirators' communal
vow, which is pivotal to the plot, 'The château, and all the race? ... The
château and all the race ...' (Bk 2, Ch. 15).

These are examples of what happens all through the novel, but the
most prominent repetition of words occurs towards the end as Sydney
Carton is deciding to replace Charles Darnay, Evrémonde, at the guillotine (Bk 3, Ch. 9). Wandering round Paris with the necessary drug in
his pocket, and thinking of death, he meditates on his ill-spent past and
his probably brief future, and there comes into his head a quotation
from the Anglican burial service which becomes a personal text of faith
and self-sacrifice: 'These solemn words arose in his mind "I am the

resurrection and the life, saith the Lord: he that believeth in me, though he were dead, yet shall he live: and whosoever liveth and believeth in me, shall never die." ' Carton heard the words at his father's funeral when he was 'a youth of great promise', but the narrator comments that Carton could easily have found 'the chain of association that brought the words home, like a rusty old ship's anchor from the deep' in a city 'dominated by the axe', but 'He did not seek it, but repeated them and went on' (Bk 3, Ch. 9). In his wandering he helps a mother and child across the road, asks the child for a kiss, and the quotation is repeated, in quotation marks but not directly placed in Sydney's memory and in a separate paragraph. Then the first seven words of the quotation recur after another three paragraphs, marking and ritualizing a moment of assertion and recovery: Sydney has identified himself with a purposeless floating eddy in the Seine, but recovers and formally dedicates himself to making the sacrifice if it is necessary.

The Resurrection text makes its last appearance in the isolated and unassigned form, taken out of the character's consciousness, as Sydney Carton waits his turn at the guillotine (Bk 3, Ch. 15). The text exactly occupies the period of his execution, after the previous number, Twenty-Two, has been counted by the knitting women and before we are given his last sensations. These are recorded in a free indirect style: 'The murmuring of many voices, the upturning of many faces, the pressing on of many footsteps in the outskirts of the crowd, so that it swells forward in a mass, like one great heave of water, all flashes away', and after that last image of the quick guillotine edge, Carton's death is counted off in another isolated phrase, his number, 'Twenty-Three'.

'The resurrection and the life' is ritualized by the repetition, to sustain Sydney during the difficult period before Darnay's final sentence, when he does not know if his sacrifice will be necessary, and the quotation is a clever implicit way of tracking the tension, irresolution and resolution. It is also of course the most solemn image of the novel's complex theme of resurrection, which sinks as low as the resurrectionists' trade practised by Jerry Cruncher, who himself makes the link between the message 'Recalled to Life' and his own grave-robbing. At the end Dickens uses the text to assimilate a Christian belief in immortality to secular hope of survival in history or memory, a hope cleverly displaced, or at least made provisional, as it is displayed. The famous lines 'It is a far, far better thing that I do, than I have ever done; it is a far, far better rest that I go to than I have ever known' contain the last repetition in the novel, and conclude the hero's projection of a future. Once more the words are not his direct speech but presented provisionally, as an imagined statement modelled on that of a woman who set down her thoughts at the foot of the scaffold, 'If he had given an utterance to his, and they were prophetic, they would have been these ...' (Bk 3, Ch. 15).

There is another repetition even more important to the political subject. It is always a pleasure to see an artist improving technique and the prison narrative of Alexandre Manette – the most genuinely affective passage in this romantic novel – shows how Dickens's internal narrative has become subtly particularized in style and structure (Bk 3, Ch. 10). The manuscript Doctor Manette hides in the chimney of his cell, written in rust, soot and blood, is pivotal in the plot because it is discovered by Defarge at the storming of the Bastille and used to indict Darnay. But it is much more than this, because as it explains the particular revenge-motive of Madame Defarge, whose sister was raped by one of the Evrémonde brothers, it provides a precise indictment of aristocratic power, striking and important in an action which spends so much energy on critique of the Revolution. The story is compassionately but quietly and plainly told from the viewpoint of the doctor commandeered by the aristocratic brothers to treat their victims, the raped woman and her brother stabbed in his attempted vengeance. The brutality and callousness are made particular and clearly generalized. Manette is listener as well as teller, imprisoned for his telling, and reports the story told him by the dying brother. The woman can only keep repeating: 'My husband, my father, and my brother! One, two, three, four, five, six, seven, eight, nine, ten, eleven, twelve', a verbless cry and count which mark the hour and the sobs of the father's death, after he has been harnessed by day and made to quieten frogs at night: 'Taken out of harness one day at noon, to feed – if he could find food – he sobbed twelve times, once for every stroke of the bell, and died ...'. The story is the heart of the novel, its poetry of enumeration a climax essential to plot and politics.

Repetition and local patterning are also prominent in *Our Mutual Friend*, and we can only guess at the reason. It is not because it is a late novel: *Edwin Drood* is later and written in spare plain prose. Stylistic assertion works effectively for the highly satiric passages, but it is not confined to them. But *A Tale of Two Cities* had established the habit of marked rhythm, and in its successor too the book and chapter titles set up theme and image clusters of their own and relate to clusters in the text. In it the patterns of language become even more assertive and stylized, and the incremental figure which recurs in *A Tale of Two Cities* becomes a repeated movement, developing more elaborately and frequently from a simile or metaphor which is analysed or explained, to become a straight identification, like a Homeric or Virgilian epithet, 'wine-dark sea' or 'pius Aeneas'.

It is used comically and seriously. For example, there is a joking comparison of Mrs Podsnap's 'bone, neck and nostrils' to the features of a rocking-horse (Bk 1, Ch. 2) which becomes a nicknaming accompaniment, with variation including her talk, 'at her usual canter, with arched head and mane, opened eyes and nostrils', and the demeanour of her daughter, Miss Podsnap, a 'young rocking-horse ... being trained in her mother's art of prancing in a stately manner without ever getting on' (Bk 1, Ch. 11). Another example is the satiric label used for the Veneerings' butler, who starts off as a 'retainer', becomes 'the Analytical Chemist', suggesting his knowledge and the quality of the Chablis he serves, and comparison grows into identification, so he is always 'the Analytical Chemist' or 'Analytical Chemist' and in later chapters 'the Analytical' (Bk I, Ch. 2; Ch. 10). There is a similar process when Bella Wilfer appropriates her father's admiring 'lovely' and acquires the habit of playfully calling herself 'the lovely woman' in her arch flirtatious style. There is a minor example, aptly small for a character flaunting insignificance, when the inarticulate George Sampson puts his walking stick in his mouth 'like a stopper' and it becomes 'his stopper' (Bk 1, Ch. 9).

Once Dickens begins an incremental comparison then drops it after finding it does not answer. He compares the police station where Wrayburn and Mortimer call after being summoned by Charlie Hexam to 'a monastery', the comparison explained by the whitewashed bare station room and the Inspector's concentrated reading of papers, and the Inspector becomes 'the Abbot' (Bk 1, Ch. 3). But when he turns out, perhaps unpremeditatedly, to have an important detective role which takes him away from his quiet room and attentive reading to the streets and river, the monk-and-monastery conceit is dropped. From time to time the narrative returns to the police station, most notably when John Harmon and Bella go there with the Inspector, and then it is referred to as whitewashed, with documents to be studied, but without clerical connotations. Dickens made careful notes about some recurrent images, like the wild waves in *Dombey*, but also worked hand-to-mouth.

A more serious image-series begins in the first chapter, where Jesse Hexam is compared to a bird of prey: 'He was a hook-nosed man, and with that, and his bright eyes and his ruffled head bore a certain likeness to a roused bird of prey', and Rogue Riderhood says, 'I a'most think you're like the wulturs, pardner and scent 'em out.' Between his first and last appearances the comparison gradually develops, from simile to identification. In Chapter 3 the narrator says the bird 'raised its ruffled

head, and looked like a bird of prey', and 'He had the special peculiarity
of some birds of prey, that when he knitted his brow, his ruffled crest
stood highest', and two sentences later Eugene speaks to Hexam and
'the bird of prey slowly rejoined, "And what might *your* name be?" ' Two
chapter titles, 'Tracking the Bird of Prey' and 'The Bird of Prey Brought
Down', carry on the naming, and after his death, 'the form of the bird of
prey – dead some hours – lay stretched upon the shore'. It reappears in
the following chapter title, 'More Birds of Prey', but this refers to
Riderhood, his daughter Pleasant and George Radfoot. We have worked
slowly towards a climax, and down from it, to see uncovered the process
of imaginative grasp and invention, in a combination of displayed art
and strong feeling.

Unlike the fanciful satiric stereotype of 'Analytic' and 'rocking-horse',
there is a way in which this bird image fixes and also frees, challenging us
to see more than the conditioned creature. When Lizzie repeatedly calls
'Father', as Wrayburn watches her knowing Hexam is dead, we feel the
power of her human naming and calling the more strongly after the
insistent and reductive bird imagery (Bk 1, Ch. 14).

There is a powerful and local pattern of repetition in the painful scene
where Bradley Headstone makes his violent declaration of love to Lizzie:

'You draw me to you. If I were shut up in a strong prison, you would
draw me out. I should break through the wall to come to you. If I were
lying on a sick bed, you would draw me up – to stagger to your feet and
fall there.'

The wild energy of the man, now quite let loose, was absolutely
terrible. He stopped and laid his hand upon a piece of the coping of
the burial-ground enclosure, as if he would have dislodged the stone.
(Bk 2, Ch. 15)

He begins with the simple present indicative 'you draw', then moves to
the conditional 'would draw' and a little later we have the permutation,
repeated six times, 'could draw', as if all the forms must be rehearsed to
imprint his meanings when he says he loves her:

You know what I am going to say. I love you. What other men may
mean when they use that expression, I cannot tell; what *I* mean is, that
I am under the influence of some tremendous attraction which I have
resisted in vain, and which overmasters me. You could draw me to fire,
you could draw me to water, you could draw me to the gallows, you
could draw me to any death, you could draw me to anything I have

most avoided, you could draw me to any exposure and disgrace. (Bk 2, Ch. 15)

Of course what strikes us first is not the repetition and variation but the imagery of compulsion itself, beginning with that prison wall: Dickens famously influenced Eisenstein and I am sure this passage was unconsciously or consciously recalled by a later Russian director, Tarkovsky, when the succubus in *Solaris*, undesired but created by the spaceman's imagination so tethered to him metaphysically and physically, on a planet inhabited by mind-made aliens who are also familiars, breaks through the metal of the cabin where he has confined her because she cannot be separated from him. The physical image of being drawn through strong barriers is repeated and reinforced by the violence, unconscious or as good as unconscious, of the man's physical wrenching at the stone, in an interplay of object and image which is typically Dickensian though there are examples in George Eliot and Henry James. Here the series of images are linked and marked by Dickens's unflagging repetition of that 'could draw' and the parallel construction of the clauses the verb governs.

Like the brief liberating activity of Sikes as he temporarily rejoins the human race, it does not ingratiate the character to the reader, indeed it renders Headstone frightening and abhorrent, as he is to Lizzie, undesiring object of his desire, and anticipates his murderous attack on Eugene and his self-destroying murder of Rogue Riderhood. It is one of Dickens's most profound imaginings of passion and desire, and like the other moments, product of an art which compels insight into human feeling and action together with an admiration of rhetoric.

In Book Four, Chapter 6, 'A Cry for Help', Lizzie rescues Wrayburn after he has been battered and pushed in the Thames by jealous murderous Bradley Headstone. After the action is announced, 'there was ... a splash, and all was done', we cut to Lizzie who hears blows, a groan and the fall; then 'Her old bold life and habit instantly inspired her.' She finds broken wood and bloody grass on the bank, sees a bloody face in the water, and the narrative's free indirect speech declares, 'Now, merciful Heaven be thanked for that old time' and she goes into action: 'A sure touch of her old practised hand, a sure step of her old practised foot ... A quick glance of her practised eye.' After recognizing Wrayburn and performing the extraordinary feat of attaching his inert heavy body to the boat, there is a third repetition of 'old' and a second repetition of the prayer: 'Now, merciful Heaven be thanked for that old time ...'. The repetitions of 'old' and 'practised' are framed by the repetitions of 'that old time' and words and phrase emphasize the exact repetition of Hexam's actions in the first chapter of the novel, when lower down the same river, he grabs the corpse and ties it up as Lizzie looks away in abhorrence.

Without Lizzie's self-esteem the marriage to Wrayburn would be a desperate solution to an insoluble social problem. We must remember the mores of the time: as is emphasized before he is attacked, Wrayburn can neither seduce her nor leave her, and he only proposes to her when he is severely injured, nearly dead. What makes her acceptance acceptable, indeed honourable, is what makes her lose the sense of social inferiority, discover self-esteem and like Scrooge and Little Dorrit, accept her whole life, past and present. It is this which is emphasized in the rescue scene, in her proud gratitude for what she has been ashamed of, the practised skill acquired in 'the old time'. The rowing was inseparable from her shame: in the fireside scene when Jenny asks what she would do if she was a lady, she says at once, 'I, a poor girl who used to row poor father on the river. I, who had rowed poor father out and home on the very night when I saw him for the first time' (Bk 2, Ch. 11). The acceptance of her old skill is an act of gratitude to her father, who began the novel by reproaching her for hating the river from whose driftwood her cradle was made. Dickens made a note that her second rowing scene should be a return to the first chapter, and so it is, in the deepest sense.

There is variation as well as repetition. The word 'old' is repeated with a difference, picked up again when Charley visits Bradley Headstone, to cast him off cruelly and formally, and he mentions the old time which is his shame, making a subtextual connection, moral and narrative. He uses the word 'old' not to cherish but to reject it; he can only live by denying the past. As with Amy and William Dorrit, Dickens is putting a positive and a negative together, pitting one against the other, to assert meaning.

Perhaps 'the old time' entered into the memory of Samuel Beckett, another artist who loves repetition, as Winnie repeats 'the old style', in a refrain sounding all through the bitter-sweet nostalgias that sustain and undermine her in *Happy Days*.

Chapter 12

Shakespeare in Dickens: *David Copperfield* and *Great Expectations*

Dickens was a great admirer of Shakespeare, on the page and the stage, saw many performances and knew many actors well, especially the great Charles Macready who was a close friend. Dickens might have been a Shakespearean actor himself, if he had not been prevented from going to a theatre audition at Drury Lane by a cold, and turned to writing instead. He occasionally acted in Shakespeare, once playing Justice Shallow, and read Shakespeare not only in popular texts but in scholarly editions in the British Museum reading room. He eventually bought a house called Gad's Hill, the scene of a famous adventure and a great comic lie, 'Falstaff's noble fancy', in *Henry IV, Part 1*. Dickens resembled Shakespeare in familial and social circumstance[1] but above all in success and fame and was often thought of as the Victorian Shakespeare and the Shakespeare of the novel, so as he was not especially modest, he may now and then have thought of Shakespeare as his rival or his peer.

In his novels he alludes to Shakespeare over a thousand times and critics have counted, catalogued and interpreted them in many ways. I intend to discuss some well-known references and two or three others which have been neglected, and which are examples of the dynamic intertextual relationship between imaginations, a two-way traffic in which the original text may be changed or look different after it has helped to create another. When we read the words of his remembered Hamlet and his intricated, even re-imagined Feste the echoes become reversed.

Although Dickens was saturated in Shakespeare and perhaps emulated his achievement, he seems to me most unlike Shakespeare in every specific aspect of art, though one can praise them both, as F. R. Leavis has done most convincingly, in *Dickens the Novelist*, for profound character-creation and original language. In some ways Dickens is closer to the comic and satiric genius of Ben Jonson in humour, stylization, social criticism, and what T. S. Eliot called Jonson's art of the surface; he admired Jonson too. Though there are tragic occasions and tragic characters in his novels, Dickens does not use the novel as a medium for tragedy, like George Eliot or Thomas Hardy, and it is generally in his comic characterization and broad satire that he owes most to Shakespeare. But Dickens is fascinated by his opposite, a dramatist excelling in tragedy and an artist who does not so much criticize society as show that political criticism is impossible or difficult – as in *Coriolanus, Henry IV* and *Antony and Cleopatra* – but whose insight into political life energizes his tragedy and comedy. The interest lies in Dickens's imaginative use of such an opposite, whose words, characters and actions he has long contemplated and assimilated. He engages in a highly concentrated dialogue with Shakespeare, because unlike other English novelists, including Thackeray, George Eliot, James and Hardy, Dickens does not engage with the older heritage of Greek and Latin literature and drama. He knew the *Arabian Nights* and eighteenth-century novelists, but it is Shakespeare who engages his attention, and provides the cultural model and tradition all artists need. He came to know Shakespeare well enough not only to remember but also to forget him, to use his characters and language consciously but also intuitively. To use the phrase he used of Venice, Shakespeare became 'a bit' of his 'brain' (*Letters* 4, 271). Dickens often approaches Shakespeare with the intention of making fun of him and this is what a large number of his thousand references to Shakespeare do – often parodying his style in the way Shakespeare did with Lyly, Marlowe and Kyd. Dickens's jokes about Shakespeare prove that nothing is impermeable to satire and comedy, neither noble language nor tragic conflict. Sometimes the joke is made at the expense of bardolatry, as when Mrs Wititterley boasts: 'I'm always ill after Shakspeare . . . I scarcely exist the next day . . . I find the reaction so very great after a tragedy, my lord . . . Shakespeare is such a delicious creature' (*NN*, Ch. 27).

Dickens's comic butt is often Hamlet, who is ridiculed at the beginning of *A Christmas Carol* – rather heavily – to tease expectation and obey Goethe's principle of narrative retardation:

If we were not perfectly convinced that Hamlet's Father died before the play began, there would be nothing more remarkable in his taking a stroll at night, in an easterly wind, upon his own ramparts, than there would be in any other middle-aged gentleman rashly turning out after dark in a breezy spot – say Saint Paul's Churchyard for instance – literally to astonish his son's weak mind. (Stave One)

Some of the comedy is more serious: when Wopsle alias Warvengraver asks for an opinion of his performance, Herbert Pocket prompts Pip with 'massive and concrete', and though this is used to evade the truth and compliment the actor, it probably represents Dickens's sense of a good performance of Shakespearean character (*GE*, Bk 2, Ch. 12).

Dickens uses Shakespeare most variously in *David Copperfield*. Hamlet inspires a bizarre joke when David reports a party at the Waterbrooks, where he encounters a lady in a black velvet dress and huge black velvet hat, like a relative of Hamlet's, 'say an aunt', developing the comparison until it becomes fixed like the bird of prey in *Our Mutual Friend* and she is always 'Hamlet's aunt' (Ch. 25). (In one of his fairly frequent self-quotations, and an uningratiating move from art to life, Dickens carried on this joke when his mother was old and failing, saying her affectation of sables turned her into a female Hamlet.) The character who is most Shakespeareanly 'massive and concrete' is Wilkins Micawber, always called Mr Micawber by the narrator, and a rich source of Shakespearean allusion which he compounds by combining the roles of Shakespearean character, reader and admirer. His language teems with creative sug-gestiveness, reflexive in more ways than one, exemplifying Dickens's assimilations.

Like Falstaff, Micawber is a genial optimist, wit, stylist, careless with money and fond of food and drink, like Polonius he delivers moral 'precept' fo be 'stored' by the young, and like Don Armado in *Love's Labours Lost* he is a florid rhetorician and a great letter-writer. To these massive and concrete models Dickens added Samuel Johnson with his many layered periodic sentence, and his own feckless, good-natured and grandiloquent father. When Micawber quotes Shakespeare he is so Shakespearean that it is as if Falstaff or Polonius were to comment on their own creation – and draws attention to the way Falstaff does just this when he plays himself in Hal's production and Polonius when he draws attention to his art and wit. Some of Micawber's references are amus-ingly bathetic, like his deflating praise of his father-in-law: 'Take him for all in all, we ne'er shall – in short, make the acquaintance, probably, of anybody else possessing, at his time of life, the same legs for gaiters, and able to read the same description of print, without spectacles' (Ch. 12), an *hommage* to Hamlet's devout – and premature – 'A was a man, take him for all in all / I shall not look upon his like again' (1.2). Dickens's parody is controlled by Micawber's tag-phrase 'in short', which allows him to be talkative, self-restrained, and draw to a conclusion.

Micawber is sufficiently clever and deep in Shakespeare to mix his allusions, and when he is wound up for the unmasking of Heep, he comments that he is speaking 'Shakespearianly', flourishing the grand word as he joins a quotation from the witches in *Macbeth* (1.3), 'dwindle, peak, and pine' with Hamlet's 'worse remains behind' (3.4), referring to 'the philosophic Dane' and mentioning the 'universal applicability' which distinguishes the 'illustrious ornament of the Elizabethan era' (Ch. 52). Micawber's range includes Thomas Gray, the Homeric tag 'men and ways' and the dialect of Burns, but his dialogue is with Shakespeare.

Micawber is pompous but genuine, in almost every way, and he is a Shakespearean who shows off but has knowledge to show off. When he produces his evidence against Heep, in the great unveiling scene at Canterbury, he shows his Falstaffian blend of self-dramatization with sincerity. The sincerity is not invariable and does not make either character virtuous, but the moral mixture is part of their massive concrete reality. Micawber might have been more Shakespearean if he had not made such a success of emigration, but if we agree with Chesterton that his author shipped him off to Australia because he was too vivacious and incorrigible to handle, we can see Dickens emulating Hal's dismissal of Falstaff.

On another occasion Micawber makes a subdued and teasing allusion:

If any drop of gloom were wanting in the overflowing cup, which is now 'commended' (in the language of an Immortal Writer) to the lips of the undersigned, it would be found in the fact, that a friendly acceptance granted to the undersigned, by the before-mentioned Mr Thomas Traddles, for the sum of £23 4s. 9½ d. is overdue ... (Ch. 28)

The reference is to Macbeth's, 'This even-handed Justice / Commends th' ingredience of our poison'd chalice / To our own lips' (1.7). The reader who does not know the context will get a sense of the grand style, and the reader who does will see the irrelevance of the deep context, and read Micawber as a promiscuous Shakespearean show-off. (It is just possible that Dickens intended an extra layer of meaning in the reference to poison, hinting at Micawber's routine suicide threat, but that seems unlikely.)

Some of the half-buried references are allusions which go deep in feeling as well as language. Not all of them may be deliberated but because of Dickens's saturation in Shakespeare, may be unconscious memories. Earlier in the novel Micawber writes another letter to David, in a similar mood of despair and style of extravagant rhetoric, making a jumbled allusion: 'The die is cast – all is over. Hiding the ravages of care with a sickly mask of mirth I have not informed you, this evening, that there is no hope of the remittance! ...' (Ch. 17). The proverbial phrase 'the die is cast' was suggested by the word 'cast' from the other line alluded to, in *Hamlet* (3.1): 'the native hue of resolution / Is sicklied o'er with the pale cast of thought', from which 'sickly' is taken; Dickens is also remembering Hamlet's mask and the loss of 'mirth' that he confides to Rosencrantz and Guildenstern in Act 2, Scene 2. Dickens may be appreciating Micawber's knowledge and wit or mocking grandiose jumble but either interpretation depends on us catching the references.

Accidentally or deliberately, Dickens makes David Copperfield accidentally jumble Shakespeare too, when in Chapter 38, 'A Dissolution of Partnership', he describes his 'almost heart-breaking' struggle with shorthand and says, 'It might have been quite heart-breaking, but for Dora, who was the stay and anchor of my tempest-driven bark', adapting Sonnet 116 in another subdued, teasing and perhaps unconscious reference, where adaptation is resonant and ironic – if we notice it:

O, no, it is an ever-fixed mark,
That looks on tempests and is never shaken;
It is the star to every wand'ring bark ...

David sees Dora as a 'star' in his rhapsodic story of love at first sight but Dickens's catachresis – a tempest-driven bark cannot be anchored – is based not only on the sonnet but conflates it with the weird sisters' chanted curse from the third scene of *Macbeth* in which there is another sailor, another ship and another tempest, all connected, 'Though his bark cannot be lost, Yet it shall be tempest-tost'. (As I have said, the chant is quoted later in the novel by Micawber, whose 'dwindle, peak, and pine' line comes immediately before 'Though his bark ...', and may have been a link (1. 3).) It seems unlikely that this elision and medley was consciously intended as David's version, super-subtly placed as a pre-Freudian slip to show David's unconscious qualms about a marriage which was not one of true minds, and it looks like an unconscious error on Dickens's part. If so, and the jumbled quotation comes from Dickens's buried memory, it works better than he knew to show his character's emotional confusion: David is romantically appropriating Shakespeare's love poem at this immature stage in his sentimental education. But if we dig deeper in the spirit of Mr Curdle, it may be true to what Dickens 'actually' felt not only for Maria Beadnell but also for Catherine Hogarth. There is a life-link: *David Copperfield* was published between 30 April 1849 and 31 October 1850, long before his separation from his wife in 1857, but it contains a fictionalized version of his old haunting undefined unhappy feeling (see Forster, Bk 8, Ch. 2, where one of the running titles is 'One Happiness Missed'). In Dickens's accounts of the estrangement from his wife, he denied that he had ever felt love for Catherine, which seems a falsification, or that they had ever had anything in common, which may have been true – though they discussed his work. The sonnet-jumble may be not David's but Dickens's pre-Freudian slip. Dickens wrote about his mistake in marriage more harshly than David writes about Dora, who of course was conveniently disposed of by death, and more gently than the wife in 'The Bride's Chamber' (1857). In any case, the quotation from Shakespeare's most wonderful lyric of love and affinity, if a trifle garbled, helps to engage the reader's sympathy for Dora.

When David first calls Agnes his 'good Angel', in Chapter 25, 'Good and Bad Angels', she responds by warning him 'against [his] bad Angel' and at the back of this imagery may be another Shakespeare sonnet (144) – 'Two loves I have, of comfort and despair' – in which there is a bad and a good angel. David echoes 'comfort', saying he is 'comforted' by his good angel Agnes, and denies that he has a bad angel: the bad angel of the sonnet is the dark lady, but since the subject is the influence and conflict of two friends, and since Dickens evidently had the sonnets in mind, Shakespeare's opposed angels may be at the back of his mind. The lovers in Shakespeare's passion-triangle are not at all like David's, except that David's bad angel is Steerforth, and he has a deep feeling for him which survives the discovery that Steerforth is a treacherous liar and seducer, not all that remote from the sonneteer's ambivalent feelings for his man friend, and like it, not subjected to analysis. This is Dickens's most confessional novel, full of Shakespearean echoes.

These examples are intricate small allusive tricks of the conscious and unconscious play of creative mind, but there is one deep Shakespearean allusion in *David Copperfield* which is intricately woven into the affective fabric and form of the novel. It occurs in Chapter 55, which has the Shakespearean title 'Tempest', and though it has no overt or covert connection with *The Tempest* it cannot have been used without a memory of Shakespeare's play, especially as its first paragraph has two or three Shakespearean allusions:

I now approach an event in my life, so indelible, so awful, so bound by an infinite variety of ties to all that has preceded it, in these pages, that from the beginning of my narrative, I have seen it growing larger and larger as I advanced, like a great tower in a plain, and throwing its forecast shadow even on the incidents of my childish days.

Here Dickens is invoking Enobarbus's praise of Cleopatra's 'infinite variety' (2.2) and Othello's recall of Brabantio's request for his reminiscences, 'I ran it through, even from my boyish days' (1.3). The forecast shadow of the tower on a plain, 'growing larger and larger' sounds like a faint echo of Nestor's speech in *Troilus and Cressida*, 'the baby figure of the giant mass / Of things to come at large' (1.3). The paragraph is image-crammed, musical and impassioned, a lyrical preface to the tragic scene which follows. The narrative is given extra emphasis when David tells us he has often re-lived it in vivid dreams, and is brought back to it by stormy wind or the 'lightest mention of a seashore'. He speaks of effort, 'I will try to write it down', though as so often, his story is a vision: 'I do not recall it, but see it done; for it happens again before me.' The introduction is very personal and very literary.

Except for the tempest none of the images has a thematic connection with *David Copperfield* but Dickens is recalling two, perhaps three, of Shakespeare's orators, for a strongly reflexive introduction, with references to preparation and expectancy, as if he is calling on Shakespeare – consciously or unconsciously – to act as Muse or model for his indelible, awful and long-expected storm. In these conflations, echoes and fragments Dickens looks forward to T. S. Eliot and other modernists.

The chapter invokes Shakespeare for this prologue and most thrillingly for its crisis point. After all those irreverent jokes, Dickens makes his most serious, resonant and moving allusion to *Hamlet* which no one seems to have noticed, not because it is deeply buried but because it does not use Shakespeare's words. Before going to his death in the duel with Laertes, Hamlet says to his old friend Horatio, in evenly balanced lyrical prose:

Not a whit. We defy augury. There is a special providence in the fall of a sparrow. If it be now, 'tis not to come; if it be not now, yet it will come. The readiness is all. Since no man of aught he leaves knows aught, what is't to leave betimes? Let be. (5.2)

Before going to his death, to attempt the rescue of the drowning man he does not know is Steerforth, Ham is also given a rhythmically ordered lyric prose, in which he says to his old friend David: 'Mas'r Davy ... if my time is come, 'tis come. If 'tan't, I'll bide it. Lord above bless you, and bless all! Mates, make me ready!' So just before their deaths these two strikingly different characters, one a magnificent, learned, eloquent and witty Prince, the other an uneducated, inarticulate fisherman, are not only identical in their attitudes to Providence, but similar in their language and their feeling, and most plausibly: they have in common the New Testament, a conscious apprehension of mortality and an unforced religious faith, and can speak of these intimately, to a friend. There are only two actual repetitions of the Hamlet speech in Ham, 'ready', the first two syllables of 'readiness', and "tis', right for Ham's and for Elizabethan abbreviation. Both men need to be made ready, in accoutrements as well as spirit, and there is a subdued connection of revenge, since both are going, with imperfect knowledge, to confront an enemy. Ham has premonitions: David says he looks out to sea in 'a certain wild way' and Peggotty says, 'it's fur from being fleet water in his mind' (Ch. 46); Hamlet says 'how ill's all here about my heart'. It is Steerforth whose body is carried by fishermen on a bier and covered with a flag, if not honoured as a prince, respected as a gentleman. David Copperfield, like Horatio, is to speak a message to the living. And we cannot ignore the semantic link, between their names, Ham echoing Hamlet. The correspondence is woven of many threads, and accordingly strong. It makes one of those deep moments, particular but generalized, ritualized and re-inforced by companion instances, as in the death of Milton's Lycidas, the Hades scene in Joyce's *Ulysses*, the sea, music, son and father of *The Tempest* in *The Waste Land*. In these last examples the resonance is large, structural and general, while *David Copperfield* uses the correspondence for a powerful local effect: to be reminded of Hamlet's readiness for death in Ham's is to be moved by a startling and profound association of two very different characters. To bring Hamlet and Ham together is to be textually and humanely imaginative.

In *Great Expectations* here is a similarly local and similarly lyrical allusion. At the beginning of Volume 2, Chapter 20, Pip announces, with formality, 'I was three-and-twenty years of age'. He is living in chambers near the river, in the Temple, and his high rooms make him feel he is in a lighthouse on a night of bad weather, 'stormy and wet, stormy and wet', with high wind and heavy rain coming up river from the east. As usual, Dickens makes poetry out of his city knowledge and one rhythmical paragraph is almost a reprise of the weather descriptions in the 'Tempest' chapter in *David Copperfield*, with weather reports, detail of conditions in town and surrounding country, lead roofs stripped off high buildings, trees uprooted, shipwreck and death at sea, veils of driving cloud, and 'mud, mud, mud deep in all the streets'. (It echoes the

November start of *Bleak House*, also in the Temple.) Here the wind and rain announce and mark the turn in the action, with the arrival of Magwitch and Pip's discovery that his great expectations have been great illusions.

Of course the wind and rain are symbolic and synecdochic, the storm scenes external and internal, physical and psychic: Pip is lonely, disappointed and in deep gloom, and the scene is set for mood and mind by the wind and rain, with the reality and the metaphor lyrically emphasized in rhythm and repetitions. Both metaphor and musicality are reinforced by a memory of the song sung by Feste the Clown at the end of Act Five in *Twelfth Night*:

> When that I was and a little tiny boy
> With hey, ho, the wind and the rain,
> A foolish thing was but a toy,
> And the rain it raineth every day.

In this chapter, the wind and rain are combined, either at different points in the same sentence, as in 'violent blasts of rain had accompanied these rages of wind', or linked, as 'in the teeth of such wind and rain'. The word wind occurs three times before it is joined by rain, in 'such wind and rain', and 'before the wind like red-hot splashes in the rain', then twice more before Magwitch's entry. The pattern is almost symmetrical, the combination of wind and rain used five times but only as an exact echo, 'the wind and the rain', in the middle of a conversation, when Pip recognizes Magwitch and returns to their past:

> Even yet, I could not recal [*sic*] a single feature, but I knew him! If the wind and the rain had driven away the intervening years, had scattered all the intervening objects, had swept us to the churchyard where we first stood face to face on such different levels, I could not have known my convict more distinctly than I knew him now, as he sat in the chair before the fire. No need to take a file from his pocket ...

In this sentence 'the wind and the rain' are imagined as forces with power over time, going back to the day when Pip was a little tiny boy looking up at the tall man.

At the end of the chapter, where the lyricism is intensified, the wind and rain are repeated: 'In every rage of wind and rush of rain, I heard pursuers' and in the last sentence: 'and the wind and rain intensified the thick black darkness'. In a metaphor which may be picked up from *David*

Copperfield Pip says, 'I began fully to know how wrecked I was and how the ship in which I had sailed was gone to pieces.' The chapter ends: 'When I awoke, without having parted in my sleep with the perception of my wretchedness ... the wind and rain intensified the thick black darkness.' There is another exact quotation towards the end of the next chapter: 'I doubt if a ghost could have been more terrible to me, up in those lonely rooms in the long evenings and long nights, with the wind and the rain[2] always rushing by' (Vol. 3, Ch. 1).

So 'the wind and the rain' make a running motif. Pip is taken back to when he was a little boy, and here at last he comes to 'man's estate', in no way the estate he has been expecting. The term is formally used of David Copperfield at his conventional coming of age (Ch. 43) but Pip at 23 has arrived at the age decreed by his unknown benefactor for coming into his property. Magwitch has turned up in person, having crossed the world to give Pip his estate. And he is the agent and occasion of Pip's maturing, as he comes to be accepted, at first reluctantly, but soon humanely, fully and imaginatively. Pip grows up, and grows out of illusion, out of self-centredness, out of the expectation of great estate into man's estate. He comes of age.

Dickens's first conception of the novel was the idea of a 'foolish' man and a boy, but it is Pip who is the fool, and the potted life of Shakespeare's clown or fool relevant to his encounters with thieves and knaves and his coming 'to wive'. Its song's deep melancholy suits Pip's moods and the night's life-spanning memories. At the end of the play, Feste, who has always been outside the great households where he sings and jests, is singing in solitude, after all the lovers have been paired off, and Dickens had intended to leave Pip solitary and unmated. Even with the revised ending, much of the last part of the novel is marked by his loneliness, and his meeting with Estella is stamped with a grave melancholy.

If *Twelfth Night* were echoing somewhere in Dickens's memory, it may not have been the only Shakespearean hooked atom. A snatch of the Fool's song was repeated in the storm scene of *King Lear*, slightly changed but with the same refrain, its metaphors of the wind and the rain finding literal and symbolic point of reference in the storm – also a storm in nature and in the mind of a man, both created by art, in the most famous act of sympathetic weather in English literature. There are new lines introduced in deference to Lear's madness:

He that has and a little tiny wit
With heigh-ho the wind and the rain

Must make content with his fortunes fit,
Though the rain it raineth every day. (3.1)

This fits Pip even better. He has to make content with his new fit for-tunes. And for him too there is a real storm and a storm in his mind.

Both songs would have been originally sung by the actor Robert Armin, and Shakespeare's self-quotation is an astonishing bit of inter-textuality, which – consciously or unconsciously – Dickens compounds, enriching and deepening scene, character, feeling and morality. It may be that Dickens would have written this chapter of wind and rain in much the same way had he not read *Twelfth Night*, but I find it impossible not to have the Fool's wry poetry in mind as I read the chapter. And like the allusion in *David Copperfield* – also in a storm scene – the Shakespearean moment, deeply buried and far from obvious, shows Dickens's imagination reaching out to companionable model and ancestry.

There are many more obvious Shakespearean parallels which have been discussed in detail. *The Old Curiosity Shop* has been compared with *King Lear*, but the links are superficial and obvious. Nicholas Nickleby is a young hero who plays Romeo and is involved in a family feud, but there are no deep resemblances. Steerforth is briefly shown as tor-mented in conscience before he commits his sin, deceitful and destructive seduction, identifying with Macbeth when he says David is breaking in 'like a reproachful ghost', and speaks of himself as breaking up the feast, having a fit of conscience but recovering, 'Why, being gone I am a man again'. In this moment, and in his offence against hospitality, he is like Macbeth, but in nothing else. Such resonances and connec-tions show Dickens's absorption in Shakespeare, but I think few if any are as emotionally deep and complex as those Shakespearean moments in the imagined lives of Ham and Pip. At some point in Dickens's intensely emotional and moral conception of the death of Ham, and later in his intensely emotional and moral conception of Pip's meeting with Magwitch, the Shakespeare connection was made.

Notes

¹ Alfred Harbage makes interesting comparisons of the social and familial circumstances of Shakespeare and Dickens in *A Kind of Power*. In her invaluable *Shakespeare and Dickens*, Cambridge: CUP, 1996, Valerie Gager lists four examples of Dickens quoting the special providence passage, all direct,

unmistakable and facetious: two are jokes in letters; the other two refer jok-
ingly to Wopsle and Pecksniff. She lists two references to the wind and the
rain, again facetious, one in a letter and one in an article (pp. 294, 368).

  [2] Dickens first wrote 'east wind' and the excision is interesting.

Chapter 13

Dickens in the Twentieth Century

Like Shakespeare's, Dickens's creativity was posthumous as well as contemporary. Like Shakespeare, Dickens was original and popular enough to affect his successors in a thousand ways, inspiring imitation, homage, critique and deep assimilation. He had a strong influence, general and specific, on traditional social novels like those of H. G. Wells and Evelyn Waugh, who would not have been what they were without his fiction, but he also inspired and encouraged those experiments in form and language we call modernist, the new free narratives and styles of James Joyce, T. S. Eliot, Samuel Beckett and Virginia Woolf.

Ulysses, Penelope, Hamlet, Shylock and Tartuffe are strong characters who are sufficiently representative and sufficiently individualized to attain the stature and status of myth, and Dickens created a large number of such high-profile creations, usually comic or satiric characterizations like Pickwick, Fagin, Pecksniff, Micawber, Scrooge, Mrs Gamp and Mr Gradgrind, grotesque, simplified, fascinating, larger than life and with a speech of their own.

The simplest kind of response to Dickens is the recall of these characters in a typological shorthand used for different effects. In Henry James's most Dickensian novel, *The Princess Casamassima*, for example, we only have to be told that a man leaning out of a window reminds somone of Micawber to identify the shabby London ambience where would-be revolutionary Christina Light chooses to live for a while. Angus Wilson in *Anglo-Saxon Attitudes* invokes class privilege and incompetent bureaucracy in the figure of Tite Barnacle, cites the crook and capitalist Merdle and in *The Old Men at the Zoo* calls someone Quilpish; in *Point Counter Point* Huxley mentions the self-seeking canting hypocrite Stiggins and Mr Mantalini turning the mangle.

Dickens's symbolic climate, cities and buildings are identification points too, when Evelyn Waugh calls a Glasgow fog Dickensian, George Orwell dwells on the dust and pollution of *1984*'s London and Kafka represents an imaginary unattainable castle in *The Castle*, and replaces Sleary's circus by a theatre in *America*, a self-styled but obscure version of

David Copperfield. There is no need to multiply examples because Dickensian types and symbols still crop up in books, everyday speech, news-
papers, radio and television. His objects, words and situations have
entered into the language – gamp, umble, Humbug!, What larks!, asking
for more. Every Christmas has its unreconstructed Scrooge, any school
can become Dotheboys Hall, even modern elections may be Eatanswills,
and the Circumlocution Office is all around us.

   H. G. Wells found Dickens a congenial genius, like himself lower-
middle class, highly intelligent, politically idealistic and with a Portsmouth connection. His admiration is made explicit in the novel *Marriage*
when he speaks of Dickens as a social reformer using a comic medium:
the message 'we need another Dickens' is addressed – a little ambigu-
ously – to a literary charlatan, the author Mr Mantel. And three of Wells's
popular novels are conspicuously Dickensian.

   Wells was conscious of his Dickensian model when writing the rambling and high-spirited *History of Mr Polly* and it makes many references
to Dickens, including snappy expressive peculiar names like Polly and
Garrace, some actual echoes of Dickens's names like Podger, Larkins
and Voules. Mr Polly, the uneducated jolly shopkeeper hero with a
jaunty suggestive name, is given an eccentric reading list which includes
a reservation about Sterne perhaps reminiscent of David Copperfield's
care about identifying with 'a child's' 'Tom Jones':

> Sterne he read with a wavering appreciation and some perplexity, but
> except for the 'Pickwick Papers', for some reason that I do not
> understand, he never took at all kindly to Dickens. Yet he liked Lever,
> and Thackeray's 'Catherine', and all Dumas ... I am puzzled by his
> insensibility to Dickens, and I record it, as a good historian should,
> with an admission of my perplexity. (Ch. 7)

This may be a false trail to tease Dickensians expecting Dickens to
appear on a Dickensian character's curriculum, or the anxiety of influence, or a complication of his extrovert, larky character or a shrewd
realization that the ordinary comic-romantic hero would not admire
someone who wrote novels about people like himself – probably all four.

   There are Dickensian words like 'Humbug' and 'lark', and an imitation of Jingle's telegraphese in a scene where the young Polly is showing
off: 'Stout elderly gentleman – shirt sleeves – large straw waste-paper
basket sort of hat – starts to cross the road – going to the oil-shop –
prodic refreshment of oil-can' (Ch. 5). The 'prodic' is one of the
ambitious Dickensian errors – not as funny or clever as Gamp's – which

are his style-mark and include 'Zealacious commerciality' (Ch. 7) and 'convivial vocificerations' (Ch. 6).

Mr and Mrs Polly, and the plump innkeeper woman he ends up with, remind us of Dickensian characters in their comic stereotyping and high spirits but are lightweight in comparison, and do not open out to surprise us like Betsy Trotwood and the Micawbers.

Tono-Bungay is a fictionalized autobiography of its author and a first-person rambling novel by a fatherless narrator who marries unwisely, finds his true love, and is a novelist, but unlike David Copperfield, writes only one novel – this one. Like *Great Expectations* it is set in Kent, near Rochester, has a poor hero, George Ponderevo, who falls in love when very young with a well-born lady, fights rough with a boy from a higher class – his Herbert Pocket – rises in the world with the aid of a not wholly scrupulous self-made man, and satirizes social climbing, financial success, and the origins of wealth. It contains characters who may be called Dickensian, especially the hero's 'grandiloquent' uncle Teddy Ponderevo and his aunt Susan, an eccentric Wellsian revisionist, a Birkbeck student and a kind of feminist. She and her husband have comic idiolects with speech-tags, Polly's tendency to inspired error and loose flowing talkative narrative. The story makes full use of the geography of London's river, with a detailed account of sailing down to the Thames estuary, and ends with the symbolic flow of river into ocean.

Kipps is something else, something even closer to Dickens, a twentieth-century revision of *Great Expectations*. An earlier discarded central figure was called Waddy, Dickensian but not as Dickenisan as 'Kipps' which includes 'Pip'. To tell the story is to bring out similarities in plot and social situation, with some differences: a working-class orphan boy, of whose parentage we are told next to nothing, is brought up by an uncle and aunt in the marsh country of Kent; one of his childhood friends is a working-class boy – no Herbert Pocket – with whom he fights, and he is a little in love with the girl next door, the boy's sister. During his apprenticeship – not to a village blacksmith but a small-town draper – he suddenly comes into a large fortune and is taken up by mercenary social superiors, including a beautiful educated young woman to whom he has a romantic attachment. He has immense problems adapting to middle-class culture, which are treated seriously and comically, and eventually leaves his fiancée for his old love, the novel's version of Biddy. He gives up middle-class culture, is swindled out of his fortune, buys a bookshop, regains some money from an unexpectedly successful play he has backed and chooses to stay in the lower-class world, doing a little self-improvement, as indeed he did before coming into his fortune, because

Wells knew enough about working-class culture to show him enjoying books and going to art classes. The connection of name is unlikely to be coincidental because Wells was interested in names and draws attention to the oddity 'Kipps', dropping a clue in an 'Anagram Party' where one of the hero's agonized social trials is a game of jumbled names. Like his predecessor, Kipps suffers from shame, and guilt about the shame, though he is not guilty of anything like Pip's betrayals, and his moral and psychological experience is treated superficially. But Wells is not at all superficial about class, culture and money.

Great Expectations is incomparably the greater novel but the shallower imitation – in the Renaissance sense, with no suggestion of plagiarism – has its points as social history. Indeed, the particularized detail of Kipps's aspirations, fear and humiliation as he tries to improve his speech and grammar to join the ceremonies of the chattering classes, shows exactly what Dickens glosses over or leaves out. Pip's language-shame is illustrated tersely when Estella mocks his use of 'jacks' for 'knaves' but Kipps's fruitless struggles not only with lexis but more formidable problems of aspirate, grammar and polite idiom are solidly specified. Pip's education and acquisition of culture are treated in a summary account of lessons with Matthew Pocket, an unspecified love of reading and a library which provokes Magwitch's request that he read aloud from books in foreign languages. Wells's new *Great Expectations* is like the old in showing pathetic awkward attempts at style and dress, but in Kipps, the central character. Farcical details of wearing slippers at dinner in a hotel and not knowing what to do with your hat, remind us of Joe Gargery, not Pip, who is never shown, and only once reported, to speak or behave clumsily – on his first visit to Satis House. The cultural shift is painless: all Pip needs are one or two tactful lessons in table manners from kind Herbert Pocket. What Wells dwells on is what Dickens neglects: the hero's lack of polite manners and high culture and his agonized attempts to acquire them. Wells includes an alternative, meritocratic social mobility and self-improvement, in Kipps' friend and brother-in-law Sid, who rises by skill and inventiveness, without favour or fortune, has an interest in politics and no worries about class – in some respects like his author. Wells enters into a tacit political dialogue with Dickens, as an author sharing his varied social experience and humane ideals but also as a sociological thinker documenting cultural change, in details of language, education, conversation, and class culture. *Kipps* is an *hommage* and a critique drawing attention to questions of class-consciousness which Dickens ignores or simplifies.

Another novelist who drew directly and indirectly on Dickens is Evelyn

Waugh, in class-origin and politics at the other extreme from the low-born and socialist Wells. Waugh also alludes to Dickensian types and myths, once or twice comments on Dickens, shows obvious and oblique traces of influence, and thought he was modelling some of his novels, for instance *Decline and Fall*, on the autobiographical books *David Copperfield* and *Great Expectations*. He was also influenced by another Dickensian, T. S. Eliot, the only modernist he seems to have admired, who used Sloppy's mimicry in newspaper reading, 'He do the police in different voices', as a working title for the multi-vocal *Waste Land*, imitated Podsnap for The Rum Tum Tugger's 'he will do as he do do', in *Old Possum's Book of Practical Cats*, and perhaps suggested the title of Waugh's best and most Dickensian novel, *A Handful of Dust*, which used for its epigraph four lines from the first section of *The Waste Land* including 'I will show you fear in a handful of dust'.

Waugh scatters Dickens stereotypes: in *A Handful of Dust* Pecksniff's architecture is invoked to describe the Last family's Gothic pile; in *Officers and Gentlemen* the daughter of a classics master asks 'How is Dotheboys Hall?' (Bk 1, Ch. 3); in *The Ordeal of Gilbert Pinfold*, the story of a paranoid breakdown, the novelist hero has a Dickens-like name, is a Roman Catholic whose knowledge about Nonconformists comes from Chadband, and believes that all novelists, even 'the most daemonic masters' like Dickens and Balzac, have in them 'the germs of only one or two novels, and all the rest is trickery'.

There are larger connections. If *Kipps* is Wells's *Great Expectations* then *Decline and Fall* is Waugh's *Pickwick Papers*. Both are first novels, illustrated, picaresque, with comic or serio-comic scenes of sport, duelling, prison, and male camaraderie with much drinking. (I think Waugh and some critics are wrong in suggesting a resemblance to *Great Expectations*.) As well as its illustrations, *Decline and Fall* has a structural feature rare in the twentieth century, the inset narrative, in Waugh's case a comic mirror of the larger novel and rivalling the tall tales of Jingle and Sam Weller. Like Pickwick, the hero Paul is a good listener and always being told stories, including one about a man courtmartialled for trying to shoot himself after being left with a pistol, a decanter of whiskey and the injunction to behave like a gentleman, but released with the words, 'It won't do to shoot an old Harrovian.'

Waugh is urbane on the surface, unnerving and iconoclastic at heart, and though he tends to separate his serious and comic stories, unlike Dickens, who after *Pickwick* finely merges serious and comic tones, Waugh can now and then achieve a similar affective blend, as he does in *A Handful of Dust* (1934), where the dust heaps from *Our Mutual Friend* –

for which there is no place in Waugh – may have reinforced the title and the epigraph from Eliot. His direct invocation of Dickens is for the grotesque fate of Tony Last, one of Waugh's most sympathetic high-life characters. After losing love, child, wife and trust in human relationships, Tony travels to find life-meaning and a lost city in South America, only to be sentenced for life to read and re-read Dickens to a mad illiterate Dickensian, Mr Todd:

> You see, they are the only books I have ever heard ... I have heard them all several times by now but I never get tired; there is always more to be learned and noticed, so many characters, so many changes of scene, so many words ... I have all Dickens's books here except the ones that the ants have devoured. It takes a long time to read them all – more than two years. (Ch. 6)

Todd's origins are various. On his South American travels Waugh encountered a boring religious maniac and then a priest who lent him Dickens, whom he enjoyed after disliking him for years. His father Arthur Waugh was a ardent Dickensian, a managing director of Dickens's old publishers Chapman and Hall and member of the Dickens Fellowship, who regularly read the novels aloud to his family. This episode has been seen as a parody of Dickensians, and Todd weeps, laughs, and makes wonderfully painful comments, like 'I think the Dedlock is a very proud man' and 'Mrs Jellyby does not take enough care of her children' (Ch. 6), but the satiric text is overridden by the novel's pessimistic vision and black humour. There is a humiliating end for the betrayed romantic Victorian, pinning hopes on a dream of the good city – which may owe something to the rise and fall of Dorrit's cloud-castle – a dreadfully apt nemesis, in a unique literary hell:

> We will not have any Dickens today ... but tomorrow, and the day after that, and the day after that. Let us read *Little Dorrit* again. There are passages in that book I can never hear without the temptation to weep. (Ch. 6)

More deeply Dickensian, but only locally, in one episode, is the death scene of Lord Marchmain in *Brideshead Revisited*. The novel was first published in 1944, and revised for the 1959 edition where the death scene was made more realistic and less poetic, to cut what had been criticized as over-written.[1] To my mind, the original version of this scene is superior to the second which loses introspection, and reduces the part played by the coupling of inner drama in Marchmain and Charles Ryder.

Dickens's deathbeds must, at some level, have influenced the presentation of Marchmain's slow and dramatic death, which Waugh said was written in a more poetic and less realistic mode than the rest of the novel. During the scenes of his dying we see several points of view. The dying man is revealed during the first stages of his homecoming at Brideshead but his point of view is withdrawn towards the end, when his consciousness is critically in question: Marchmain is a Catholic convert and apostate who at the moment of death is watched closely by his two daughters and mistress (one good and two bad Catholics) a priest and the unbeliever Charles. Appearing to have finally lost consciousness, he makes the sign of the cross after the sacrament of extreme unction has been ministered – against his last spoken wish. This was apparently based on a real Catholic deathbed occurrence interpreted by Waugh as a miracle. We see Marchmain through the close observation of the narrator, artist and agnostic Charles Ryder and just as Dickens represented David Copperfield's life as he observed and related the lives of other people, so we see Ryder's destiny as his imagination grasps the meanings of Marchmain's death, and he tells his story.

All Dickens's major deathbeds, from Nell's to Dorrit's, are marked by a locally dominant object or image which binds the scene in unity and tension, registers the process of dying and is psychically internalized: green plants for Nell, river and wild waves for Paul Dombey, a cart for Jo the crossing-sweeper, a castle in the air for William Dorrit. The only other novelist I know who uses a similar device is Waugh, also one of the few modern novelists to do a big death scene. It is obviously significant that his death scene is a religious crisis, but it is also significant that he was saturated in Dickens.

Lord Marchmain has chosen what the sectionalized chapter title, removed in revision, calls 'Death in the Chinese drawing-room', announcing the image which dominates the scene and his dwindling lonely consciousness: a set of ornate gilded figures decorating the Chinese fireplace. (This imagery is kept in the revision.) The figures occupy and obsess the dying man just as the waves and the cart obsessed Paul and Jo, tracking a sick, exhausted but imaginative process in which the dying mind is oddly but naturally engaged, and which also serves a symbolic purpose, as it represents dying, death, and like Nelly's green plants and Paul's flowing river, an afterlife. Waugh wrote a Preface explaining – in response to adverse criticism – that Marchmain's 'dying soliloquy' was not 'intended to report words actually spoken' and belong to a different way of writing from, say, the early scenes between Charles and his father: 'I would not now introduce them into a novel which elsewhere aims at verisimilitude' (see Penguin edition, 1959).

I believe his imagination was haunted by Dickens's 'different way' and as a consciously naturalistic novelist he was uneasy about it. Perhaps this was an unconscious factor in the revision. Dickens too had thought of himself as replicating real life, though with less sophisticated awareness of other modes and genres and a greater tolerance of fantasy. Fantasy is what links the two writers, in their scenes where a dying derangement of the senses and mind calls out the lyricism and symbolism of poetry. Waugh unconsciously recalls Dickens's animation of the object world as he destabilizes the senses of dying character, as Dickens did for Paul and Jenny Wren in their pain, for Paul and Jo in their dying. The 'grotesque, chinoiserie chimney-place' (Bk 3, Ch. 5) is in the great room Marchmain has chosen to die in, and the pictures of the grotesque gold or yellow men obsess the dying mind, blurring pathology and poetry in transformative visions. Paul sees odd shapes in the wallpaper and waves of light on the ceiling and Marchmain sees the little men come to life. The fantasy, as in Dickens, is made strange and poetic, as Waugh said, but also controlled and realized because it is clearly and delicately pathologized. In spite of the novelist's demurral there is no genre clash between his realism and his poetry. The figures provide light and company, as the interpreting narrator observes, 'Next to death, perhaps because they are like death, he feared darkness and loneliness. He liked to have us in his room and the lights burnt all night among the gilt figures' (Bk 3, Ch. 5). The figures change and become animated by his observation and imagination, in a creative dying which changes perspective – like Paul's approach to the sea:

> Better today. Better today. I can see now, in the corner of the fireplace, where the mandarin is holding his gold bell and the crooked tree is in flower below his feet, where yesterday I was confused and took the little tower for another man. Soon I shall see the bridge and the three storks and know whether the path leads over the hill. (Ch. 5)

A little later in the chapter, Waugh brilliantly invokes the imagination and its image-pattern to dramatize the mental and physical effort and pain of dying. Like Paul struggling through sand and Jo dragging the cart up the last stretch of hill, the disoriented breathless man articulates his sensations through the figures on the fireplace. Their animation can turn nasty: 'Who would have thought that all these little gold men,

gentlemen in their own country, could live so long without breathing?
Like toads in the coal, down a deep mine, untroubled' (Bk 3, Ch. 5).
Later still, when he has been given oxygen, Marchmain makes a last
speech in which the little men are no longer gold, and at their most
menacing: 'Is that why they've locked me in this cave, do you think, with
a black tube of air and the little yellow men along the walls, who live
without breathing?' (Bk 3, Ch. 5). This is just how Dickens manipulates
his structural imagery when he turns river and sand malignant for Paul's
hard dying.

Brideshead Revisited is a didactic Catholic novel, and Waugh uses two
image patterns in this scene, one to mark Marchmain's slow God-
directed dying and another (reduced in revision) to show Charles
Ryder's slow God-directed move towards Catholicism: seeing the good
death begins Ryder's conversion and ends his engagement to Marchmain's divorced daughter Julia. The play of the narrator's sharp and
sceptical central consciousness – the imagination of the artist in the
novel – is young and active as he observes passive age and fatigue, and is
given structure and motion by dynamic imagery. For him the dominant
and dynamic image is an arctic hut, with a trapper inside, threatened
and eventually destroyed by an avalanche slowly moving down from the
high mountain. The story is told and felt from Charles's point of view,
from the moment when the snow and rocks start to move until they
destroy the man in his hut: 'The avalanche was down, the hillside swept
bare behind it; the last echoes died on the white slopes; the new mound
glittered and lay still in the silent valley' (Ch. 5). The moving avalanche
is the Providential motion, its crash the end of profane and the beginning of sacred love.

In the revised version there is only that one last image in Chapter 5,
and the other avalanche image is separated from the death scene, placed
at the end of Chapter 4. The first image is also different in emphasis,
describing snow piling up against the hut door, rather than threatening
from high up the mountain. Altogether, the changes make the structure
of the scene more diffuse and weaken the dynamism of gradual inex-
orable process and providential pattern.

It is the final chapter of the novel's retrospect, before we return to the
Epilogue and the war, where the novel and Charles Ryder's flashback
began. The avalanche story shows divine grace at work in several people,
subsumed in a larger theme, secular and religious, the coming of war
and the death of the old life. *Brideshead Revisited* is a deeply conservative
novel, religiously and politically tendentious, but what is fascinating, for
those who do or do not share Waugh's faith, is the way the structure of

imagery is used to describe and dramatize imaginative experience. In a note printed in the Penguin edition Waugh says that he regarded 'writing not as investigation of character but as an exercise in the use of language, and with this I am obsessed'. It is Dickens's imaginative poetry, used to figure imagination, that seems creatively active at the end of this fictitious first-person memoir purporting to be written by an artist, partly but not entirely about his art, and described – like *David Copperfield* – as the writer's memory. In *A Handful of Dust* Dickens is deliberately invoked for a grotesque tragic humiliation, and in *Brideshead* unconsciously recalled for a redemptive dying.

The most Dickensian modern novelist is James Joyce, whose admiration was on the cool side of idolatry. As part of a qualifying test for a teacher of English, in Zurich, he was set an essay on Dickens, and wrote that Dickens had entered into the English language more than any writer except Shakespeare, that to praise him for 'greatness of soul' was as inept as to criticize him for 'claptrap', that Thackeray was perhaps in some ways the greater novelist, and that he admired Dickens's grasp of London and the city.[2] Dickens certainly enters into Joyce in many ways: in allusion, imitation, rejection and influence, locally and largely, in particular and in general. His Dickens re-namings are critical, comic, erotically knowing and entirely Joycean: 'meetual fan', *The Old Cupiosity Shape* and 'Dovert Covertfilles' adopt the confusions and conflations Dickens played with in Mrs Gamp's inspired errors, Betsy Trotwood's joke about the 'murdering' woman, and the awful Mrs Crupp who calls David 'Mr Copperfull'. The parodies are congenial since Dickens himself liked to use Gampian wordplay in his letters to friends, and as I have mentioned, affectionate nicknamings like 'the Plorn' for one of his sons, and 'the Patient' and 'the little reason' for Ellen Ternan.

Joyce's more formal pastiche is weak, like all attempts I know to imitate Dickens: Micawber the writer of letters and mixer of punch is part of the disappointingly feeble voice in the imitations of English prose style for 'The Oxen of the Sun' in *Ulysses*, where Joyce also quotes Dora's 'Doady'. There is a profound critique of Dickens's sentimentality in *Dubliners*, where the lyrical nostalgic 'Distant Music' in 'The Dead' is repeatedly associated with his wife Greta by Gabriel Conroy and echoes David's lyrical nostalgic feeling for Agnes: 'I could listen to the sorrowful, distant music and desire to shrink from nothing it awoke. How could I, when blended with it all, was her dear self, the better angel of my life?' (Ch. 60).[3] The buried allusion is finely equivocal: Joyce is placing the nostalgic self-indulgence of Gabriel's sentimental moment, to be rejected by his wife and his own wiser self, by ironically invoking and

delicately criticizing the nostalgic sentimentality of David – and Dickens.
It is what we expect from Joyce who imitated sentimental novelettes for
Gerty MacDowell and adapted Meredith's great definition of sentimen-
tality in *The Ordeal of Richard Feverel* for a telegram read out by Buck
Mulligan: 'The sentimentalist is he who would enjoy without incurring
the immense debtorship for a thing done' (*Ulysses* 9, 'Scylla and
Charydis').

Dickens's major contribution to modernist language and narrative was
the inner monologue or stream of consciousness, tried in *A Portrait of the
Artist as a Young Man*, developed throughout *Ulysses,* flourished in Molly
Bloom and extended most poetically and subversively in *Finnegans Wake.*
It has other sources but none I think as marked as the style of Dickens's
garrulous woman.

The imitation of the conscious and the unconscious mind in *Finnegans
Wake* represents dead Finnegan's wake and begun-again Finnegan's
awakening, as it elides 'Finn' and 'again'. Both aspects of mind figure in
Molly Bloom and the Liffey goddess Anna Livia Plurabelle: Joyce's
stream of consciousness, like Dickens's, was used to impersonate women,
but not patronizingly or misogynistically. Dickens kept the voluble loose
flow for women but Joyce used it for men too, intensifying its lyricism for
the poet Stephen Dedalus in the last section of *Portrait of the Artist* and
combining it with Jingle's staccato for Leopold Bloom. Finally, he used it
in a highly musical and surreal flow for the most lyrical section of *Finnegans Wake,* where two Irish washer-women celebrate Anna Livia but
transcend gender as they become tree and stone and Anna Livia
becomes Liffey water, geographically specific and symbolic like Dickens's
Thames as it leaves banks and estuary to join the ocean. At the beginning
of the Anna Livia section the strongly punctuated but fluid prose urges
on the listener in elided dialogue and colloquial poetry that knows what
it is doing: 'Well, you know Anna Livia? Yes, of course, we all know Anna
Livia. Tell me all. Tell me now. You'll die when you hear ... Tuck up
your sleeves and loosen your talk-tapes' (*FW*, 196). *Finnegans Wake* is the
unconscious mind and the imagination dreaming, and for the end of
the section the rhymes, neologisms, puns, repetitions and musical word-
blurrings articulate the lack of boundary in nature, sea, sleep and story-
telling:

Can't hear with the waters of. The chittering waters of. Flittering bats,
fieldmice bawk talk. Ho! Are you not gone ahome? What Thom
Malone? Can't hear with bawk of bats, all thim liffey-ing waters of. Ho,
talk save us! My foos won't moos. I feel as old as yonder elm. A tale told

of Saun or Shem? All Livia's daughter-sons. Dark hawks hear us. Night!
Night! My ho head halls. I feel as heavy as yonder stone. Tell me of
John or Shaun? Who were Shem and Shaun the living sons or
daughters of? Night now! Tell me, tell me, tell me, elm! Night night!
Telmetale of stem or stone. Beside the rivering waters of, hither-
andthithering waters of. Night! (*FW*, 215–6)

When the psychoanalytic feminists Hélène Cixous and Luce Irigaray
praise the looseness and freedom of *l'écriture féminine* they recognize that
it is not confined to female talk and text but nevertheless claim a privileged derivation from the woman's body and a political function of
freeing language from patriarchal hegemony. There is no better example of the loose fluid self-aware style than Joyce's Dickens-inspired Anna
Livia passages, women's talk which Mrs Gamp, like the Wife of Bath and
Erasmus's Moria, can help us to see as man's invention. It is Joyce's
particular version of Romain Rolland's 'oceanic feeling'[4] and for this
too, as style and concept, Dickens must be given some credit, since he
established the oceanic symbol and a language which breaks boundaries
of syntax and sense, and aspires to the condition of music.

Molly Bloom's drowsy monologue is more legible than the poetry of
Anna Livia's water-cronies: even as she is falling asleep her babble makes
good common-sense, like Flora Finching's 'if the organ-boys come away
from the neighbourhood not to be scorched nobody can wonder being
so young and bringing their white mice ...' (Bk 2, Ch. 9). We hear Mrs
Gamp in 'Covertfilles' and 'Lawn Tennyson' and Mrs Nickleby and Flora
in Molly, Joyce's version of Penelope, Homer's definer of dreams:

a quarter after what an unearthly hour I suppose theyre just getting up
in China now combing out their pigtails for the day well soon have the
nuns ringing the angelus theyve nobody coming to spoil their sleep
except an odd priest or two for his night office or the alarm clock next
door at cockshout clattering the brains out of itself let me see if I can
doze off 1 2 3 4 5 what kind of flowers are those they invented like the
stars the wallpaper in Lombard street was much nicer the apron he
gave me was like that something only I only wore it twice better lower
this lamp and try again so as I can get up early Ill go to Lambes there
beside Findlaters and get them to send some flowers to put around the
place in case he brings him home tomorrow today I mean no no
Fridays an unlcky day first I want to do the place up someway the dust
grows in it I think while Im asleep then we can have music and
cigarettes I can accompany him first I must clean the keys of the piano

with milk whatll I wear shall I wear a white rose ... (*Ulysses*, 18, 'Penelope', p. 642)

Joyce inherits Dickens's fluid affective language, his confusions and fusions of appreciation, curiosity, hope, sympathy and pleasure, using them all to create Molly, tell the story of the Blooms, and recall Homer. He said Molly's stream of consciousness was inspired by his wife's lack of punctuation, but because Molly is meditating – as when Flora is talking – the informality and flow are less a misogynist critique and joke than the anarchic and creative motion of mind. These talking women may be used to mock women's immethodical speech and writing but they use and express the artistic experience of two men – Dickens self-educated, Joyce formally educated – and their knowledge of creative relaxation, self-generative form, flow and affect. Of course that experience took in, critically or appreciatively, the actual speech of the women they knew, less educated and empowered mothers and wives, but it entered the literary tradition as the writing of men, inherited by Dickens and Joyce, both in the line of Chaucer, Erasmus, Shakespeare, Sheridan and Sterne.

Virginia Woolf claimed that the women's 'sentence' was invented by Dorothy Richardson, but the claim is qualified:

> She has invented, or if she has not invented, developed and applied to her own uses, a sentence which might be called the psychological sentence of the feminine gender. It is of a more elastic fibre than the old, capable of stretching to the extreme, of suspending the frailest particles, of enveloping the vaguest shapes. Other writers of the opposite sex have used sentences of this description and stretched them to the extreme. But there is a difference. Miss Richardson has fashioned her sentence consciously, in order that it may descend to the depths and investigate the crannies of Miriam Henderson's consciousness. It is a woman's sentence, but only in the sense that it is used to describe a woman's mind by a writer who is neither proud nor afraid of anything that she may discover in the psychology of her sex.[5]

'... if she has not invented, developed and applied': the imputed purpose, 'to describe a woman's mind', does not quite fit Richardson, who now and then describes men's minds too, though Woolf may not have read all the relevant passages. Richardson never uses interior monologue as her prevailing style like Woolf or Joyce. Woolf's account of gendered language is vague, but Richardson herself is more precise. In her 1938

Foreword to the *roman fleuve, Pilgrimage* – where Miriam has amusing reflections on Dickens titles, including the feeling that she couldn't read a novel called *Nicholas Nickleby* – she links two 'writers of the opposite sex', Dickens and Joyce, as 'delightfully ... aware' of women's unpunctuated prose, explaining that she herself used commas sparingly in her experimental narratives. Her lightly punctuated interior monologues, full of dashes, are used sporadically for passages of reverie, but they are usually smooth and single-themed. A typical stream of consciousness from the first book, 'Pointed Roofs', dissolves miscellaneous events in Miriam's memory but it is not hugely capacious or 'elastic' and only seems unconventional – for its time, 1915 – because of elided syntax, dashes and the many omission points:

> ... her mother's illness, money troubles – their two years at the sea to retrieve ... the disappearance of the sunlit red-walled garden always in full summer sunshine with the sound of bees in it, or dark from windows ... the narrowing of the house-life down to the Marine Villa ... with the sea creeping in – wading out through the green shallows, out and out until you were more than waist deep – shrimping and prawning hour after hour for weeks together ... (Ch. 2)

Such sentences show emotional 'depths' and 'crannies' but Woolf's 'more elastic fibre ... capable of stretching' better describes the freer miscellaneous monologues of Flora Finching, Molly Bloom and Mrs Dalloway. (The metaphor suits *Tristram Shandy*'s digressive flow too, and when Joyce was being attacked for writing nonsense in *Finnegans Wake*, he mentioned Sterne as a precedent.) Though Woolf may have been influenced by Richardson, the stream of consciousness in *Jacob's Room* and the later novels is much more like that of Joyce. It may have been because of her feminism that she emphasized Richardson and underplayed Joyce, though sexual politics did not stop her praising the elasticity of Byron's *Don Juan*: 'Its what one has looked for in vain – a[n] elastic shape which will hold whatever you choose to put into it' (*The Diary of Virginia Woolf*, Vol. 1). The suppression of Joyce may also have been an anxiety of guilt and influence, because she and Leonard Woolf rejected *Ulysses* for the Hogarth Press but her narrative syntax changed radically after it was published. Whether she knew it or not, the subversive woman's sentence which she developed in her own brilliant style, owes something to him and through him to Dickens. She used the elastic sentence to record the smallest particles and vaguest shapes in men's

minds as well as women's, in normal experience and in imaginative
derangements she knew at first hand:

> Love – but here the other clock, the clock which always struck two
> minutes after Big Ben, came shuffling in with its lap full of odds and
> ends, which it dumped down as if Big Ben were all very well with his
> majesty laying down the law, so solemn, so just, but she must
> remember all sorts of things besides – Mrs Marsham, Ellie Henderson,
> glasses for ices – all sorts of little things came flooding and lapping
> and dancing in on the wake of that solemn stroke which lay flat like a
> bar of gold on the sea. Mrs Marsham, Ellie Henderson, glasses for ices.
> She must telephone now at once. (*Mrs Dalloway*, 141)

and

> ... cabs were rushing round the corner, like water round the piers of a
> bridge, drawn together, it seemed to him, because they bore people
> going to her party ...
> The cold stream of visual impressions failed him now as if the eye
> were a cup that overflowed and let the rest run down its china walls
> unrecorded. The brain must wake now. The body must contract now,
> entering the house, the lighted house, where the door stood open,
> where the motor cars were standing, and bright women descending:
> the soul must brave itself to endure. He opened the big blade of his
> pocket-knife. (*Ibid.*, 181)

and

> But they beckoned; leaves were alive; trees were alive. And the leaves
> being connected by millions of fibres with his own body, there on the
> seat, fanned it up and down; when the branch stretched he, too, made
> that statement. The sparrows fluttering, rising, and falling in jagged
> fountains were part of the pattern; the white and blue, barred with
> black branches. Sounds made harmonies with premeditation; the
> spaces between them were as significant as the sounds. A child cried.
> Rightly far away a horn sounded. All taken together made the birth of
> a new religion – (*Ibid.*, 26)

The first passage shows a woman's mind, the second a man's, both
healthy imaginations moving from inside to outside, but the third passage shows the enclosed schizophrenic mind of Septimus Warren. All

three minds take in outside impressions and draw them together. In all three the elastic style shows a mind in the process of ordering and selecting, making and unmaking. A frequent feature in Dickens's images of imagination is the sense of effort and difficulty, betrayed by Mrs Nickleby's uncontrolled random swerves and Flora's uncontrolled speed and digressions, the painfully troubled mind of dying Paul and the restlessness of the night-wandering Uncommercial Traveller. Various kinds of imaginative effort are visible here in the mental-affective flow of the constructing and dissolving consciousness of Mrs Dalloway, Peter Walsh and Septimus Warren.

All three are dealing with fragmented experience. There is a very fine line separating what we might call the healthy from what we might call the unhealthy imagination, detectible only in the last mad interpretative movement of Septimus Warren's paragraph. At the end of his trajectory of feeling and sense-impression, his act of ordering is the most creatively inclusive of the three: Mrs Dalloway picks from the medley her social routine, Peter sees everything related to her party, and is drawn in too, but Septimus converts all his sensation to a larger vision. We may decide that Clarissa Dalloway and Peter are healthily combining reverie with selective humane practical living while Septimus is suffering from religious delusions, with no base in actuality, and we may even go on to understand why they choose life and he will choose suicide. But we may feel we are being invited not to make a distinction between normal and abnormal creative construction, but to see what they have in common, or even to prefer the mad to the sane, as more ambitious though less practical. In any case, as with Vardon and Barnaby, Nell and Quilp, all the imaginations are imagined by the novelist, all in one mind.

The imaginative effort and difficulty which Woolf's three sensibilities here embody is characteristic of creative composition, as in Coleridge's words the mind 'dissolves, diffuses, dissipates, in order to recreate; or, where this process is rendered impossible, yet still, at all events, it struggles to idealize and to unify' (*Biographia Literaria*, Ch. 13). What Joyce and Woolf – but Dickens before them – admit and illustrate, is the complex creative trial-and-error, its efforts, erasures, revisions, hit-or-miss invention, relaxation, recovery, and self-generative flow.

The poets knew it as well as the prose poets like Dickens, Joyce and Woolf: Emily Dickinson – like Dickens and Woolf a lover of dashes – said 'the Possible' has a 'slow fuse lit by Imagination'; and in 'The Wreck of the Deutschland' Hopkins assimilates essay and effort into the poem: 'But how shall I ... make me a room there: / Reach me a ... Fancy come faster ...'. William James analysed and imaged the mind's attempt to grasp, give up, and try again, and so does Woolf when Mrs Ramsay reaches out 'to get hold of something that evades her'. Dickens assimilates his experience of imaginative and compositional effort in the hesitations, vaguenesses and repetitions of his talkers, in Mrs Nickleby's 'by the bye', Knag's gasping 'hem', and Micawber's 'in short', which jog inspiration, apply the brake to eloquence, mask failure, and pause before dashing on, drawing attention to effort and success.

Dickens's talkative women demonstrate a wild free-for-all power, working through random and revisionary association, error, doubt and vagueness to get effects which are critical and comic within their novels, but mirroring mind at its most inventive, showing poesis in its Platonic sense, bringing into existence something that had not existed before. His loquacious talkers and tellers are walking oxymorons, brilliant stupidities, unstructured forms, subversions of rule that create new precedents. They anticipate and encourage dislocation, freedom, fracture, collision, defamiliarization, openness. They embody what Yeats praised as the wildness of imagination. As twenty-first-century readers we see misogyny in the talkative women but in them Dickens dramatized creative imagination, freed to write his wild text for the Victorian novel and the modern tradition.

The talkative woman is in one way a solipsist of the imagination, out to engross the listeners within the novel, but she also embodies her author's negative capability, embracing strange and fragmentary experience, open to new language. It is in fractures of rule and reason that such models are inspirations for later writers, but though we may privilege the extreme images of creativity in Dickens because they have changed our language, in his work they take their place in a range of creative images and imaged creators, some of them showing the imagination hard put to order and unify experience, like Master Humphrey looking at the curiosities, David in a brown study outside the Highgate house, Francis Goodchild watching the depressed man and Dickens remembering the frozen dead.

Notes

[1] For biographical information about Waugh see Martin Stannard's biographies of Waugh, and David Wyke, *Evelyn Waugh: A Literary Life*. For a different opinion of the *Brideshead* revision, see Frank Kermode's introduction to the Everyman text.

² 'The Centenary of Charles Dickens', *Journal of Modern Literature*, 5, no. 1, February 1976.

³ Don Gifford, *Joyce Annotated.*

⁴ 'Romance and the Heart', review of *Revolving Lights* by Dorothy Richardson in *Nation and Athenaeum*, 19 May 1923, reprinted in *Contemporary Writers.*

⁵ This chapter is a revision of a lecture given for a conference on *Dickens: A Man for all Media* in July 2002 at the University of London Institute of English Studies.

Sources

Books and Articles

Ashton, Rosemary (1991), *G. H. Lewes. A Life.* Oxford: OUP.

Beckett, Samuel (1978), *Happy Days: O Les Beaux Jours* (ed. James Knowlson). London: Faber.

Butt, J. and Tillotson, K (1957), *Dickens at Work.* London: Methuen.

Carey, J. (1973), *The Violent Effigy.* London: Faber.

Coleridge, S. T. (1975), *Biographia Literaria.* London: Dent.

Coleridge, S. T. (1969), *Collected Works of Samuel Taylor Coleridge.* London: Routledge and Kegan Paul.

Collins, Wilkie (1961), 'Queen Mab's Chariot among the Steam Engines; Dickens's Fancy', in *English Studies*, No. 42.

Connor, Steven (1985), *Charles Dickens.* Oxford: Blackwell.

Cross, J. W. (1885), *George Eliot's Life As Related in Her Letters and Journals* (3 vols). Edinburgh and London: Blackwood.

Davis, Earle Rosco (1964), *The Flint and the Flame: The Artistry of Charles Dickens.* London: Gollancz.

De Quincey, Thomas (1998), *Confessions of an English Opium-Eater and Other Writings.* Oxford: OUP.

Eliot, George (1968), *Essays of George Eliot* (ed. Thomas Pinney). London: Routledge and Kegan Paul.

—— (1943), *Old Possum's Book of Practical Cats.* London: Faber.

Eliot, T. S. (1971), *The Waste Land. A facsimile & transcript of the Original Drafts* (ed. Valerie Eliot). London: Faber.

Forster, John (1928), *The Life of Charles Dickens* (ed. J. W. T. Ley). London: Cecil Palmer.

Gager, Valerie (1996), *Dickens and Shakespeare.* Cambridge: CUP.

Garis, Robert (1965), *The Dickens Theatre. A Reassessmemt of the Novels.* Oxford: Clarendon Press.

Gifford, Don (1982), *Joyce Annotated.* Berkeley, Los Angeles and London: University of California Press.

Gray, Beryl (2001), 'Tattycoram and Caterina Sarti', in *George Eliot Review*, No. 32.

Haight, G. S. (1968), *George Eliot. A Biography.* Oxford: Clarendon Press.

Harbage, Alfred (1975), *A Kind of Power. The Shakespeare/Dickens Analogy*. Philadelphia: The American Philosophical Society.

Hardy, Barbara (1964), *The Moral Art of Dickens*. London: Athlone.

—— (1975), *Tellers and Listeners*. London: Athlone.

—— (2006), *George Eliot: A Critic's Biography*. London: Continuum.

Harvey, Stephanie (2002), 'Dickens' Villains: A Confession and Suggestion', in *The Dickensian*, No. 4658, Vol. 98, Winter.

Hillis Miller, J. (1958), *Charles Dickens. The World of his Novels*. Oxford: OUP.

Housman, A. E. (1993), *The Name and Nature of Poetry*, the Leslie Stephen Lecture. Cambridge: CUP.

Huxley, Aldous (1928), *Point Counter Point*. London: Chatto & Windus.

Jackson, T. A. (1937), *Charles Dickens. The Progress of a Radical*. London: Lawrence and Wishart.

James, William (1890), *Principles of Psychology*. London and New York: Macmillan.

James, Henry (1947), *The Art of the Novel: Critical Prefaces*. New York and London: Charles Scribner's Sons.

—— (1950), *The Princess Casamassima*. London: John Lehmann.

Johnson, Edgar (1953), *Charles Dickens: His Tragedy and Triumph*. London: Gollancz.

Joyce, James (1944), *Portrait of the Artist as a Young Man*. London: Jonathan Cape.

—— (1948), *Finnegans Wake*. London: Faber.

—— (1976), 'The Centenary of Charles Dickens', in *Journal of Modern Literature*, 5, No. 1, February.

—— (1986), *Ulysses*. Harmondsworth: Penguin.

—— (1967), *America*. Harmondsworth: Penguin.

Kafka, Franz (1971), *The Castle*. Harmondsworth: Penguin.

Leavis, F. R. and Q. D. (1970), *Dickens the Novelist*. London: Chatto and Windus.

Lettis, Richard (1989), *The Dickens Aesthetic*. NY: Ams Press Inc.

—— (1990), *Dickens on Literature*. NY: Ams Press Inc.

Lewes, G. H. (1872), 'Dickens in Relation to Criticism', in *Fortnightly Review*, February.

Mann, Thomas (1988), *Selected Stories*, trans. David Luke. Harmondsworth: Penguin.

Richardson, Dorothy (1938), *Pilgrimage*, 3 vols. London: Dent.

Sanders, Andrew (1982), *Dickens Resurrectionist*. London: Macmillan.

Schlicke, P. (1984), *Dickens and Popular Entertainment*. London: Allen and Unwin.

Slater, Michael (1983), *Dickens and Women*. London: Dent.

—— (1999), *An Intelligent Person's Guide to Dickens*. London: Duckworth.

Spencer, Herbert (1904), *Autobiography*. London: Williams and Norgate.

—— (1982), *Evelyn Waugh: No Abiding City*. London: Dent.

Stannard, Martin (1986), *Evelyn Waugh: The Early Years*. London: Dent.

Stone, Harry Stone (1994), *The Night Side of Dickens: Cannibalism, Passion, Necessity*. Columbus: Ohio State University Press.

Thackeray, W. M. (1852), *The History of Henry Esmond*, 3 vols. London: Smith, Elder and Co.

Tomalin, C. (1991), *The Invisible Woman, The Story of Ellen Ternan and Charles Dickens*. London: Penguin.

Trembling, Jeremy (1995), *Dickens, Violence and the Modern State*. London: Macmillan.

Waugh, Evelyn (1962), *Decline and Fall*. London: Chapman and Hall.

—— (1910), *Marriage*. London: Nelson.

—— (1934), *A Handful of Dust*. London: Chapman and Hall.

—— (1945), *Brideshead Revisited*. London: Chapman and Hall.

—— (1993), ——. London: Everyman; Random House.

—— (1959), ——. Harmondsworth: Penguin.

—— (1962), *The Ordeal of Gilbert Pinfold*. Harmondsworth: Penguin.

—— (1971), *Officers and Gentlemen*. Harmondsworth: Penguin.

Wells, H. G. (1946), *The History of Mr Polly*. Harmondsworth: Penguin.

—— (1946), *Kipps*. Harmondsworth: Penguin.

—— (1946), *Tono-Bungay*. Harmondsworth: Penguin.

Wilson, Angus (1957), *Anglo-Saxon Attitudes*. London: Secker & Warburg.

—— (1961), *The Old Men at the Zoo*. London: Secker & Warburg.

Wilson, Edmund (1952), *The Wound and the Bow*. London: W. H. Allen.

Woolf, Virginia (1933), *Mrs Dalloway*. London: Hogarth Press.

—— (1976), 'Romance and the Heart', review of *The Grand Tour* by Romer Wilson and *Revolving Lights* by Dorothy Richardson, in *Nation and Athenaeum*, 19 May 1923, reprinted in *Contemporary Writers*. New York: A Harvest Book, Harcourt Brace Jovanovich.

—— (1977), *The Diary of Virginia Woolf*, Vol. 1. London: Hogarth Press.

Wyke, David (1999), *Evelyn Waugh. A Literary Life*. New York: St Martin's Press.

(Publication details refer to editions used for reference.)

Film and Television

Spellbound (1945), Alfred Hitchcock, director; Salvador Dali, sequence director; United Artists.

Solaris (1972), Andrei Tarkovsky, director; from the novel by Stanislaw Lem; Mosfilm.

Don't Look Now (1973), Nicholas Roeg, director; Paramount and British Lion.

Steptoe and Son (1962–74), Ray Galton and Alan Simpson, writers; Duncan Wood *et al.*, directors; BBC.

Index

All the Year Round 12, 13, 23, 28–9, 45, 112, 118

American Notes 6

Arabian Nights, The 1, 13, 37, 45, 63

Arnold, Matthew xiv

Austen, Jane 65, 68, 111, 125n

Barnaby Rudge 5–6, 20, 24, 39–40, 75–8,

Beadnell, Maria *see* Winter

Beckett, Samuel 46, 144

'Black Veil, The' 20, 35

Bleak House 10–11, 54–6, 72–3, 103–4, 163

'Bride's Chamber' Story, The 106, 108n, 150

Brookfield, Jane 23

Browne, Hablot Knight (Phiz) 3

Bulwer Lytton, Sir Edward 30

Burdett-Coutts, Angela 10, 12, 13, 91

Butt, John xviii

Byron, George Gordon, Lord 170

Carey, John xviii, 91

Carlyle, Thomas 137

Carroll, Lewis 75

Cervantes, Savvedra, Miguel de 37, 67, 87

Chaplin, Charlie 33

Chaucer, Geoffrey 61

'Chatham Dockyard' 27–8

Chesterton, G. K. 9, 10–11, 88, 148

Chimes, The 7, 43–4, 122

Christmas Carol, A 7, 44, 45–6, 98–100, 146

Cixous, Hélène 168

Coleridge, Samuel Taylor xvn, 34, 63, 68, 75, 172

Collins, Philip xvn

Collins, Wilkie 12, 13, 23–4, 80, 106–7

Connor, Steven 135

Cross, John Walter 21–2

Cruikshank, John 34, 36

Dali, Salvador 73

Dante, Alighieri 11

David Copperfield 8–10, 46–54, 74–5, 88–90, 91–4, 116, 147–52, 155, 166–7

Davis, Earle Rosco 69n

De Quincey, Thomas 73, 80

Dickinson, Emily 172

Dickens, Alfred (brother) 1

Dickens, Alfred (son) 13

Dickens, Augustus (brother) 1

Dickens, Catherine, *née* Hogarth (wife) 1, 3, 12–13, 17, 19–21, 149

Dickens, Charles (son) 4, 13

Dickens, Dora (daughter) 10, 13

Dickens, Edward or Plorn (son) 13

Dickens, Elizabeth, *née* Barrow (mother) 1–2, 63

Dickens, Frances or Fanny, later Burnett (sister) 1

Dickens, Francis (son) 13

Dickens, Frederick (brother) 1, 6

Dickens, John (father) 1, 2, 10, 147

Dickens, Kate, later Perugini
    (daughter) 13, 85n
Dickens, Letitia, later Austin (sister) 1
Dickens, Henry (son) 13
Dickens, Mary or Mamey, (daughter)
    13
Dickens, Sydney (son) 13
Dickens, Walter (son) 13
Dickinson, Emily 172
Diderot, Denis 43
Doctor Marigold's Prescriptions 45
Dombey and Son 8, 73, 94, 100–3, 163–5
Donne, John 34
Don't Look Now 123
Dostoevsky, Fyodor 91
Dryden. John 34

Eco, Umberto 112
Eisenstein, Sergei 143
Eliot, George 21–2, 38, 41, 48, 88,
    95–6, 109, 110, 111, 112, 120, 125,
    125–6n, 130, 137
Eliot, T. S. 145, 152, 161
Erasmus, Desiderius 61

Fielding, Henry 48
Fields, Annie 16
Fildes, Luke 16
Flaubert, Gustave 130
Forster, John 1, 2, 11, 16, 19, 20, 21,
    22, 24, 28–30, 50, 67, 81, 85n
Freud, Sigmund xvin, 20

Gager, Valerie 155–6n
Garis, Robert xvin
Gaskell, Elizabeth 10, 11
Goethe, Johann Wolfgang, von 146
Gray, Beryl 95
Great Expectations 14–15, 24, 29–30, 45,
    56–9, 73–4, 132–4, 152–6, 159–60

Harbage, Alfred 155n
Hard Times 11, 104–6, 127–32
Hardy, Thomas 89n, 98

Hitchcock, Alfred 73
Hogarth, George (father-in-law) 3
Hogarth, Georgina (sister-in-law) 12,
    16
Hogarth, Mary (sister-in-law) 4, 20
Household Words 11, 12 , 13, 14, 28,
    106–8
Housman, A. E. xiii, 24–5
Holme, Constance 68
Homer 62, 141
Hopkins, Gerard Manley 172
Hunt, William Holman 35
Huxley, Aldous 157

Ibsen, Henrik 109
Irigaray, Luce 168

Jackson, Thomas A. 133
James, Henry 49, 83, 100, 109, 110,
    112, 120, 125, 157
James, William 27, 172–3
Jerrold, Douglas 67
Johnson, B. S. 43
Jonson, Ben 145–6
Joyce, James xvin, 26, 27, 47, 62, 67,
    90–1, 126, 152, 166–70

Kafka, Franz 12, 124, 157–8,
Kant, Emmanuel 119
Keats, John 119
Knights, L. C. 63

Lamert, James 1
Lawrence, D. H. 47, 89, 94, 119
Lazy Tour of Two Idle Apprentices, The
    13–14, 106–8
Lear, Edward 75
Leavis. Q. D. 47
Leavis, F. R. 115, 119, 120, 125n, 145
Lettis, Richard xvin
Lever, Charles 30
Lewes, G. H. 21–2, 38–9
Little Dorrit 11–12, 14, 27, 67–8, 78,
    94–5.102, 109–25, 168

Macready, William Charles 6
Mann, Thomas 25, 47
Martin Chuzzlewit 6–8, 16, 66–7, 88
Marx, Karl 5, 11–12
Master Humphrey's Clock 4–6, 40–3
Matisse, Henri 30
Meredith, George 167
Milton, John 87, 152
Molière (Jean-Baptiste Poquelin) 7
Mystery of Edwin Drood, The 15–16, 80–5
Nicholas Nickleby 4, 63–6, 75, 155

'Night Walks' 25–6, 71

Old Curiosity Shop, The 5, 40–3, 87–8,
    90–1, 95, 125, 155, 163
Oliver Twist 3–4, 37–9, 97–8
Orwell, George 157
Otway, Thomas 75
Our Mutual Friend 15, 90, 127, 134–5,
    140–4

Pictures from Italy 7–8.114, 115, 117,
    119, 122
Pickwick Papers 3, 4, 34, 36–7, 50, 61–3,
    87, 158, 161
Piranesi, Giovanni Battista 73. 85n
Poe, Edgar Allan 7
'Poor Relation's Story, The' 121
Proust, Marcel 120

Reade, Charles xvn
Richardson, Dorothy 69, 169–70
Rolland, Romain 168

Scott, Sir Walter 6
Seymour, Robert 3
Shakespeare, Wllliam 42, 61, 63, 68,
    90, 106, 146–56, 157
Shaw, George Bernard 11–12
Sheridan, Richard Brinsley 7
Sketches By Boz 3, 20, 31–6
Slater, Michael xvin, 108n

Smith, Arthur 13
Solaris 143
Sophocles 41, 74
Spencer, Herbert 21–2
Spellbound 73
Stendhal (Henri Beyle) 93
Steptoe and Son 3
Sterne, Laurence 43, 64, 170
Stone, Harry xvin, 108n
Storey, Gladys 13
Swift, Jonathan 88

Tale of Two Cities, A 14, 71–2, 78–9, 109,
    127, 137–40
Tarkovsky, Andrei Arsenyevich 143
Ternan, Ellen 12–14, 16, 106n, 166
Thackeray, William Makepeace 15, 22,
    23, 34, 44, 48, 95–6, 130
Thousand and One Nights, The
    see *Arabian Nights*
Tillotson, Kathleen xvin, 40, 76
Tomalin, Claire 16
Trembling, Jeremy 85n

Uncommercial Traveller, The 25, 71,
    118

Virgil 141

Waugh, Evelyn 157, 160–166
Watson, Mrs Richard 19, 26–7
Wells, H. G. 158–61
Wilde, Oscar 5, 93
Wills, W. H. 13
Wilson, Angus 157
Wilson, Edmund xvin, 41
Winter, Mrs Henry *née* Beadnell 2, 17,
    149–50
Woolf, Virginia 69, 169–73
Wordsworth, William 6, 74, 75–6, 99,
    120

Yeats, W. B. 76–7, 111